BIRDS and MEN

BIRDS and MEN

American Birds in Science, Art Literature, and Conservation, 1800–1900

Robert Henry Welker

THE BELKNAP PRESS OF HARVARD UNIVERSITY PRESS

Cambridge 1955

DISTRIBUTED IN GREAT BRITAIN BY
GEOFFREY CUMBERLEGE, OXFORD UNIVERSITY PRESS, LONDON

LIBRARY OF CONGRESS CATALOG CARD NUMBER 55-11608
PRINTED IN THE UNITED STATES OF AMERICA

To my good friends and mentors

Ludlow Griscom
Ornithologist and Writer
and
Howard Mumford Jones
Teacher, Author, and Critic

I am happily privileged to dedicate this book

Contents

Illustrations

Introduction

Sumer is i-cumen in
Lhude sing, cuccu!
Groweth sed and bloweth med
And springth the wude nu.
Sing cuccu;

Awe bleteth after lomb,
Lhouth after calve cu;
Bulluc sterteth, bucke verteth;
Murie sing cuccu.
Cuccu, cuccu!

Wel singes thu, cuccu,
Ne swik thu naver nu!

Middle English lyric, c. 1300

From the beginning men have taken note of birds. In his concern with them, the fourteenth-century English poet singing of the cuckoo was a late comer indeed. A century earlier another poet had written *The Owl and the Nightingale*, seventeen hundred lines of argument between a spitfire songster and a grumpy bird of night; and as early as the eighth century had appeared the Anglo-Saxon riddle "A Swan." About that time also *Beowulf* had mentioned the swan, the eagle, and the raven. Centuries before, there had come to Europe the Physiologus tales, drawing upon nature lore of Greece and the Middle East, in verse and prose; and before them, the *Naturalis Historia* of Pliny the Elder, who in turn looked back to Aristotle for much of his material — but who scarcely aspired to his mentor's standards of critical scientific inquiry. A century before Aristotle, Aristophanes had peopled his ideal state of Cloudland with political birds; and Aesop, yet another century earlier, had assembled his winsome animal tales, many of them with birds as speaking characters.

By Aesop's time, or earlier, the Hebrew singers had written:

> For, lo, the winter is past, the rain is over and gone;
> The flowers appear on the earth; the time of the singing
> of birds is come, and the voice of the turtle is
> heard in our land;

and

> Behold, thou art fair, my love; behold, thou art fair;
> Thou hast dove's eyes within thy locks:

and

> My beloved is white and ruddy, the chiefest among ten
> thousand.
> His head is as the most fine gold, his locks are bushy,
> and black as a raven

and

> My dove, my undefiled is but one; she is the only one of
> her mother, she is the choice of her that bare her.

And the ravens had fed Elijah the Tishbite, and the lawgivers had forbidden the eating of nineteen "birds of abomination" (Leviticus 11:13–19), and the quails had come up to the camp of the Israelites fleeing Egypt.

The land from which they fled had been for many centuries rich in bird lore. Painted, carved into frieze and hieroglyph, or drawn on papyrus, birds had appeared centrally in Egyptian culture; and in Egypt had arisen the idea that the bird is symbolic of the human soul. In other great civilizations of the eastern Mediterranean — the Cretan, the Corinthian, the Laconian, the Chaldean, the Boeotian, the Attic, the Etruscan — bird art also had developed.*

It was not here, however, among these peoples of known history, that the earliest bird artifacts were produced. Perhaps as early as the thirty-fifth millennium before Christ, Paleolithic man, carving or painting on the walls of caves in France and Spain, drew the first birds (so far as we know) ever recorded by human hands.† And he drew them well enough that today we know them in our own scientific terms; we can assign the family, or even the genus or species, to sev-

* See Claus Krüger, *Der fliegende Vogel in der antiken Kunst bis zur klassischen Zeit* (Quakenbrück, 1940).

† See Jean Anker, *Bird Books and Bird Art* (Copenhagen, 1938), p. 1. See also Alcalde del Rio, Breuil, and Sierra, *Les Cavernes de la région cantabrique, peintures et gravures murales des cavernes paléolithiques* (Monaco, 1911), pp. 230–237.

eral of his birds. By these tokens we know that the human creature even in the Age of Stone was aware of birds, and observed them in critical detail.

But to return across three hundred and fifty centuries to the *Cuckoo Song*. One might suppose that so slight a lyric would count for very little by way of observation of nature. In fact, however, its honesty shines forth amidst the gloom of its time; for if the poem observes little, it observes truly, and if its truth is unimportant, at least the verse does not lie. Elsewhere in this period we can find avowed "natural history" enough—the Physiologus tales mentioned above, with their offspring, the bestiaries; and scarcely a page of them can be read today without incredulity, amusement, or dismay. For in the course of time these tales had lost all pretense to scientific truth; what had been originally an accurate observation of a bird or a mammal was now wrenched askew to fit some churchly saw, and what had begun as fabulous lore was now further debauched by grotesque moralizing. With natural science thus captive to the ecclesiastics, one turned to the *Cuckoo Song*, to *The Owl and the Nightingale*, or a little later to *The Parliament of Fowles*—in short, to the poets—to learn more truly of birds.

About the time of the *Cuckoo Song*, however, there was circulating in Europe a notable ornithological work by one of the most remarkable men ever to wear a crown. It was *De Arte Venandi cum Avibus* by Frederick II of Hohenstaufen. Frederick, Holy Roman Emperor, the Christian ruler who often dressed as an Arab; who established a great university in his capital, Naples; who brought thither scholars from all over the Moslem and Christian worlds; who introduced the study of the great Arab philosopher Ibn Rushd, and who rejuvenated the study of Roman law; who often defied papal authority, and suffered more than one excommunication—this man was the foremost ornithologist of the Middle Ages. *The Art of Falconry* was primarily concerned with hawks and their uses, of course; but in addition to the sections on falconry there were passages on the structure and habits of birds in general, and as originally circulated in manuscript, the work was illustrated by many colored drawings, showing various species of birds.* Here, then, was a genuine work of ornithological

* An excellent modern reproduction of *De Arte Venandi cum Avibus* is that of

science and art, in an age which viewed independent inquiry into nature as tainted with heresy.

❧ ❧ ❧

De Arte Venandi cum Avibus, the Physiologus tales, the *Cuckoo Song*: a medieval triad which has relevancy to man's interest in birds for any era. Frederick's work is bird science; many of the tales are bird myth and superstition (or, more broadly, popular lore); the poem is bird literature. In a wide sense, these three—science, art, and popular attitudes—are always with us; man's concern with birds commonly may be listed under one or another rubric. Whatever the century, there are those persons to whom the bird is a subject for dispassionate study; those who see birds as creatures of beauty and inspiration; and those who, disclaiming science or art, have their own notions of birds and their uses.

Such an analysis is suggestive, not exhaustive, nor are the rubrics mutually exclusive; but this book, in broad outline, will apply these divisions to a study of the place of birds in nineteenth-century America. Science, literature and painting, and popular attitudes will be taken up both separately and in combination; each bears upon the others, and none is independent of any other. Nor may these matters properly be isolated from the larger culture of the country and the period; they exist within the general framework, which gives them whatever relevancy and importance they may possess. Similarly, the major figures are to be studied not merely for their work with birds, but more broadly also, for their place within American society.

Immediately, however, a contradiction suggests itself. Assuming the general validity of the foregoing, how justify so arbitrary a concept as a century, an artificial span of one hundred years, within which to confine the discussion? And further—how defend the national limits imposed, especially in a pursuit so truly international as natural science?

No doubt the best answer to these questions is *nolo contendere*. But as to the first: by a happy accident, the coming of the nineteenth

---

Casey A. Wood and F. Marjorie Fyfe, editors and translators, *The Art of Falconry* (Palo Alto, California, 1943).

century coincided almost exactly with the arrivals in the United States of the man who was to be its first modern ornithologist, Alexander Wilson, and of John James Audubon, who was to be its most renowned. Toward the middle of the century, when the work of these two men had been completed, interest in birds divided and spread into various specialized phases of ornithological science, and into our finest nature literature. It also impinged upon new states and territories, new railroads, new surveys of resources — in short, it was involved with the westward movement of the young republic. Shortly it appeared in the realm of agricultural economics, and then in the gaudy domain of feminine fashion. By the end of the century, concern with birds had so broadened its base within the population that two national organizations for bird study and protection had been formed and were taking an increasing part in the new conservation movement, which reached a high point early in the twentieth century with the work of that devoted birdwatcher, Theodore Roosevelt. So to employ the one-hundred-year convention is not, in this case, to imply a symmetry wholly false.

Then as to the imposing of national limits: immediately it can be argued that because the avifauna of North America is so distinct from that of Europe, the limitation is more natural than arbitrary. In addition, concern with birds in America took its own distinctive course, one consonant with American times and situations. Finally, whatever significant influences came from abroad (especially in the early development of natural science) I hope to speak of, or at least to acknowledge. Parts of the first and second chapters are devoted to this purpose.

and other land birds during the period when his ships were on the high seas; and on September 20 "a bird . . . which was like a jay: it was a river-bird and not a sea-bird and had feet like a gull." None of these events is wholly implausible; land birds and other nonpelagic species are frequently seen from ships crossing the Atlantic, and one migration route for North American birds extends far to sea, past Bermuda. But the impression is strong that at times Columbus was seeing what he wanted to see, not what was actually there. Similarly, in the well-known letter to Gabriel Sanchez (1493) he claimed he had heard a nightingale sing on the island of Cuba — a statement based not on strict observation but on inadequate evidence buttressed by what an Italian scholar has called "un'illusione letteraria." *

So it would be with those who followed Columbus. They described birds, compiled lists, and dispatched to Europe bird skins or captive birds (the turkey prominent among the latter); but they larded their first-hand observations with fanciful tales and superstitious lore, attempting to explain the New World in terms then current in Europe, where ornithology was scarcely beyond its infancy. Seldom were these men scientists; but even when their motives were broadly scientific — that is, when they were looking for facts, and not advertising their own exploits or the marvels of the new lands — their equipment was faulty, their preconceptions were too strong, their systems were inadequate. Thus the New World in the sixteenth and seventeenth centuries produced little that was new in the study of nature. Bird science in America had to wait upon scientific developments elsewhere. In the history of ornithology these early recorders have scarcely more than antiquarian importance.

Yet they have a broader significance, one which escapes the narrow confines of science. Almost from the first, these explorers and the colonists who followed them recorded certain broad truths about American birds. Even when they gave erroneous European names to the new species — the robin, the blackbird, the sparrow hawk — they noted the distinctiveness and diversity of our avifauna; and especially they

* Leonardo Olschki, in *Storia letteraria delle scoperte geografiche* (Firenze, 1937) devotes an entire section to "the nightingale of Columbus," indicating how the discoverer employed not so much scientific standards as poetic ones in his accounts of the new lands. See especially pp. 19, 20. The same writer again discusses the matter in "What Columbus Saw on Landing in the West Indies," *Proceedings of the American Philosophical Society,* LXXXIV (July 1941), 633–659.

noted the prodigal abundance of such species as the passenger pigeon, the Carolina paroquet, the heath hen, the turkey, and various shore and water birds. More surprisingly, however, before the seventeenth century had passed, at least two colonial observers were noting the growing scarcity of certain species.

Both early abundance and subsequent decline were recorded by William Bradford, governor of the Plymouth colony. Writing of the year 1621, he noted "ther was great store of wild Turkies, of which they tooke many"; but speaking of waterfowl, "of which this place did abound when they came first," he commented that these birds "afterward decreased by degrees." Thomas Morton, whose May-pole merrymaking sorely tried the Christian patience of the good Bradford, was in agreement with the governor on one point at least, concerning the vast numbers of wild turkeys to be found in New England. He claimed these birds "divers times in great flocks have sallied by our doores," and upon asking the Indians how many turkeys might be seen in the woods in a single day, he was told "Neent Metawna, which is a thousand."

William Wood, another early New England writer, agreed with Morton and Bradford as to the abundance of wild turkeys, and of the passenger pigeon he said: "I have seen them fly as if the Ayerie regiment had beene Pigeons; seeing neyther beginning nor ending, length, or breadth of these Millions of Millions." From a vast nesting area thirty miles from the settlement he noted that "the *Indians* fetch whole loades" of these birds. Because Bradford was writing some years after the events he described (he began the history "aboute ye yeare 1630" and continued till 1646) we may assume that he refers to birds of later seasons when he says "but afterward decreased by degrees." Wood, whose book was published in 1634, also mentioned the prospect of scarcity—and immediately denied it:

> But me thinkes I heare some say that this [abundance of birds] is very good if it could be caught, or likely to continue, and that much shooting will fright away the fowles . . . yet they are not much affrighted. I have seene more living and dead the last yeare that I have done in former yeares.

The historian John Josselyn, however, was not deceived. Writing forty years after Wood, he clearly copied most of the latter's section on the passenger pigeon; but his conclusion had little in common with Wood's optimism: "But of late they are much diminished, the English taking them with Nets." Concerning the wild turkey he was even less sanguine:

> I have also seen three-score broods of young turkies on the side of a marsh, sunning of themselves in a morning betimes. But this was thirty years since; the English and the Indians having now destroyed the breed, so that 'tis very rare to meet with a wild turkie in the woods.*

Here, then, are two opposing attitudes already set forth: a notion of a new continent abounding with inexhaustible supplies of birds, and a concern for the future of certain birds under the impact of white settlement. From one attitude sprang the exploitation which would burgeon in the following centuries; and from the other, the conservation movement.

American ornithological science could not depend for its growth on the uninstructed and often incidental observations of the early colonists. Natural science is a systematic endeavor, and a mere list of birds will not suffice, however accurate the separate notes appended to the list. It was necessary to establish a taxonomy, a system of classification whereby any bird might be placed in its proper relationship within the total avifauna. The system in use today originated in the eighteenth century, with the work of Linnaeus (1707–1778); but a century earlier, in 1678, there appeared in England *The Ornithology of Francis Willughby*, edited and translated by John Ray. This work, with its systematic arrangement of species, its detailed data on anatomical structure, its careful notes on habits, and its generally superior plates, was in the newly developing spirit of scientific inquiry. It had little to do directly with North American birds, mentioning very few

* The quotations in this section are from the following: *Bradford's History "Of Plimoth Plantation,"* from the Original Manuscript (Boston, 1928), p. 127. Thomas Morton, *The New English Canaan* (1637), with Introductory Matter and Notes by Charles Francis Adams, Jr. (Boston, 1883), pp. 192–193. William Wood, *New England's Prospect* (1634; Boston, 1865), pp. 31–32, 35. John Josselyn, *An Account of Two Voyages to New England* (1674; Boston, 1865), p. 79. John Josselyn, *New-Englands Rarities* (1672; Boston, 1860), p. 144.

of them; but because it shows clearly the advances being made in ornithology, it helps to explain why the volumes of Mark Catesby (1682–1749?) were superior to anything previously done on our avifauna.

Catesby's *The Natural History of Carolina, Florida, and the Bahama Islands* comprised two sumptuous folios, published by sections in London between 1731 and 1743, with an appendix added to the second volume in 1748. With its large, vivid plates and its wide range of observations, it was a remarkable work by any standard; and it included not only many birds and plants, but also insects, crustaceans, fish, turtles, snakes, lizards, a saurian, amphibians, and mammals. (Among the amphibians was "Rana maxima Americana Aquatica," the bullfrog, now called *Rana catesbiana* in Catesby's honor.) As indicated by its title, the work was designed to encompass natural history generally, within the area specified. Concerning the birds, for example, Catesby said: "I believe very few Birds have escaped my Knowledge, excepting some Water Fowl and some of those which frequent the Sea." He was quite wrong, of course; neither with birds nor with any other class of vertebrates did he succeed in describing more than a fraction of the indigenous species. Yet however short it fell of its grandiose objective, Catesby's work was a notable scientific achievement; Linnaeus based at least one third of his American bird descriptions on the data furnished by these volumes.

In his efforts to discover, name, describe, and paint the birds of the southeastern colonies and the islands "between the 30th and 45th degrees of latitude" Mark Catesby made two extended visits to America, from 1712 to 1719, and from 1722 to 1726. It is apparent that he wanted a great deal of first-hand experience with the living creatures and that he chose not to employ earlier records. Such records were available, as they were in New England. In the area which was to be North Carolina, for example, Captain Barlowe recorded his discovery in 1584 of "cranes" (no doubt egrets) along the coast, Thomas Hariot a few years later noted "four score and six" Indian names of "all sorts of fowl" to be found in the vicinity, and John Lawson in 1714 devoted ten pages of his *History of North Carolina* to lists of birds and descriptions of some of them. John White, an artist who had visited the Roanoke colony, did watercolors of some American birds in 1585;

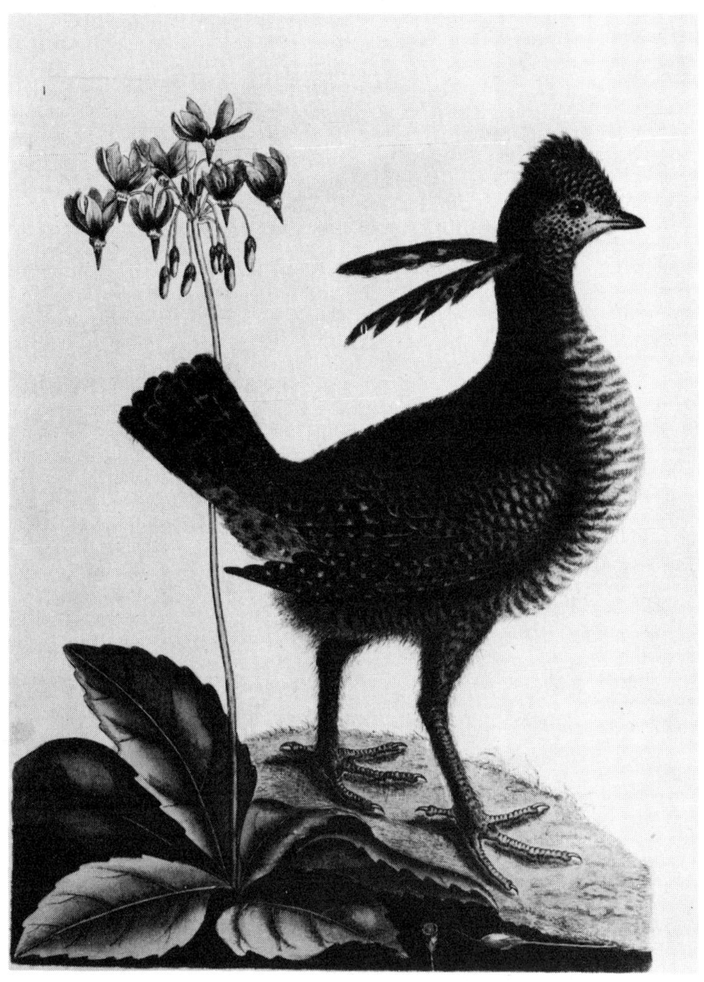

1. THE HEATH HEN, an eastern race of the prairie chicken or pinnated grouse, was a locally abundant species when this illustration appeared in Mark Catesby's *Natural History of Carolina* in 1748. But it was destined to be one of several birds exterminated by white settlement. A New York law of 1708 established a closed season for it; later other states extended protection. Yet excessive shooting in the restricted habitat of this bird caused its disappearance from the mainland by 1870, with the last of the race surviving only on Martha's Vineyard off the Massachusetts coast. In 1928 only three birds were left on the island; in 1933 the last one died and the race became extinct, having failed to adapt its ways well enough to survive.

Edward Topsell, famous English naturalist, included nine American birds (under Indian names) in his illustrated *Fowles of Heauen* about 1614; and the flamboyant John Smith named in English about twenty birds in his *A Map of Virginia with a Description of the Country* in 1612.

Of such works Catesby may have been unaware; or he may have dismissed them as of little use. In any event, he generally disavowed them when he said: "Very few of the Birds having Names assigned to them in the Country, except some which had *Indian* Names; I have call'd them after European Birds of the same Genus, with an additional Epithet to distinguish them." In Latin his system of nomenclature tended to produce simply short verbal descriptions (as with the bullfrog—"largest American aquatic frog") rather than specific designations as later understood. In English, however, it had one good effect, in establishing generic relationships between American and European birds regardless of superficial resemblances. Thus Catesby correctly called the robin "The Fieldfare of Carolina"—an attempt to link scientific classification with a proper vernacular name, and also an attempt (however unsuccessful) to remove the implication of generic relationship between our reddish-breasted thrush and the robin redbreast of England.

But Catesby cannot properly be judged by his nomenclature, which is pre-Linnaean and therefore by modern standards archaic. The more important question concerns Catesby's qualifications as a scientist generally—his freedom from hearsay or superstition and his devotion to the observable fact. In these respects he qualifies remarkably well, considering his time. To be sure, he thought American birds were scarce because they had trouble reaching the New World after Noah's flood; he said paroquet guts were "certain and speedy poison to cats"; he believed passenger pigeons roosted on one another's backs; he thought that the turkey vulture found carrion by sense of smell, and that the nighthawk's booming was produced by its wide mouth. But these are details. Catesby's general attitude is that no common opinion is to be credited unless it can be verified by observation.

Consider for example his straightforward accounts of American snakes. No creature is so obscured by fearsome folklore as the serpent; but Catesby abjured the shadows and saw most of his snakes in the light of day. Under the "Water Viper" (moccasin) he wrote at some length to deny that the snake's horny tail-tip ("This harmless little thing") is poisonous and capable of destroying life with a single stab. An Indian superstition concerning the powers of the coachwhip snake he called "their silly Belief." He repeated the bird-charming story at the end of his account of the rattlesnake; but he specifically denied having witnessed any such occurrence himself, and the rest of his comments on this species were straightforward and generally accurate. He mentioned that some persons thought the "Blue tail Lizard" (skink) to be venomous, but insisted that he himself could not confirm the notion. Similarly with the hog-nosed snake: he believed the creature to be "of the venomous Tribe, till searching in his Mouth for the hollow Viper's Fangs," he could find none, and concluded by admitting he was not sure.

Catesby showed a similar spirit in observing and speculating upon birds. For example, concerning the winter habitat of the "American Swallow" (chimney swift) he said:

> Their periodical retiring from, and returning to *Virginia* and *Carolina*, is at the same seasons as our Swallows do in *England*; therefore the place they retire to from *Carolina* is I think most probably *Brazil*, some part of which is in the same latitude in the southern hemisphere, as *Carolina* is in the northern.

Here we have not only an implicit denial of the popular theory that swallows and swifts hibernate in the mud of ponds, but also a shrewdly reasoned conjecture as to the actual winter quarters of those birds. By such clarity and scientific acumen Mark Catesby merited the title of the founder of American ornithology. At separate points his data may have been inaccurate or incomplete; but generally and in spirit he was a true scientist of nature.

He was also an artist who strove conscientiously to present his natural creatures in terms both scientifically and pictorially valid. Only a generous critic would say he succeeded. Perhaps Catesby's most effective illustrations are of fishes; but these creatures are presented *in vacuo*, not in natural surroundings as part of a larger artistic conception. When Catesby attempts to join birds, plants, and perhaps insects in a single plate, his reach exceeds his grasp. Now and again his patterns are arresting—for example, in the case of the golden crowned kinglet, the cedar waxwing, the Bahama titmouse. Yet even here he fails to place his birds persuasively, to "locate" them in a natural and organic way within the plant pattern.

As an artist, therefore, Catesby is important for his aspiration and direction, not for his achievement. In attempting to paint birds as part of a larger decorative pattern of flowers and plants, he was breaking new ground. Earlier ornithological illustrations had used no plants at all, or had thrust them into the composition as meaningless or incidental accessories. It was Catesby (by profession as much a botanist as an ornithologist) who first attempted the artistic synthesis which would be perfected by Audubon a century later.

Catesby's birds, strictly considered, are seldom painted with complete accuracy. If they lack the glassy stare, the dragonlike claws, and the scaly plumage of medieval bird drawings, nevertheless they also lack persuasiveness in more modern terms. At least seven of his species are superficially unrecognizable. Others are drawn in the distorted poses of birds either patently dead or badly mounted. Seldom does Catesby pay close attention to plumage pattern; his renditions are approximate, not precise. In these particulars he represents not advance but regression; in Ray's edition of Willughby, the birds were frequently drawn with scrupulous attention to pattern and stance. Yet again the comparative failure of Catesby is in part the result of a bold and novel conception. Ray's birds seldom have animation; Catesby's often do, even at the cost of precision. When Catesby drew the kinglet, the chat, the blue jay, the flicker, the bald eagle and many others in unconventional, even distorted poses, he produced poor works of ornithological illustration; but in taking single birds and placing them in attitudes of active life within a large and colorful painting, he again anticipated the masterworks of Audubon.

* * *

Catesby lists in his preface a number of "Encouragers of this Work." So large and ambitious an undertaking as these volumes evidently needed sponsors. Among the scientists, Catesby's most important patron was Sir Hans Sloane, biologist and physician, and the founder of the British Museum. Among the "encouragers" in America were Lord Baltimore, "John Bertram," William Byrd of Virginia, Robert Johnson of South Carolina, "Thomas Pen, Esq., Proprietor of Pensylvania," and Sir John Randolph of Virginia. Once again Catesby foreshadowed later things; something akin to the patronage indicated here (often accompanied by real interest in natural history) was to continue among highly placed Americans, manifesting itself both in subscriptions for the expensive works of Wilson and Audubon, and in specimens or observations offered to supplement their studies.

Benjamin Franklin, Benjamin Thompson, and John Bartram, the great Quaker naturalist, were three Americans who achieved the honor of international scientific reputation in the eighteenth century. Linnaeus called Bartram the greatest natural botanist of his time. Franklin placed him second on the list of founders of the American Philosophical Society. Bartram carried on correspondence with many eminent scientists of Europe, including Peter Collinson, John Frederick Gronovius, Peter Kalm, and Linnaeus himself. He founded and carried forward the first strictly botanical garden in America, and welcomed many distinguished persons there. His devotion to nature inspired his son William, who became America's earliest nature essayist. It was only fitting that such a man should appear among the encouragers of Mark Catesby.

The name of Benjamin Franklin does not appear, but there is good reason to think that Franklin knew of Catesby's work. Although Franklin's scientific genius asserted itself most notably in his important studies of electrical phenomena, his was a wide-ranging mind, and the philosophical society he founded was to be made up of "virtuosi, or ingenious men, residing in the several colonies," and not confined to specialists in any single endeavor. That Franklin had read ornithological works is clearly shown by a portion of a letter he wrote to his daughter, Mrs. Sarah Bache, from Passy in 1784:

> For my part, I wish the bald eagle had not been chosen as the representative of our country; he is a bird of bad moral character; he does not get his living honestly; you may have seen him perched on some dead tree, where, too lazy to fish for himself, he watches the labor of the fishing-hawk; and, when that diligent bird has at length taken a fish, and is bearing it to his nest for the support of his mate and young ones, the bald eagle pursues him and takes it from him.

> With all this injustice he is never in good case; but, like those among men who live by sharping and robbing, he is generally poor, and often very lousy. Besides, he is a rank coward; the little king-bird, not bigger than a sparrow, attacks him boldly and drives him out of the district. He is therefore by no means a proper emblem for the brave and honest Cincinnati of America, who have driven all the *kingbirds* from our country; though exactly fit for that order of knights which the French call *Chevaliers d'Industrie.*
>
> I am, on this account, not displeased that the figure [appearing on the Order of Cincinnatus medal] is not known as a bald eagle, but looks more like a turkey. For in truth, the turkey is in comparison a much more respectable bird, and withal a true original native of America. Eagles have been found in all countries, but the turkey was peculiar to ours; the first of the species seen in Europe being brought to France by the Jesuits from Canada, and served up at the wedding table of Charles the Ninth. He is, besides, (though a little vain and silly, it is true, but not the worse emblem for that,) a bird of courage, and would not hesitate to attack a grenadier of the British Guards, who should presume to invade his farmyard with a *red* coat on.*

There are errors here, of course. The kingbird is nearly twice the size of some sparrows, and considerably bigger than the largest of them. The turkey had been introduced into Europe nearly a quarter of a century before the birth of Charles IX in 1550; and the bird's antipathy toward the color red, however useful to Franklin's purpose, is doubtless folklore. But the accuracies of Franklin's account far outweigh the mistakes. The bald eagle's habit of robbing the osprey is put forth much as it is recorded in Catesby, and the account of the kingbird's rout of the eagle follows Catesby even more closely. Concerning the turkey's alleged anger at seeing red, Franklin may have been thinking of John Ray's words: "The antipathy this Fowl hath against the red colour, so as to be much moved and provoked at the sight thereof, is very strange and admirable." Whatever the sources—and one may not rule out direct observation by Franklin himself—the notable thing about the letter is the use the author makes of ornithological data, showing that he took an intelligent interest in birds.

Another maker of revolution, Thomas Jefferson, should be mentioned here, although his main contributions to natural history come

* John Bigelow, ed., *The Works of Benjamin Franklin* (New York, 1889), X, 279–280.

early in the nineteenth century. In this same year, 1784, Jefferson was issuing his *Notes on the State of Virginia*, which included ninety-three birds listed under Catesby's system, with "Linnaean Designation," "Popular Names," and "Buffon Oiseaux" (the latter by number only) added. To these Jefferson appended thirty-two more, and commented that there were "doubtless many others which have not yet been described and classed." Even as President, Thomas Jefferson would have much to do with the discovery of new American birds, and would follow with interest the work of Alexander Wilson, "Father of American Ornithology."

In the last year of the eighteenth century appeared an unusual and emblematic work, *Fragments of the Natural History of Pennsylvania*, by Benjamin Smith Barton. As projected, this work was to include various branches of nature study, but only the section devoted to birds saw print. Something more than a convenient year of publication makes it symbolic. Barton's work is truly transitional, looking back to the scientific spirit of the past, yet foreshadowing much that was to come.

Its affinity for the past may be noted, first, by considering Barton himself. America had yet to produce a professional ornithologist; those who had written of birds up to this time were amateurs, and Barton was no exception. Beneath his name on the title page he listed membership in the Society of Antiquaries of Scotland, the American Philosophical Society, The American Academy of Arts and Sciences of Boston, the Massachusetts Historical Society, the Physical Society of Jena, and the Linnaean Society of London; and then appeared his professional title, Professor of Materia Medica, Natural History and Botany in the University of Pennsylvania. A highly educated and gifted amateur Barton was, to be sure — but an amateur nevertheless.

As a natural consequence to his wide learning and diverse attainments, this work has a leisurely way about it, and at times an almost antiquarian air. Barton quotes from Virgil and Milton, he mentions Columella and Pliny, he has a scholarly footnote on a verb used by

Caesar and Cicero and defended by Erasmus; he draws upon Hernandez and Piso and the Abbé Clavigero; at one point he launches into a discussion of the time wasted in American schools in learning classical languages. Even his main subject, bird migration, is blurred and dissipated by erudite musings and scholarly qualifications. His general conclusions are scientific enough, but along the way he temporizes and hesitates. His mind reveals itself as subtle rather than incisive. In short, Barton lacked the vigor and lucidity of outlook which would so distinguish Wilson and Audubon.

Yet this work is, after all, a detailed and painstaking inquiry into a single aspect of bird behavior. Indeed, it may be called the first ornithological monograph written by an American. It depends for its conclusions not on diffused data and general observations, but on separate notes taken on migrating birds over the period of a full year, March 1791 through February 1792. Correlated with these notes are temperature readings, weather conditions, foliage development, and miscellaneous pertinent comments; and the inference he draws – that birds depend upon conditions of temperature and food supply in their migrations – is based on these correlations. Moreover, Barton's general system is valid; he employs the nomenclature of Linnaeus and Gmelin, and although he mulls over the testimony of ancient authorities and contemporary informants, he depends for his more important references on such proper authorities as Edwards, Catesby, and Pennant. In all these particulars, Barton's work belongs with the ornithological science of modern times.

2 *Pioneer and Prophet: Alexander Wilson*

> I am most earnestly bent on pursuing my plan of making a Collection of all the Birds of this part of N. America. Now I dont want you to throw cold water as Shakespeare says on this notion, Quixotic as it may appear. I have been so long accustomed to the building of Airy Castles and brain Windmills that it has become one of my comforts of life a sort of rough Bone that amuses me when sated with the dull drudgery of Life.
>
> *Alexander Wilson, March 12, 1804*

It was not for Alexander Lawson, the Philadelphia engraver to whom these lines were addressed, to throw cold water on Wilson's "Quixotic" notion. Lawson was in part responsible for the notion; in the same letter Wilson speaks of "that Itch for Drawing which I caught from your honourable self." Alexander Lawson had helped Wilson to learn to draw, and was soon to lend the prestige of his position as a leading engraver to the proposed work. For many years he was to be a central figure in the organization and issuance of the completed project. Among the many Philadelphians interested in the work only John Bartram's son William, himself a noted naturalist and writer, and Charles Willson Peale, the painter and amateur scientist, deserve more credit than does Lawson for bringing to birth Wilson's *American Ornithology*.

To a disinterested observer, however, the notion might have appeared quixotic indeed. In 1804 Alexander Wilson, immigrant weaver, peddler, versifier, and schoolmaster, had almost no training, either scientific or artistic, for his proposed great task. Moreover, he had practically no funds. Although he lived near Philadelphia, then the scientific center of the republic, he had at that time few friends among the learned. The state of his ornithological training is indicated in a letter to Bartram (with bird drawings enclosed) dated March 29, 1804: "I have now got my collection of Native Birds considerably enlarged and shall endeavour if possible to obtain all the smaller ones this summer. Be pleased to mark the Names of each with a pencil as except 3 or 4 I dont know any of them." Despite the fact that he had been many months at work, collecting his birds and drawing them, he still had virtually no knowledge of proper nomenclature. Nevertheless he persevered, and four years later the first of his nine volumes came from the press.

Although in this instance, as often again, Wilson turned to William Bartram for help, there was relatively little Bartram could teach him of strict ornithological science. The famous *Travels Through North and South Carolina, Georgia, East and West Florida* (1791) had listed two hundred and fifteen species of birds, but Bartram had frequently given them his own Latin names (making the exact species uncertain), and even his Linnaean designations were occasionally employed in a confusing way. The *Travels* may have contained "the first important contribution by an American to American ornithology," as J. A. Allen stated,* but the book contributed little to Wilson's scientific training. Bartram's place is not as ornithological mentor, but as friend and sponsor, and as contributor of many separate observations of bird habits and places of occurrence.

Yet if Bartram's writings did not serve Wilson's scientific education, there was no other American work which could. Again from J. A. Allen: "When Alexander Wilson, the 'Father of American Ornithology,' began his great work . . . probably not a dozen species of American birds had been scientifically described by American writers, and almost nothing had been published relating to their distribution or habits." Only in the work of European scientists did Wilson find the systematic treatment upon which to model his own standards of classification. That he adopted the general plan provided

* "Progress of Ornithology in the United States during the Last Century," *The American Naturalist*, September 1876, p. 536. The quotation in the following paragraph is from p. 548.

by the British ornithologist John Latham is less important than the fact that he found no "usable past" in this aspect of science in America.

Because the subject of ornithological classification will recur elsewhere, the problem should be briefly discussed here. In carrying out his plan to make "a Collection of all the Birds in this part of N. America," Wilson needed more than a quick fowling piece, an observant eye, an accurate brush, and a fluent pen. He needed what the ornithologist Ludlow Griscom has called "a graduated series of pigeonholes in the great desk of Natural History" * — that is, a system by which a distinguishing name could be assigned to each bird, and relationships established between one kind of bird and another. Plainly, vernacular names would not serve even the first of these requirements. To take but one example: Wilson's "Gold-winged Woodpecker." the common and distinctive flicker, was known then (as it is now) by various local names — in the "Dutch country" around Philadelphia as Gehlschpecht, Grieschpecht, or Holsschpecht, elsewhere as High-hole, Hittock, Flicker, Piut, or Yucker. Common names follow no clear system. In designating the bird *Picus auratus* Wilson was giving it a pigeonhole labeled "golden," thereby separating it from all other species included under the generic label "woodpecker" (*Picus*). Admittedly, Wilson was scarcely an expert taxonomist, and much of his nomenclature was changed by subsequent editors; but he was the first American ornithologist to unite the Linnaean binomial system with verbal descriptions of each bird's appearance, habits, and distribution, and also with colored illustrations of the species so described and classified.

Thus it was one of Wilson's main concerns to choose among Latin names already given by European ornithologists to our birds — or, if a bird turned out to be a nondescript and new to science, to discover its place among the orders and genera, and give it his own designation. However, of Wilson's two hundred and sixty-two species, only thirty-nine were new; the remainder had been classified by Europeans working from live specimens, from skins, or from such early descriptions as those of Catesby. Most of the original work had been done, and therefore classification as such was the least arduous of Wilson's tasks

* Ludlow Griscom, in *Modern Bird Study* (Cambridge: Harvard University Press, 1945), p. 164.

(although, as also with Audubon and many ornithologists since, it remained a vexatious problem).

Wilson's greater efforts and more important contributions were made elsewhere, in those investigations of bird life which are best accomplished on the scene, with the birds in sight and hearing. For such a task there is no substitute for direct observation. As Wilson himself said:

> It is only by personal intimacy, that we can truly ascertain the character of either [men or birds], more particularly that of the feathered race; noting their particular haunts, modes of constructing their nests, manner of flight, seasons of migration, favourite food, and numberless other minutiae, which can only be obtained by frequent excursions in the woods and fields, along lakes, shores, and rivers, and requires a degree of patience and perseverance, which nothing but an enthusiastic fondness for the pursuit can inspire.*

In such investigations Wilson was far more on his own than he was in the matter of classification. Such European studies as had been made of the habits of American birds were quite incomplete and very often in error, depending as they did on information largely secondhand. The more important of these works should nevertheless be mentioned.

Aside from Catesby's volumes, already considered, one of the earliest British works to which Wilson referred was George Edwards' *A Natural History of Birds* (1743–1751), a study of world birds which contained fifty-seven colored drawings and verbal descriptions of circumpolar or distinctively North American species. At times both common and scientific names were misapplied, and Edwards occasionally entertained quaint notions of bird habits; but inasmuch as the author had not visited this continent, he was forced to use the data of others for American birds. Perhaps to engender the desired spirit of scientific curiosity, he said in the Preface to Volume I: "It would be very proper for all Travellers into foreign Parts, to take notice of what Birds and Beasts they find, and at what Seasons of the Year they find them, and at what Times they disappear, and when they appear again." However commendable in spirit, such observations were likely to be fragmentary and inaccurate in substance; and therefore those

* Alexander Wilson, *American Ornithology* (9 vols., Philadelphia, 1808–1814), I, 4.

sections in Edwards devoted to American birds (even when the notes were contributed by so famous a naturalist as John Bartram) could not be taken at face value by a later investigator like Wilson.

John Latham's *A General Synopsis of Birds* (1781–1785), upon which Wilson generally based his classification, was a technical work with few illustrations. Fundamentally it was a systematic handbook, with synonymy of each species from Ray, Brisson, Buffon, Linnaeus, Catesby, Edwards, and others, and short accounts under the headings "Description" and "Place," and perhaps "Female," "Young," "Manners," "Food," and "Migration." Two dozen American birds were first described here, many from data gathered from various American observers, including the bird artist John Abbot of Savannah, who later was to help Wilson himself. For Wilson, however, the chief value of the work lay not in its treatment of particular species, but rather in its systematic completeness.

Similarly valuable was William Turton's *A General System of Nature . . . by Sir Charles Linné* (1806), a rendering into English of "the last edition of the Systema Naturae of Linné, by Gmelin, amended and enlarged by the improvements and additions of later naturalists." It seems fortunate that such a translation of Linnaeus appeared just as Wilson was well launched on his study, since it made available to a man not skilled in foreign languages the basic text for modern classification. When Bartram sent a new specimen to Wilson, the latter could respond confidently, "It is the Rallus Virginianus of Turton and agrees exactly with his description." Of the rail genus he could say, "Turton mentions 4 species as inhabitants of the United States. I myself have seen 6." * As with other European sources, Wilson could not depend blindly upon Turton; but he could and did use the work as a guide in identifying new birds.

Another British publication, Thomas Pennant's *Arctic Zoology* (1784–1785), considered hundreds of American birds, and was perhaps the work most often cited by Wilson in *American Ornithology*. However, Pennant depended on the accounts of travelers and explorers, none too well trained in observing birds, and the result was much inaccuracy. There are species in Pennant which later were dis-

* All quotations from Wilson's letters are taken from the originals in the collection of Wilsoniana in the Museum of Comparative Zoölogy, Harvard University.

covered to be nonexistent, and observations which owe more to imagination than to close study. Wilson needed to be cautious in accepting any statement based solely on the text of *Arctic Zoology*.

A work somewhat different from those mentioned was Thomas Bewick's *History of British Birds* (1797–1804). Often quoted or cited by Wilson, these two modest volumes represented something new in British bird books. Exotic species were not featured (except for domesticated birds such as the turkey and the guinea fowl), since Bewick diverged from the practice of most earlier ornithologists in confining himself to the birds of his own country. In addition, he was little concerned with classification, simply listing his birds according to Linnaeus and Buffon. His main concern was to tell about each bird, giving a detailed description and some account of its ways and times and places of occurrence. His text was concise, his diction simple and rather quaint—and enlivened by both warmth and humor. His descriptions were aptly complemented by beautifully detailed and accurate woodcuts of most of the birds discussed; his humor was reinforced by charming and often scatological vignettes. It is plausible to suppose that Wilson received from Bewick stylistic hints as well as ornithological data.

Of continental works Wilson mentioned especially those of Brisson and Buffon. Brisson's *Ornithologie* (1760) was essentially a book of taxonomy, containing a synonymy of terms from Gesner, Aldrovandus, Linnaeus, Catesby, and others, plus a detailed description of each bird's physical features and plumage but not of its habits or distribution to any extent. Here again was a book to be used by Wilson as a technical manual. Far different, however, was the other French work, by Brisson's contemporary Georges Louis Leclerc, Comte de Buffon.

Briefly, Buffon was not so much a scientist as a writer for the French court, who took all zoological knowledge to be his province. On birds alone his output was prodigious; the *Histoire naturelle des oiseaux* (1771–1786) comprised ten ponderous folios, and included nearly a thousand full-page colored plates (by Martinet and others) with twelve hundred figures. In keeping with such sumptuousness, the format was appropriately rich and the style properly grand. Indeed, it is by virtue of his style and his courtly renown that Buffon survives; his reputation as a scientist, once so towering and resplendent, has long since fallen before critical assailants—among them Alexander Wilson.

Perhaps the initial quarrel between Wilson and Buffon was over classification. As he began learning his ornithologist's trade, Wilson found that Buffon had rejected the binomial system which stemmed from Linnaeus, and had boldly asserted that in nature there are no systems, only individuals. Whatever the philosophical merits of such a stand, for scientific purposes it was barren. But there were deeper causes for conflict between the two men. While rejecting modern classification with cavalier assurance, Buffon imposed on living creatures a system of his own, based on patent anthropomorphism. Thus the lion was first among beasts, being the noblest; and among birds, "the first species is the great eagle which Belon, following Athénée, has called *the royal eagle* or *the king of birds*." It followed logically that the first volume of Buffon's birds should be devoted to the "noble" and "warlike" species, the birds of prey—which meant lumping together the eagles and hawks with such distant relatives as the owls and shrikes.

However, Buffon's anthropomorphism went a good deal further than the imposition of social classes on the birds. No single passage of Buffon called forth more derision from Wilson than the following, concerning the woodpecker:

> Of all the birds which nature forces to live by the chase, she has assigned to none a life more harsh and laborious than that of the woodpecker; she has condemned it to labor, to a perpetual life of the galley slave, so to speak; while other birds may employ pursuit or flight, the ambush or the attack, where they may utilize courage and address, the woodpecker is assigned a harsh task, able to secure his nourishment only by piercing the bark and the hard wood of the trees which conceal it; engaged without respite in this necessary labor, the woodpecker knows neither relaxation nor repose; often indeed he sleeps and passes the night in the strained posture of the day's task . . . His movements are brusque, he has an inquiet air, a rude countenance and harsh features, a savage and surly nature . . . and when the physical needs of love force the woodpecker to seek a mate, he does so with none of the graces which love inspires in all beings that experience this sentiment with a responsive heart.

After demolishing point after point of this argument, Wilson concluded:

> It is truly ridiculous and astonishing that such absurdities should escape the lips or pen of one so able to do justice to the respective merits of every species; but Buffon had too often a favorite theory to prop up, that led him insensibly astray; and so, forsooth, the whole family of Woodpeckers must look sad, sour, and be miserable, to satisfy the caprice of a whimsical philosopher, who takes into his head that they are, and ought to be so!

Buffon of course deserved censure for such ludicrous notions, and for similar passages elsewhere in the work, applying grossly human standards to the life of birds. But note Wilson's particular cavil: that Buffon failed "to do justice to the respective merits" of woodpeckers, and *not* that he wrote of birds in human terms. It was the imputation of misery and hardship which offended Wilson, not the anthropomorphic bias. He himself was quite willing to write of birds in terms of human sentiment and morality; he objected to Buffon's strictures as reflecting upon avian felicity and by implication upon the perfection of Creation. Wilson was not notably religious, but he deeply loved the natural world and its most charming creatures, the birds—and he would not see them traduced.

In yet another respect Buffon and Wilson were at odds. It was the Count's firm belief that new-world creatures were descended from European forms which had made their way to this hemisphere by a northern route, degenerating in the process. Thus the song thrush of Europe had become one of the American thrushes, with a cry now harsh and unpleasant, "as are the cries of all birds that live in wild countries inhabited by savages." Again, the American redstart differed from the European form only because it had undergone a similar degenerating process. Such nonsense was more than Wilson could abide:

> This eternal reference of every animal of the New World to that of the Old, if adopted to the extent of this writer [Buffon], with all the transmutations it is supposed to have produced, would leave us in doubt whether even the Ka-te-dids of America were not originally Nightingales of the Old World, degenerated by the inferiority of the food and climate of this upstart continent.

Wilson was expressing here more than a scientist's scorn at foolish theorizing; he was also revealing outraged patriotism. The country which this Scotch weaver had adopted in 1794, in the twenty-eighth year of his age, was and remained for him—despite early discouragements and periods of nostalgia—a blessed land. Always a democrat, a stern individualist, a shrewd and sardonic social critic, and an ardent Jeffersonian, Wilson could not but be affronted by these Buffonian notions, as offensive to the patriot as they were ridiculous to the scientist.

For all his absurdities, however, Buffon may not be simply dismissed. His reputation as an ornithologist has long since been laid low; but his influence extended far beyond strict science. The renown he enjoyed helped "natural history" to gain respectability, social prestige, and patronage; in his time he was an ornament in the world of the rich and learned. If only in grandeur and weight, these volumes of Buffon from the royal printery excelled any work ever before issued on birds; they would be superseded in this respect only by Audubon's elephant folios. In literary style also Buffon foreshadowed Audubon and many another writer, to whom the bird world provided less scientific than artistic inspiration. This book concerns them too.

❧ ❧ ❧

In the light of the numerous references Wilson made to the bird works of Europe, it seems an act of ingratitude that he should have said, "Such is the barrenness of the best European works on the feathered tribes of the United States . . . that little has been, or indeed can be, derived from that quarter." He appeared to be on much firmer ground when he similarly dismissed American authorities:

> From the writers of our own country the author has derived but little advantage. The first considerable list of our birds was published in 1787, by Mr. Jefferson in his celebrated "Notes on Virginia" . . . The next, and by far the most complete that has yet appeared, was published in 1791, by Mr. William Bartram, in his "Travels through North and South Carolina," &c. in which 215 different species are enumerated . . . Dr. Barton, in his "Fragments of the Natural History of Pennsylvania," has favored us with a number of remarks on this subject: and Dr. Belknap, in his "History of New Hampshire," as well as Dr. Williams in that of Vermont, have each enumerated a few of our birds. But these . . . can be considered only as cata-

logues of names, without the detail of specific particulars, or the figured and colored representations of the birds themselves.

It was indeed true, as has been noted earlier, that American writers had produced few books of ornithological value. Yet formal writing by no means fixed the bounds of the resources upon which Wilson could draw, and this fact is emphasized by numerous references in his work. There were many individuals (including the President of the United States) who contributed notes and observations; there were institutions whose proceedings provided data; there were bird collections both public and private which were available for study; and there was even a federal party of exploration which sent back new birds for Wilson's use.

"My venerable friend, Mr. William Bartram" is a phrase which appeared again and again in the *American Ornithology*, nearly always to introduce an observation by the Quaker naturalist on bird habits or distribution. Some of these notes were taken from the *Travels*, but many others were contributed personally—as Wilson, with a touch of vanity, reminded the reader by such footnotes as "Letter from Mr. Bartram to the author." The relationship between the two men was both personally and scientifically fruitful. Wilson was a moody and sensitive man, but a difference of nearly thirty years in age and the older man's unstudied kindliness and patience helped smooth the asperities which others found trying in dealing with Wilson. Bartram's friendship gave Wilson his initial impulse toward the serious study of birds, and reinforced an attitude toward nature already implicit in the poetic side of his temperament. Another naturalist might have made of Wilson a "closet ornithologist," a trafficker in dried skins and taxonomy. Bartram's emotional and reverential outlook encouraged Wilson to observe and write of the living bird in the beauty of its natural environment.

William Bartram had the special virtue of being a naturalist by choice and calling. Thus the aid he gave Wilson came not from hours of avocational study, but from a lifetime of observing and relating. He helped Wilson especially in dealing with the rich avifauna of the southern states, which he knew from extensive travels both alone and in the company of his father, the pioneer naturalist John Bartram. The birds of the middle states he also knew very well, and could supplement Wilson's own broad experience there. No man living in America knew more of nature than did Bartram, and none was more willing to impart his knowledge.

John Abbot, an English entomologist, ornithologist, and painter who had settled in Georgia before the Revolution, was the only other professional naturalist enlisted to aid Wilson. Abbot made part of his living by collecting insects and birds. His arrangement with Wilson was to sell him observations and specimens of birds not readily obtainable in other areas. Such phrases as "according to Mr. Abbot of Savannah" or "Mr. Abbot informs me" occur throughout the *American Ornithology*, and presumably other notes from this source were incorporated without being identified.

Another sort of observer is typified by Dr. Benjamin Barton, the Philadelphia scientist mentioned earlier, whose *Fragments* and less elaborate studies are occasionally cited by Wilson. The list of such contributors includes Dr. Samuel Latham Mitchill, the brilliant and versatile New York physician who founded *The Medical Repository*; Judge John Joseph Henry, justice of the supreme court of Pennsylvania; Dr. Nathaniel Potter, professor of medicine at the Medical College of Maryland, sometime editor of *The Baltimore Medical and Philosophical Lyceum*, and authority on yellow fever; and of course Thomas Jefferson, political philosopher, amateur naturalist, and President of the United States. Contributions by such members of the learned gentry lent a certain style to Wilson's volumes; and they indicate to the later student that an interest in birds might well have been one of the intellectual pursuits of enlightened gentlemen of the young republic.

For Wilson's purposes, one of the particular benefits of this interest was the fact that such persons might make available private collections of bird skins or mounted specimens, or at least might send Wilson such birds as came their way. Thus the Little Auk (dovekie) was killed at Great Egg Harbor and was sent to Wilson "as a great curiosity"; the Great Footed Hawk (peregrine) was sent from the same place; the roseate spoonbill was presented by the family of Wilson's "late benevolent and scientific friend, William Dunbar, Esq." of Natchez; and the Gray Phalarope was found "preserved in Trowbridge's Museum, at Albany." Among many references in Wilson's letters concerning aid received, the following from a letter to Daniel H. Miller, October 12, 1808, is notable:

> I waited on a Mr. Alsop of the town [Middletown, Conn.] to whom I had been recommended . . . He also furnished me with a good deal of information respecting the Birds of New England being himself a great sportsman, a man of fortune and education and had a considerable number of stuffed Birds some of which he also gave me besides letters to several gentlemen of influence in Boston.

For the greatest number of specimens made available for study, however, Wilson was indebted neither to a country gentleman nor "a man of fortune," but to the great Charles Willson Peale, one of America's early painters and founder of Peale's Museum in Philadelphia. This extraordinary man, whose portraits of Revolutionary leaders rank with those of Stuart and Copley, had begun his museum in 1784 with a stuffed paddlefish, an angora cat contributed by Benjamin Franklin, some mastodon bones, and many of his own paintings. As the collection grew, it was moved to the hall of the American Philosophical Society and then to a part of Independence Hall. By 1805 the museum contained seven hundred and sixty types of birds in one hundred and forty cases, "the insides of which [were] painted to represent appropriate scenery, Mountains, Plains, or Waters, the birds being placed on branches or artificial rocks." * Peale, who did much of the collecting and mounting of specimens, delivered lectures on many aspects of natural history. He also engaged the interest of notable persons in his project. Thomas Jefferson served for a time as president of the museum, and among its prominent visitors were Washington, Madison, Hamilton, and Robert Morris.

So again the accident of residence near Philadelphia worked to the benefit of Alexander Wilson. In Peale, as in Bartram, he found a friend both helpful and well-informed; a man of considerable renown and authority, but without arrogance or side; and one whose interest was enthusiastic but not importunate. Toward him Wilson's gratitude apparently was warm and unfeigned. In the first volume he spoke of "Mr. Charles W. Peale, proprietor of the museum in Philadelphia, who, as a practical naturalist, stands deservedly first in the first rank of American connoisseurs, and . . . has done more for the

* See Witmer Stone, "Some Philadelphia Ornithological Collections and Collectors," *The Auk*, April 1899, p. 168.

promotion of that sublime science than all our speculative theorists together"; and in the last volume from his pen, he mentioned certain specimens "preserved in the superb museum of my much respected friend, Mr. Peale, of this city." Of course Wilson could take pride in the fact that the relationship here was not parasitic but symbiotic; while he received much benefit from his studies in the museum, he turned over his own collection of birds to it, and by his work reflected upon it great credit.

It was by virtue of its close association with Jefferson that the museum received in 1809 an unusual group of specimens, those collected by Lewis and Clark on their journey of exploration to the Pacific between August 1803 and September 1806. This was the expedition which both William Bartram and André Michaux, the botanist, had been urged to accompany. It was a great loss to science that neither man was able to go; for the burden of recording and collecting the flora and fauna of the vast new territory then fell upon the two leaders, neither of them properly qualified (despite instruction from Jefferson himself) for the task. No formal account of the natural history work of the expedition was ever put together; and the material on birds (other than notes in passing) was limited to a section of twenty-three pages, written by Clark. A few of the birds, such as certain grouse, the California condor, and Lewis' woodpecker, were described at length, but most of the accounts were brief and often unclear as to species. These pages make plain the fact that Clark was no more than an interested and dutiful observer, with so little formal training that he confused a wren with a flycatcher, a bat with the class of birds, a cormorant and a coot with the ducks. Nevertheless, Wilson gleaned a dozen references (mostly on distribution) from oral or written accounts of the expedition.

Such delicate articles as the skins of birds were not easily preserved during the long months of travel and storage incident to this arduous journey, and only three new species reached Peale's museum in a condition permitting mounting. These three, the western tanager, Lewis' woodpecker, and Clark's nutcracker, were described and illustrated in Wilson's third volume, published in 1811. They were of course new to science, and therefore bestowed prestige on the work in which they first appeared.

Apparently there was a disagreement between Wilson and Peale over priority in publishing figures of these birds. We have only Wilson's side of the dispute, so that the situation is not entirely clear. Writing to Lawson from Lexington, Kentucky, on April 6, 1810, Wilson said:

> I did not think Mr. Peale would have acted as he has done. I sincerely believe that the publication of these 3 of Clark's birds in the Amer. Orn. [*American Ornithology*] would be advantageous to his work; but if they think otherwise and prefer Peale's drawings, I am satisfied. I shall find subjects enough in the vast regions I have yet to traverse. I will not beg from Man what the God of Nature has scattered around me in such abundance.

Perhaps because of the question evidently raised by Peale, Wilson in his text for the Lewis' woodpecker made this unequivocal statement: "It was the request and particular wish of Captain Lewis, made to me in person, that I should make drawings of such of the feathered tribes as had been preserved, and were new." However, any ill-feeling engendered by this incident seems to have passed away quickly, as Wilson only a few pages later referred to the "noble collection" of "Mr. Peale of this city."

One further resource of Philadelphia should be included in the list of aids to Wilson. The American Philosophical Society for Promoting Useful Knowledge, formed in 1769 by the union of the American Philosophical Society and the Junto, was of course concerned with numerous fields of learning, natural history being only one of them. A list of subjects taken from the early volumes of *Transactions* includes these: a live worm in a horse's eye, how to quill a harpsichord, observing the transit of Venus, fixing smoking chimneys, construction of a "Sub-marine Vessel," raising the common logarithm of any number immediately, and "A Memoir on the Discovery of certain Bones of a Quadruped . . . in the Western Parts of Virginia, by Thomas Jefferson, Esq." Joseph Priestley, Caspar Wistar, Benjamin Barton, Samuel L. Mitchill, "C. W. Peale and his son Raphaelle," David Rittenhouse, and other prominent men appear among early contributors. Since only Barton among the American correspondents had any detailed knowledge of ornithology, it would be rash to assert that Wilson derived much primary help from the work of the society;

his references to it were few and not wholly complimentary. Its usefulness was found not in its particular contributions to bird science, but rather in its purpose, outlook, and membership. Here were learned and often highly placed Americans joined in the fellowship of intellectual curiosity, seeking enlightenment among diverse (and occasionally rather singular) pursuits. Here was a society which would not find a birdman strange; on the contrary, these cognoscenti would welcome the work of America's first notable ornithologist, and at length honor him with election to their company.

3 *The "American Ornithology"*

All the help in the world would have availed Wilson little, had he not possessed the gifts, the will and the courage to carry through his project. However numerous his references to the work of others, however steadfast his friends and collaborators, the *American Ornithology* was Wilson's own. He observed, collected, and mounted most of the birds, and painted them all; he composed the text, whether the material was derived from others or from his own observations; he saw nearly all his volumes through the press, and sold the necessary subscriptions; and at last (if we may credit Audubon) he perished "under the lash of a bookseller," his work within sight of completion.

The first volume of *American Ornithology* appeared in September 1808; the eighth was in the press when Wilson died in August 1813; both this volume and the ninth and final one were issued in 1814 under the editorship of George Ord. This first edition was of imperial quarto size, with seventy-six color plates distributed nearly uniformly throughout. Three hundred and twenty figures of birds appeared, representing two hundred and sixty-two species. From Wilson's original watercolors, the plates were engraved on copper by four men — Lawson did fifty, J. G. Warnicke twenty-one, George Murray four,

B. Tanner one—were lettered by Harrison and Vallance, printed, hand-colored by Alexander Rider and others, bound with the text and issued by Bradford and Inskeep, Philadelphia.

Reviews of this work appeared as the volumes were issued, notably in the *Port Folio* and *The Medical Repository*. In general they consisted of warm praise, extensive quotation, and little critical discussion. They are of slight use in indicating the strictly scientific reception of Wilson's work; but they are interesting social documents, because they generally argue that the *American Ornithology* was something the nation could be proud of. Consider these words of Mitchill:

> For the further recommendation of this publication, it ought to be constantly borne in mind that the exquisite paper, the distinct type, the correct engraving, and the fine colouring, are all domestic; and the same American character belongs to the press-work, the binding, and the other mechanical parts of the work: the colours alone are exceptions; these are chiefly of foreign preparation. It is nevertheless expected that this dependence will not last long: our country abounds in native ingredients for paints; its inhabitants are making rapid improvements on them by processes of art; and, in a reasonable time, it may be foretold, that chemistry will render them wholly independent of all foreign supplies.*

This was an extreme statement of the patriot's view, of course—but extreme mainly because it went into such amusing detail to prove the general thesis that Wilson had demonstrated America's superiority to the world. As indeed, in a sense, he had.

Charles Lucien Bonaparte, nephew of Napoleon and an ornithologist of international reputation, said in 1825, "We may add, without hesitation, that such a work as he [Wilson] has published in a new country is still a desideratum in any part of Europe." Not only had Wilson pioneered in America with his work; he had also produced an ornithology which for coverage of a particular avifauna, and for colored illustrations combined with extensive text, had not yet been equaled elsewhere. Most of the European works already mentioned failed on one or another count; either they tried to encompass the world (as did the huge tomes of Buffon, for example) and therefore lacked the concentration and relative completeness of Wilson's

* Samuel L. Mitchill, in *The Medical Repository*, Series III (1811), vol. II, p. 48.

work, or they were technical works which lacked the appeal of Wilson's vivid writing and colorful painting. Bewick's work of the previous decade was the nearest approach to the particular virtues of Wilson, but Bewick's excellent woodcuts were uncolored and the entire work was on a more modest and restricted scale.

To assert that Wilson has an engaging style is not to imply that his text is an exercise in literary expression after the manner of Buffon. Generally he combines a rather formal diction with succinctness and precision. His shorter discussions of one or another species tend toward the matter-of-fact; only in longer passages is he likely to reveal the personality behind the prose. One of the birds briefly discussed is the winter wren. The opening lines exemplify his shorter treatments:

> This little stranger visits us from the north in the month of October, sometimes remaining with us all the winter, and is always observed, early in spring, on his route back to his breeding-place. In size, color, song, and manners, he approaches nearer to the European Wren (M. troglodytes) than any other species we have. During his residence here, he frequents the projecting banks of creeks, old roots, decayed logs, small bushes, and rushes near watery places; he even approaches the farmhouse, rambles about the wood pile, creeping among the interstices like a mouse. With tail erect, which is his constant habit, mounted on some projecting point or pinnacle, he sings with great animation. Even in the yards, gardens, and outhouses of the city, he appears familiar and quite at home.

Casual as this passage seems, it nevertheless abounds in exact information about the wren's appearance, actions, migration, and song, and includes a shrewd guess as to its close kinship with the common wren of Europe. The paragraph is enlivened by touches of affection, but they are subordinated to the main purpose of conveying information.

The yellow-breasted chat, aptly characterized by Wilson as "a very singular bird," receives a longer and more personalized treatment, part of which follows:

> When he has once taken up his residence in a favorite situation, which is almost always in close thickets of hazel, brambles, vines, and thick underwood, he becomes very jealous of his possessions, and seems offended at the least intrusion; scolding every passenger as soon as they come within view, in a great variety of odd and uncouth monosyllables, which it is difficult to describe, but which may be readily imitated, so as to deceive the bird himself, and draw him after

> you for half a quarter of a mile at a time, as I have sometimes amused myself in doing, and frequently without once seeing him. On these occasions, his responses are constant and rapid, strongly expressive of anger and anxiety; and while the bird itself remains unseen, the voice shifts from place to place, among the bushes, as if it proceeded from a spirit. First is heard a repetition of short notes, resembling the whistling of the wings of a Duck or Teal, beginning loud and rapid, and falling lower and slower, till they end in detached notes; then a succession of others, something like the barking of young puppies, is followed by a variety of hollow, guttural sounds, each eight or ten times repeated, more like those proceeding from the throat of a quadruped than that of a bird; which are succeeded by others not unlike the mewing of a cat, but considerably hoarser. All these are uttered with great vehemence, in such different keys, and with such peculiar modulations of voice, as sometimes to seem at a considerable distance, and instantly as if just beside you; now on this hand, now on that; so that, from these manoeuvres of ventriloquism, you are utterly at a loss to ascertain from what spot or quarter they proceed. If the weather be mild and serene, with clear moonlight, he continues gabbling in the same strange dialect, with very little intermission, during the whole night, as if disputing with his own echoes; but probably with a design of inviting the passing females to his retreat; for, when the season is further advanced, they are seldom heard during the night.

Despite the involved syntax, this is vivid and evocative writing, of a sort which made the work appeal to an audience not limited to specialists in natural history.

But may it not be objected that Wilson's view of the bird is fundamentally anthropomorphic, and therefore unscientific? What of other passages in the *American Ornithology* where certain birds are even more blatantly personalized? Does not the sentimentalist here encroach upon the scientist?

These are questions which cannot be answered simply or with finality. They indicate a dilemma which every writer on birds must face, and later, in connection with literary figures, the subject will be treated at some length. For the moment, this much can be suggested: no man who concerns himself with birds can do so without having, or developing, an affection for them—and Wilson was no exception. Perhaps one may study the molds, the mollusks, or the helminths with nothing more than cold curiosity. Not so the birds, creatures too colorful, too active, too vocal, too diverse and distinctive to abide such limitation. And yet strict biological science demands that living things be viewed objectively, in terms of the facts, not in terms of human emotions, wishes, motives, or preconceptions; and hence the dilemma.

What compounds the complexity of bird science (and almost all other studies of living creatures) is that the "facts" themselves are multiform. Some can be conveyed with numerical exactitude; others depend on imprecise and connotive words for their expression. It is a fact that the average wood thrush is 8.29 inches in length — and that that it has a "song" which is "flutelike," and a distinctive note which it utters when "angry" or "alarmed." The yellow-breasted chat is hatched from an egg measuring .90 by .66 inches on the average; and the adult male makes sounds "strongly expressive of anger and anxiety" which may be "like the barking of young puppies," or "not unlike the mewing of a cat," or "like the whistling of the wings of a Duck or Teal." To make matters worse, he may utter some of this "strange dialect" while going through aerial gymnastics which seem "odd" or even "clown-like."

But ornithology is the study and correlation of all the facts about birds; and an accurate observation of the living bird, although put forth in words inevitably inexact, is no less a fact than is a datum obtained with a calibrated instrument and recorded in numerals. Wilson was not the poorer ornithologist for concerning himself with bird traits as well as times and places of occurrence, patterns of plumage, and such measurements as length and alar extent. But because he is avowedly a scientist, we may demand of him that he not falsify the record; that he not indulge in fancy at the expense of accuracy; that his birds not be made over into mere human beings; that he honor the flexible but genuine distinction between affectionate regard and sentimentality. Occasionally Wilson flouts such demands, as when he extols the "love, and faithful connubial affection" of the mourning dove, or gives us a verse in which the hummingbird "chirps his gratitude" for flower nectar. But if his outlook is not slavishly scientific, generally at least he is objective and faithful to fact.

Nowhere does Wilson's objectivity show to better advantage than in his handling of bird myths and superstitions. Consider, for example, the celebrated fiction that swallows spend the winter in the mud at the bottom of rivers and ponds. Catesby by implication had rejected the idea. Edwards had said that no swallows had been found during the winter except for a few which had suffered death by freezing. Bewick spoke of certain experiments which had been made to test the idea of hibernation, and concluded: "The result of these experiments pretty clearly proves, that Swallows . . . leave us, like many other birds, when this country can no longer furnish them with a supply of their proper and natural food." On the other hand, Jeremy Belknap in *The History of New Hampshire* (1792) had this to say of the swallow: "It was formerly supposed to migrate, but the evidences of its retiring to the water, or marshy ground, and there remaining torpid, during the winter, are so many, that this opinion is now generally received." Benjamin Barton not only communicated to the Philosophical Society a letter which offered eye-witness proof of the finding and reviving of swallows from a pond in February; he also, according to Ord, prepared a memoir supporting the idea, and then suppressed it before publication.*

Alexander Wilson's rejection of this bizarre notion was characteristically based on both empirical evidence and the promptings of reason. He could discover no valid instance of genuine hibernation, whether in hollow trees or in the mud, and he himself had made many observations to support the contrary idea, that swallows fly off to the south in the fall, migrating to regions of an assured food supply. But mere data did not satisfy him. The hibernation theory seemed to him not merely unsupported, but unreasonable, absurd, preposterous:

> I am myself something of a traveller, and foreign countries afford many novel sights: should I assert, that in some of my peregrinations I had met with a nation of Indians, all of whom, old and young, at the commencement of cold weather, descend to the bottom of their lakes and rivers, and there remain until the breaking up of frost; nay, should I affirm, that thousands of people, in the neighborhood of this city, regularly undergo the same semi-annual submersion – that I myself had fished up a whole family of these from the bottom of the Schuylkill, where they had lain *torpid* all winter; should I even publish this in the learned pages of the *Transactions* of our Philosophical Society – who would believe me? Is, then, the organ-

* Barton's communication to the Philosophical Society appears in *Transactions*, VI, 59–60; Ord's comments may be found in his *Sketch of the Life of Alexander Wilson* (Philadelphia, 1828), pp. clxxvi–cxcii.

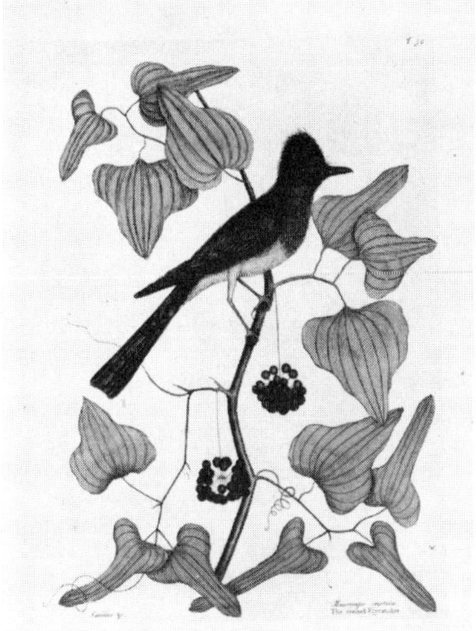

2. Catesby's crested flycatcher is poorly drawn and stiffly perched, but his pattern of smilax foreshadowed Audubon's use of the plant in his loggerhead shrike plate.

BOTH CATESBY AND WILSON (Figures 2–6) contributed important ideas to the development of American bird art — Catesby his imposing floral patterns, Wilson his scrupulous accuracy in rendering plumage, and his concern with giving his birds characteristic poses.

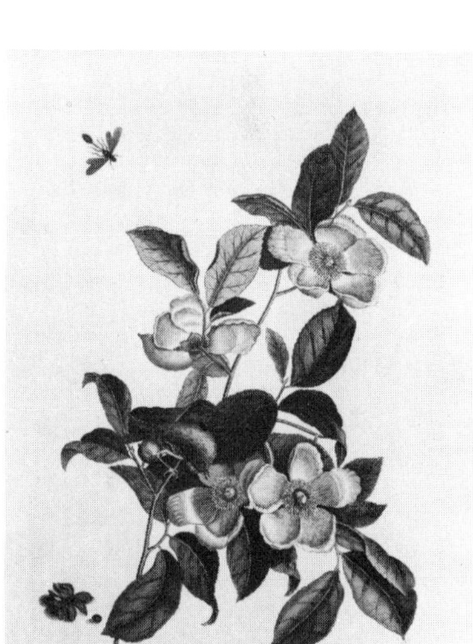

3. Perhaps the best of Catesby's floral designs was of the steuartia, upon which he perched a shriveled and twisted kinglet. Audubon, who knew of Catesby's work, used this plant in much the same manner in his plate of mourning doves.

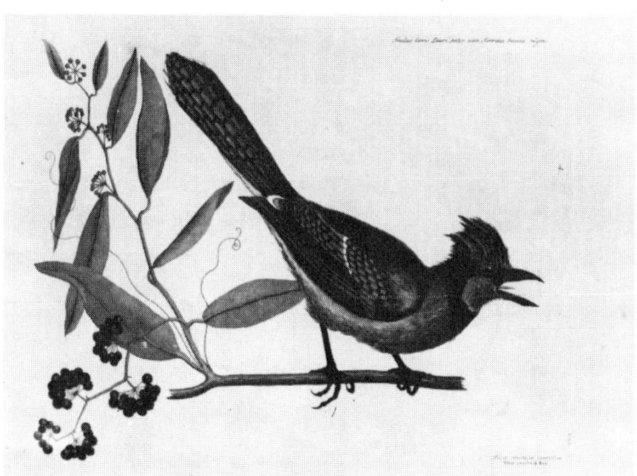

4. The "crested Jay" (bluejay) is not wholly accurate, but here Catesby succeeded in giving animation to one of his bird figures, without the distortion which was generally the penalty for such an attempt.

5. A typical Wilson plate is this of adult and immature cowbirds, a gnatcatcher, a vireo, and a warbler. The plate as a whole has a satisfactory design, and the birds are accurate and shown in lifelike attitudes; but spatially the figures have no interrelationship, and taxonomically they represent four separate genera.

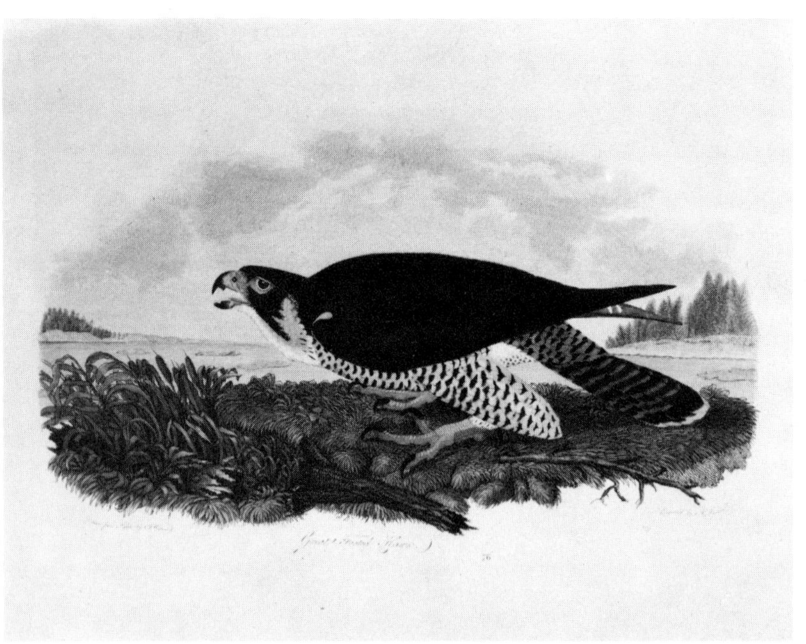

6. Wilson's potential excellence as an artist of bird life is seldom revealed in the engraved plates of his *American Ornithology*; but the last plate, of the peregrine falcon, shows how well he might have done had he been permitted to devote other plates to single species, in the manner of Audubon.

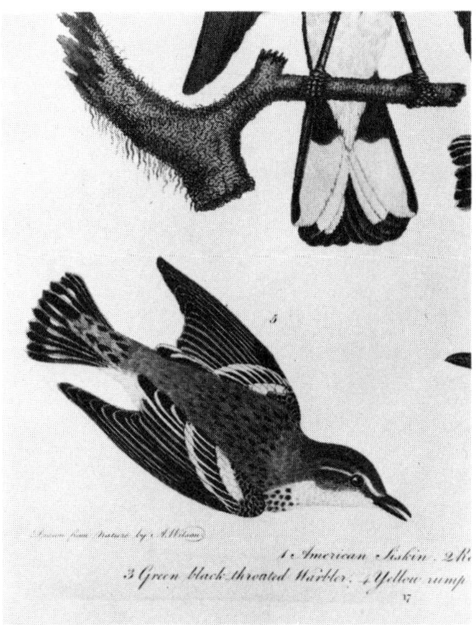

7. Wilson's male cerulean warbler.

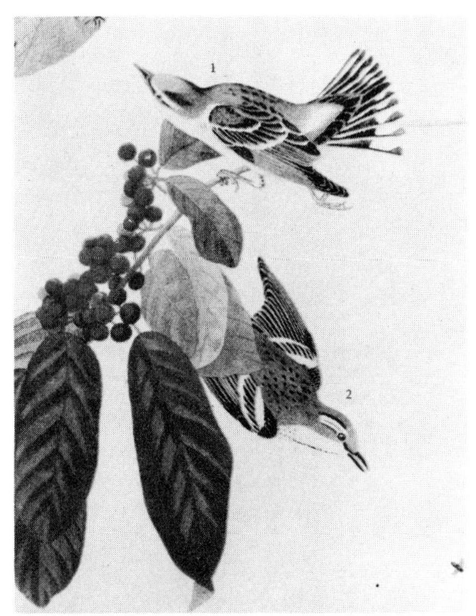

8. Audubon's "female" cerulean warbler, partially hidden behind leaves but still undeniably Wilson's.

AUDUBON'S PLAGIARISMS from Alexander Wilson show up plainly when the plates in question are compared (Figures 7–12).

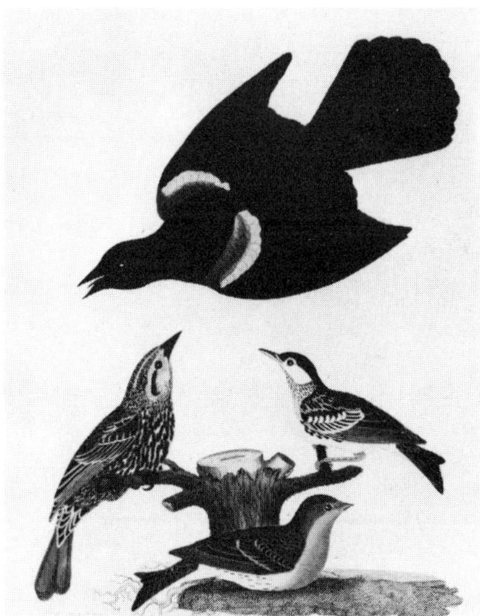

9. Wilson's redwing plate, male above and female at lower left. Two other species also appear.

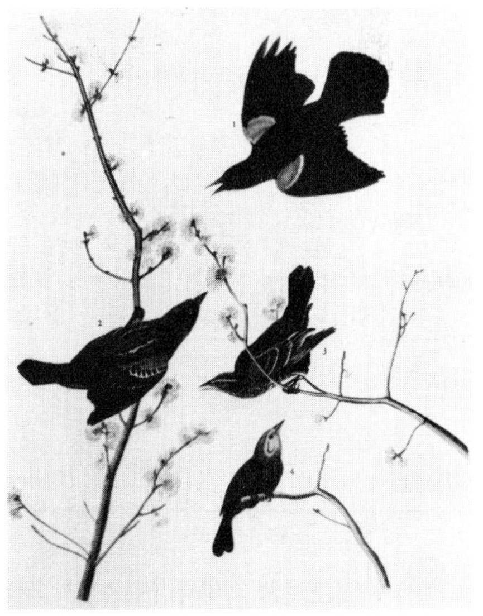

10. Audubon's redwing plate, with the lowest figure copied exactly and the uppermost showing considerable resemblance.

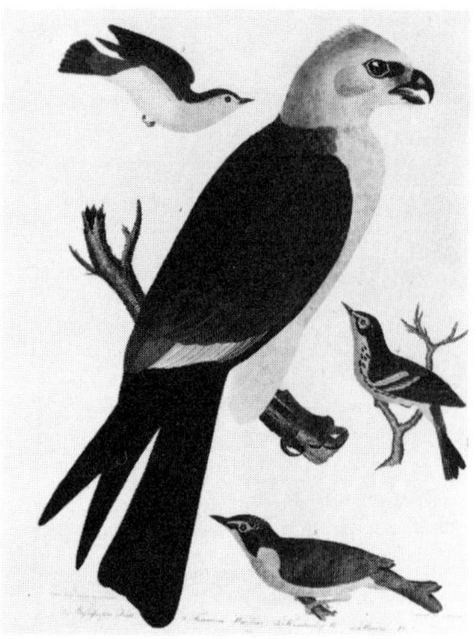

11. Wilson's Mississippi kite (with three smaller species). The bird appears life size, seldom the case with raptores in *American Ornithology*.

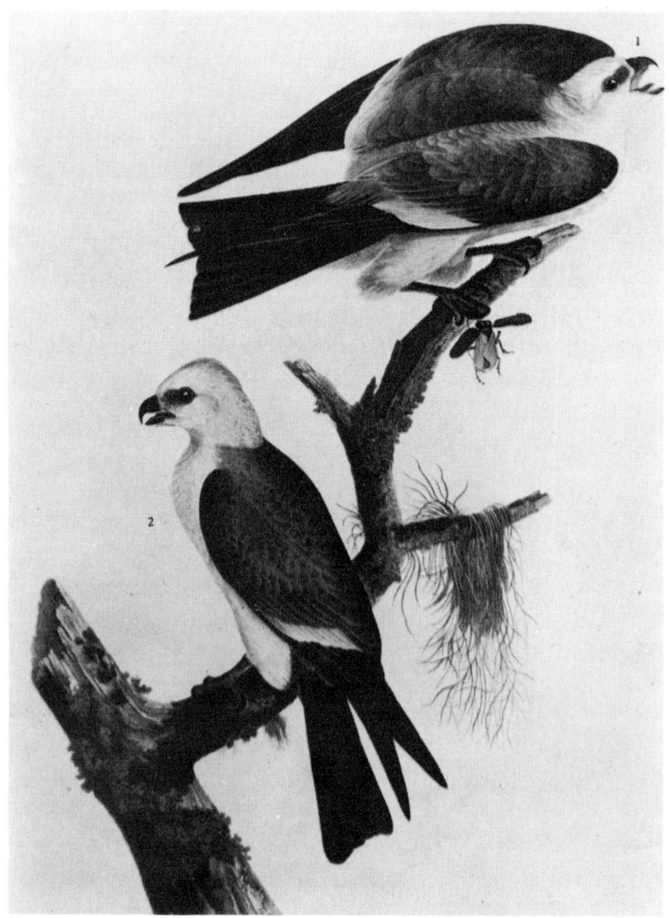

12. Audubon's "female" Mississippi kite, which is Wilson's bird reversed, with one toe missing. The two engravings superimpose perfectly.

ization of a Swallow less delicate than that of a man? Can a bird, whose vital functions are destroyed by a short privation of pure air and its usual food, sustain, for six months, a situation where the most robust man would perish in a few hours, or minutes? Away with such absurdities! they are unworthy of serious refutation!

There are many other attacks on myths and quaint notions in the *American Ornithology*, usually couched in similarly trenchant terms. The contention of Du Pratz that the summer tanager stores up "a vast magazine of maize" for the winter, Wilson puts in the same class as a story by Charlevoix, "who gravely informs us, that the owls of Canada lay up a store of live mice for the winter; the legs of which they first break, to prevent them from running away, and then feed them carefully, and fatten them, till wanted for use." One of Wilson's most eloquent passages defended the great horned owl from "ignorance and superstition" engendering "fearful awe" and "reverential horror." Far from crediting the "multitude of marvellous stories" regarding the power of the blacksnake to charm the catbird, Wilson demolished them by relating that "in all the adventures of this kind I have personally witnessed, the Cat Bird was actually the assailant, and always the successful one." He derided Buffon for accepting ancient authority in attributing "noble" traits to the eagle, and refuted him by showing the eagle to be a robber and an eater of carrion.

Perhaps the most measured of Wilson's refutations concerned the hoary fable of the barnacle goose, a bird allegedly born from a seashell adhering to a log or tree branch. In diction as well as outlook, Wilson showed himself a true son of the Enlightenment when he concluded:

> Ridiculous and chimerical as this notion was, it had many advocates, and was at that time [the sixteenth century] as generally believed, and with about as much reason too, as the present opinion of the annual submersion of Swallows, so tenaciously insisted on by some of our philosophers, and which, like the former absurdity, will in its turn disappear before the penetrating radiance and calm investigation of truth.

With such an outlook to guide him, Wilson's mistakes in the *American Ornithology* were nearly always those of insufficient learning or lack of first-hand information, very seldom those of credulity or wonderment. His difficulties with classification have already been noted, and only eleven years after Wilson's death Bonaparte began publishing his own extensive corrections and revisions. An allied problem concerned species which later investigators found either uncertain, misplaced, or nonexistent. Wilson's "Small, Green, Crested Flycatcher" is one of the four *Empidonax* which inhabit the eastern United States—which one is not clear. The bird Wilson calls the "Small-headed Flycatcher" has never been positively identified. His "Blue-green Warbler" seems to be the female of the cerulean warbler, not a separate species. Similarly, his "Pine Swamp Warbler" is the female black-throated blue. The two color phases of the screech owl confused Wilson, who named one phase the "Red Owl" and the other the "Mottled Owl." The brown-plumaged immature sharp-shinned hawk seemed to Wilson a different species from the mature bird, which he named the "Slate Colored Hawk"; and the immature golden eagle he called the "Ring-tailed Eagle," considering it distinct. On the other hand, he failed to distinguish between the two American cranes, believing the sandhill crane to be merely the whooping crane in immature plumage.

One of the ornithological mysteries in Wilson concerns the smew, a European merganser which on the water appears to be almost wholly white. Wilson drew it correctly, and his verbal description was accurate enough, but no actual specimen-in-the-hand was indicated in the text, either by reference to Peale's museum or by an account of the time and place of collecting the bird. The smew, Wilson said, was "much more common on the coast of New England than farther to the south," and was frequently seen "in the ponds of New England, and some of the lakes in the state of New York." Inasmuch as the smew is virtually unknown in the United States today (and in fact was considered very rare by Audubon, writing only two decades after Wilson), two explanations of Wilson's assertion are possible. One is that this species actually did occur in considerable numbers in the early years of the nineteenth century—or perhaps appeared for a short time only, in an irruption which has not been repeated. The other explanation, and the more probable one, is that Wilson saw some other species of white sea-bird swimming offshore, and supposed it to be the smew. The male bufflehead duck at a distance seems nearly all white, and the male old-squaw in winter plumage comes even closer to the pattern of the smew than does the bufflehead. Both of these birds occasionally appear on fresh water, but if Wilson actually saw a nearly-white bird "in the ponds of New England, and some of the lakes in the state of New York," it was probably the American merganser, despite that bird's black head and large size.

Of course there is no way of knowing exactly where the truth lies in this matter; but one good inference can be drawn from it. The question here is one of field identification. Since only a small fraction of lake or ocean birds seen can actually be shot and thus named in the hand, they must be identified as they appear on the water. Most (or perhaps all) of the birds Wilson called "Smew, or White Nun" were some other species, seen from afar. Today such a mistake would be very nearly impossible; the prism binocular and telescope have brought birds into such close range of the eye that even the interested amateur with field glasses and guide can readily distinguish the species mentioned. But Wilson had no such aid; he depended largely on the collecting gun and the naked eye, and as late as December 1811 he did not include so much as a "spy glass" in his list of possessions.

A failure not of the eye but of the ear occurred at several places in the *American Ornithology*. Although Wilson included such excellent passages on bird calls as those concerning the chat, the mockingbird, the wood thrush, and many others, he also made some noteworthy omissions. The "Ruby Crowned Wren" (kinglet), which has a remarkably sweet and vigorous song, Wilson dismissed as having "only at times a feeble chirp." The purple finch, whose common song is a pleasing warble and whose flight song much resembles the skylark's, Wilson permitted only a single *chink* note. Similarly, the "Golden-crowned Thrush" (ovenbird) was given only "a rapid reiteration of two notes, *peche, peche, peche,*" despite the ringing flight song the bird utters, generally near evening. Even more strangely, two of the most melodious of our thrushes, the hermit and the veery, were allowed only "an occasional squeak" and "a sharp chuck."

These comments do not represent an exhaustive survey of Wilson's errors—nor would such a survey be a particularly profitable undertaking. Not that the endeavor would be unworthy, a chasing of a schoolboy to his commonplaces; it would be simply gratuitous, and prove nothing more than the fact that there have been particular refinements and additions in the century and a half that separates us from Wilson. Indeed, if it is true that in science we see further each century because we stand on the shoulders of those who came before, then the very fact of Wilson's achievement allows us to criticize him. The first great work in American bird study was that of Alexander Wilson; and since continuity and at least superficial progress are characteristic of modern science, no subsequent work (not even Audubon's) could fail to build upon Wilson's massive pioneer accomplishments. Wilson has not been superseded; he has been revised and extended.

* * *

The *American Ornithology* was something new in American publishing; in order to succeed, therefore, it had to be sold to individual subscribers. Mark Catesby had been patronized by men of wealth and title; Alexander Wilson had little or no direct patronage and only such underwriting of financial risks as was assumed by Bradford and Inskeep in issuing the first volume, in two hundred copies, in September 1808. A year earlier the prospectus and sample copies of certain plates had been put out, and with these Wilson made the first of his commercial trips in October 1807, going to New York and Albany in an effort to interest booksellers. The crucial period, however, began with the appearance of Volume I. Wilson had to find subscribers or see his cherished project fail for simple lack of money.

The work was complex and costly; the plates alone, with engraving, lettering, printing, and coloring, came to nearly four dollars per volume, and the price of the complete work was put at $120 a set. When Wilson set out to collect subscriptions, he found this price to be a formidable, even a forbidding, barrier. Writing to Lawson from Albany in November 1808, when he had already canvassed the cities and towns on the route from Philadelphia to Boston, with poor financial results, he said:

> In short the Book in all its parts so farr exceeds the ideas and expectations of the first literary characters in the eastern parts of the United States as to command their admiration & respect. The only

> objection has been the *120 dollars*, which in innumerable instances has risen like my evil genius between me and my hopes. Yet I doubt not but when those subscribed for are delivered and the Book a little better known the whole number will be disposed of, and perhaps encouragement given to go on with the rest. To effect this, to me most desirable object, I have encountered the hardships and fatigues of a long, circuitous, unproductive and expensive journey with a zeal that has increased with increasing difficulties and sorry I am to say that the whole number of subscribers I have obtained amount only to 41!

Three weeks earlier, writing to the Philadelphia ironmonger Daniel H. Miller, Wilson had noted that all "the most extravagant compliments" of persons examining his sample volume he "would have very willingly exchanged for a few simple *subscriptions*," and that the complimentary reviews in newspapers of New York and Hartford "will neither purchase plates nor pay the printer—but nevertheless it is gratifying to the vanity of an author; *when nothing better can be got*." In the South, however, his fortunes improved, and he wrote to Miller in February 1809 that he had collected a total of one hundred and twenty-five subscriptions. Shortly his publishers felt it was safe to print three hundred more copies of Volume I, and beginning with Volume II, published in January 1810, five hundred copies were issued for each later volume of this first edition.

Wilson's second extended trip in pursuit of both new birds and new subscriptions came within a year of the first. He crossed Pennsylvania on foot and set sail in a small skiff down the Ohio, reaching Louisville in mid-March 1810. Early in April he was in Lexington, three weeks later in Nashville, by the third week of May in Natchez, and soon thereafter in New Orleans. He returned to Philadelphia early in September.

Such were Wilson's two principal excursions in search of subscribers. Either directly or through agents established along his routes, a total of four hundred and fifty-nine subscriptions were sold. It is interesting to note the geographical distribution of this support. Pennsylvania contributed more than a quarter of the total, Philadelphia being credited with seventy and the raw young town of Pittsburgh with nineteen. Louisville contributed nothing, but in Natchez, Wilson sold twelve subscriptions, in Baltimore sixteen, and in New Orleans sixty. From all of New England, on the other hand, came barely two dozen; and as Wilson's letters indicated, New York and New Jersey were no more generous (although New York subsequently did better than the original response would have suggested).

Despite hardships and discouragements, however, Wilson's journeys were successful in two important respects: the necessary subscriptions were secured, and new birds were discovered. The *American Ornithology* was therefore able to continue publication, and was enriched by new material. The next two years were the most productive of Wilson's life. In 1811 the third and fourth volumes appeared, in 1812 the fifth and sixth. In 1813 the seventh volume was issued, and the eighth made ready for the press; but Wilson's health, never notably good, was failing. Still carrying the major burdens of publication, together with the triple task of observing and collecting his birds, mounting and painting them, and composing the text, he was unable to withstand an attack of dysentery, and died August 23, 1813.

Had Wilson not made his commercial tours of the eastern cities and hinterlands, the Ohio and Mississippi valley frontier, and the Deep South, his long travel letters, abounding in social comment, would not have been written; and his meeting with John James Audubon, an obscure storekeeper of Louisville, would never had occurred. For the letters the student must be grateful, for they show Wilson to have been a keen and frequently sardonic observer; but for the meeting, since made so much of, one can feel little but regret.

Alexander Wilson's role of social critic is not so incongruous as might first appear. The harshness of his boyhood and youth in Scotland had sharpened both his wits and his pen; he had suffered the poverty and injustice of the mill towns, and had reacted in satiric verses, one of which he was sentenced to burn on the steps of the Paisley jail. His most famous effort, the anonymous 200-line poem *Watty and Meg* (1792), was more genial but no less perceptive. Not too strangely, Robert Burns was rumored its author. There were certain affinities between the two men. Both these humbly born Scotsmen in their writing combined sentiment with a sharp sense of satire, and both were sturdy egalitarians. Wilson was no Burns in literary promise or fulfillment, but he brought to America a keen eye for human situations, and a verbal sense already well developed.

In addition, he was an adopted son of the metropolis, Philadelphia, and so qualified to pass judgment on the hinterlands and the provincial towns. Having escaped the religiosity of Scotland, he found congenial tolerance in Philadelphia, and held trenchant opinions of religious bigots. Perhaps unfairly, he tended to compare the broad, rich Pennsylvania Dutch farmlands around Philadelphia with less favored lands elsewhere. Add to these standards of judgment Wilson's own sensitive and rather solitary nature and his unique professional status, and one need not wonder at the wit and special bias of his observations.

On his first journey, Princeton College—"this spacious sanctuary of literature"—provided him with the odd spectacle of a professor of natural history who "scarce knew a *sparrow* from a *woodpecker*"; but he added, "from what passed between us I have hopes that he will pay more attention to this department of his profession than he has hitherto done." In New York, he was attracted to the public market, where "the butchers are nearly as dirty as their stalls; and the gutters, which descend into the common sewer below the market pass among the feet of the sellers of vegetables who occupy one side of the street." It was New England, however, which inspired his most mordant comments.

Religion was first to draw his fire. The trip from New York to New Haven was by ship, and upon landing, he realized "by the stillness and solemnity of the streets [that he was] in New England and that it was Sunday." Later in the same letter he said, "A man here is as much ashamed of being seen walking the streets on Sunday unless in going and returning from Church, as many honester fellows would be in being seen going to a bawdy house." Apparently Sabbath sobriety carried over into weekdays, for at a military muster in Middletown, Connecticut, Wilson came upon a place where "the crowd had formed a ring within which they danced to the catgut scrapings of an old Negro" and noticed that "the Spectators looked on with as much gravity as if they had been listening to a sermon, and the dancers laboured with such hard working seriousness that it seemed more like a pennance imposed on the poor devils for past sins than mere frolic amusement."

Parts of the Connecticut Valley he recognized for the good farmland it was and is, but the countryside between Hartford and Boston he found rugged, barren, and poor, the people far from attractive.

> Every 6 or 8 miles you came to a meeting house painted white with a Spire and a few houses – I could perceive little difference in the form or elevation of all their steeples. The people here make no distinction between Town and Township and passengers frequently asked the driver "What town are we now in?" when perhaps we were on the top of a miserable barren mountain several miles from a house. It is in vain to reason with them on the impropriety of this. Custom makes every absurdity proper. There is scarce any currency in this country but paper, and I solemnly declare that I do not recall of having seen *one dollar* since I left New York. Bills even of 25 and 50 cents, of a hundred different Banks whose very names one has never heard of before are continually in circulation – The jargon kume, kau, kaunt &c. for come, cow, count – is also general in the country. Their boasted Schools, if I may judge from the state of the Schoolhouses are no better than our own. Their politics except in some few districts *bitterly* federal. Lawyers swarm in every town like locusts. Almost every door has the word *Office* painted over it which like the web of a Spider, points out the place where the spoiler lurks for his prey. There is little or no improvement in Agriculture – in 50 miles I did not observe a single grain or stubble field, though the country has been cleared and settled these 150 years. In short the *Steady habits* of a great portion of the inhabitants of those parts of New England thro' which I passed seem to be laziness, law bickerings and religious hypocrisy.

Remarks even more cutting were contained in a letter to Lawson a few weeks later, with a final comment on New Englanders as "snappish and extortioners lazy and 200 years behind the Pennsylvanians in Agricultural improvements."

Of course we do not turn to Wilson for a balanced or properly informed estimate of conditions in rural New England. No doubt, within the narrow bounds of his preconceptions, his observations were just and accurate enough; but he did not bring to this situation any considerable knowledge of New England history. What he was seeing, and reflecting in his astringent comments was a rural society in a state of ferment and near-dissolution. The whole country had not been "cleared and settled these 150 years"; this hill region had largely been settled in the eighteenth century, and was already declining. For easy defense, and to avoid swamps and early frosts, pioneer farmers had chosen hilltops and hillsides—land initially not favorable for good farming, and soon worn out. As the early system of "town grants" under Puritan auspices broke down, tracts were sold outright to speculators, and a good portion of Wilson's "law bickerings" no doubt arose from land litigation aggravated by rural depression. In addition, the region through which Wilson traveled was being depopulated by emigration; for decades New Englanders had been pulling up stakes for the West, the Massachusetts tract of western New York state a particular goal. Finally, the "religious hypocrisy" which Wilson decried may have been part of the ferment which recently had brought Baptist, Presbyterian, or Methodist emotionalism (the sort of thing that always aroused Wilson's scorn) into the rural areas.

A similar religious fervor had swept the Ohio Valley a few years before Wilson journeyed there, and drew similar derisive comments from him. His description of frontier coarseness, slovenliness, and poverty anticipated by twenty years the acerb strictures of Mrs. Frances Trollope; and as he traveled deeper into the South, his anger at the usages of slavery grew. It revolted him to see Negroes beaten, just as earlier he had been distressed to see "wretchedly clad blacks" put up for public sale, "people handling them like black cattle."

Although Wilson's most piquant comments are apt to be derogatory, his letters were not simply exercises in spleen. His reports from the hinterlands were never without humor; even disappointment, fatigue, and primitive conditions of travel could not stultify his keen wit. Regardless of Wilson's limitations and special prejudices, these letters are useful, if minor, social documents; and, what is more germane to the present inquiry, they reveal America's first ornithologist as a perceptive and forthright commentator on matters far removed from his scientific pursuits.

4 *A Meeting of Consequence*

On March 19, 1810, Alexander Wilson by mere chance met John James Audubon. He entered the Audubon-Rosier store in Louisville in the hope of finding a subscriber to his work, and with no notion that the handsome young fellow back of the counter was anything more than a shopkeeper. Similarly, until Wilson stated his business and opened his sample volumes, Audubon had no inkling of his visitor's identity or profession. In the history of American ornithology, such a chance encounter might have been recorded as a happy accident, something for which the student could be grateful. To the contrary: that meeting in Louisville precipitated a partisan controversy which shows no signs of settlement, nearly a century and a half after the event.

Two things should be noted immediately. There is no valid evidence that ill-feeling arose between the two men at the time; the "Wilson-Audubon controversy" is largely a creature of later and lesser persons. Just as important is the fact that we have no wholly reliable primary source giving Wilson's feelings—if any—about the meeting; and Audubon's account was written twenty years afterward, when the quarrel had already been generated.

Audubon's narrative was published in the first volume of his *Ornithological Biography* (1831) as part of an article called "Louisville in Kentucky," one of the "Delineations" which were interspersed among the bird accounts. It is fairly lengthy, but may be summarized as follows. Wilson entered Audubon's store unannounced, came quickly to the object of his visit, displayed his volumes, and asked Audubon to subscribe. Much impressed, Audubon was about to sign, when his partner, Ferdinand Rosier, spoke in French from the next room, questioning the wisdom of the transaction, especially in view of Audubon's own collection of drawings, already greater than Wilson's. Audubon reconsidered, and shortly took down his own folio of drawings for Wilson's inspection. Wilson, considerably surprised, examined the drawings carefully, and asked permission to copy certain of them. Audubon, having at that time no intention of publishing his work, assented, asking only that the source be acknowledged. Later, noting Wilson's melancholy air, Audubon introduced him to his wife and friends, and went hunting with him, "and obtained birds which he had never before seen; but, reader, I did not subscribe to his work, for, even at that time, my collection was greater than his." After some days Wilson left Louisville for New Orleans, "little knowing how much his talents were appreciated in our little town, at least by myself and my friends."

Audubon then notes that their second and final meeting occurred in Philadelphia, where he called upon Wilson, who was "then drawing a White-headed Eagle." (This would date the meeting as occurring in 1811, the year Wilson's fourth volume, containing the eagle, was published.) Wilson received Audubon with civility, and took him to the exhibition rooms of Rembrandt Peale, but "spoke not of birds or drawings." Audubon, feeling at length that his company was not agreeable, left, and never saw Wilson again.

From Audubon's standpoint, the crucial passage of his account comes at the end:

> But judge of my astonishment some time after, when on reading the thirty-ninth page of the ninth volume of American Ornithology, I found in it the following paragraph: —
>
> "March 23, 1810. — I bade adieu to Louisville, to which place I had four letters of recommendation, and was taught to expect much

> of every thing there; but neither received one act of civility from those to whom I was recommended, one subscriber, nor one new bird; though I delivered my letters, ransacked the woods repeatedly, and visited all the characters likely to subscribe. Science or literature has not one friend in this place."

It was this entry in Wilson's diary, presumably, that prompted Audubon to relate his dealings with Wilson. The entry was printed by George Ord, Wilson's editor and biographer, in the last volume (1814) of the *American Ornithology*, as part of a thirty-five page sketch of the scientist's life. In the edition of 1825, Ord enlarged the sketch to almost two hundred pages, and added several new excerpts from Wilson's diary on the subject of the Louisville visit:

> March 17. — Rained and hailed all last night, set off at eight o'clock . . . arrive at Beargrass creek, and fasten my boat to a Kentucky one. Take my baggage and grope my way to Louisville — put up at the Indian Queen tavern, and gladly sit down to rest myself.
>
> March 18. — Rose quite refreshed. Found a number of land speculators here. Titles to lands in Kentucky subject to great disputes.
>
> March 19. — Rambling round the town with my gun. Examined Mr. ——'s drawings in crayons — very good. Saw two new birds he had, both *Motacillae.*
>
> March 20. — Set out this afternoon with the gun — killed nothing new. People in taverns here devour their meals. Many shopkeepers board in taverns — also boatmen, land speculators, merchants &c. *No naturalist to keep me company.*
>
> March 21. — Went out this afternoon shooting with Mr. A. Saw a number of Sandhill cranes. Pigeons numerous.
>
> March 23. — Packed up my things which I left in the care of a merchant here, to be sent on to Lexington; and having parted, with great regret, with my paroquet, to the gentlemen of the tavern, I bade adieu to Louisville, to which place I had four letters of recommendation, and was taught to expect much of every thing there; but neither received one act of civility from those to whom I was recommended, one subscriber, nor *one new bird*; though I delivered my letters, ransacked the woods repeatedly, and visited all the characters likely to subscribe. *Science or literature has not one friend in this place.* Everyone is so intent on making money that they can talk of nothing else; and they absolutely devour their meals that they may return the sooner to their business. Their manners correspond with their features.
>
> Good country this for lazy fellows: they plant corn, turn their

> pigs into the woods, and in the autumn feed upon corn and pork—they lounge about the rest of the year.

It appears that Audubon in 1830 or 1831 had not seen this expanded version of Wilson's journal—or, if he had, he kept silent. These entries compound the problem of Wilson's visit considerably. Audubon ("Mr. ——" and "Mr. A.") is mentioned here for the first time, and the references appear genuine, not contrived by Ord to fit later events or intentions. Ord had seen Audubon's paintings in 1824 when they were brought to Lawson for possible engraving, and had helped prevent their publication; but these references in the diary can scarcely be construed as part of his campaign against Audubon, since they contain at least partially favorable comment.

But something is amiss here. The reference to seeing "Sandhill cranes" in company with "Mr. A." is difficult to explain. Audubon, writing from recollections much later, made it plain that the birds were not sandhill but whooping cranes, "of which [Wilson] had not previously seen other than stuffed specimens. I told him that the white birds were the adults, and that the grey ones were the young. WILSON, in his article on the Whooping Crane, has alluded to this, but, as on other occasions, has not informed his readers whence the information came."

To some extent, Wilson's account (in *American Ornithology*, Volume VIII) corroborates Audubon's:

> On the tenth of February I met with several [whooping cranes] near the Waccamau river, in South Carolina; I also saw a flock at the ponds near Louisville, Kentucky, on the twentieth of March . . . It is highly probable that the species described by the naturalists as the Brown Crane (*Ardea Canadensis*) is nothing more than the young of the Hooping Crane.

Apparently then Wilson had seen "other than stuffed specimens" before coming to Louisville; the reference to South Carolina checks with his itinerary a year earlier through the states of the lower seaboard. But if he also saw whooping cranes on March 20 near Louisville, why does his journal entry for the next day record sandhill cranes? Like Audubon, Wilson erroneously considered the gray crane to be merely the young of the white whooping crane, and did not use the name "sandhill" to designate any bird in his *American Ornithology*.

The solution to this puzzle seems to appear in Ord's edition of Wilson of 1825. Under the whooping crane Ord said:

> In the first edition of this work our author expressed the conjecture that the Brown and Ash-colored Crane of Edwards is nothing more than the young of the Hooping Crane. This is an error into which he was led in consequence of never having seen a specimen of the bird in question . . . Peale's Museum at present contains a fine specimen of the Grus Canadensis, which was brought by the naturalists attached to Major Long's exploring party . . . It is known to travellers by the name of Sandhill Crane.

Ord was correct in distinguishing between the gray and white cranes, and his name "sandhill" for the former has been retained to the present time. (Audubon never acknowledged the distinction, and on Plate 261 portrayed the sandhill crane as the immature whooper.) But the problem of the diary reference remains; and we are left to suppose either that Ord changed the diary to read "sandhill" or that he chose to ignore Wilson's actual reference to "a number of Sandhill cranes" when he charged that Wilson had never seen "a specimen of the bird in question." Considering other of Ord's actions, the first seems the more probable conjecture.

Finally there is the diary reference to the paroquet. According to the excerpt Ord provides, Wilson wrote ". . . and having parted, with great regret, with my paroquet, to the gentlemen of the tavern, I bade adieu to Louisville." Although Wilson's language is not entirely clear, the passage seems to mean that the ornithologist left his paroquet with the gentlemen of the tavern at Louisville. But he did nothing of the sort. His descriptive text on the paroquet (in the third volume, published 1811) relates that he carried the bird from Big Bone Lick (above Louisville) to shipboard at New Orleans; shortly after the voyage began, the bird flew overboard and disappeared in the Gulf of Mexico. A letter from Wilson to James Gibb, dated March 4, 1811, precisely corroborates this tale.

The crucial difficulty in clearing up these contradictions is the fact that Wilson's journal has disappeared. What we have of it comes by way of George Ord; and the plain truth is that Ord is not to be trusted. The first hint of this fact appears when one compares the first with later editions of the seventh, eighth, and ninth volumes of *American*

Ornithology. The later editions contain sections that refer to Wilson in the third person, but also many passages that use "I" in a confusing way—and all without proper concern for distinguishing Wilson's words from those of his editor. A closer examination reveals that Ord republished these volumes in 1824 and 1825 without acknowledging in any clear fashion his own extensive changes in Wilson's text.

A study of Ord's changes indicates that he conceived it his duty to amend and correct Wilson, not merely edit him—and indeed, he managed to eliminate an error here and there, as in the case of the golden and "ring-tailed" eagles, the sandhill and whooping cranes, the tufted and ring-necked ducks, and so forth. His niggling and pretentious scholarship, however, tends to cancel the effect of his corrections, and his arbitrary changes in common names are often more confusing than enlightening. In any event, there is no excuse for his irresponsible execution of the editor's task.

In his biographical sketch of Wilson, Ord printed a number of the ornithologist's letters—and thereby damned himself even more effectively than by his textual meddling. Not merely did Ord correct spelling, punctuation, and grammar; he altered the letters to suit himself, eliminating passages, changing meanings, inserting phrases, often without any sort of acknowledgment. Nor was he completely ignorant of proper usage in these matters; for example, in printing the letter to Daniel H. Miller (quoted above) he deleted the words "bawdy house" and "religious hypocrisy" by substituting asterisks. But elsewhere he gave no sign of his cavalier abuse of the editor's prerogatives. To cite but one instance: Wilson's line, "Their politics except in some few districts *bitterly* federal," apparently offended Ord, who dropped it entirely, and gave no sign.

Such gross mishandling of sources must cast doubt upon any statement based on Ord's authority—and especially upon the excerpts from Wilson's journal, for which there is neither a surviving manuscript nor dependable corroborative testimony (Charles Waterton's assertions scarcely falling under the latter rubric). One piece of collateral evidence, the letter Wilson wrote to Lawson from Lexington on April 6, would tend negatively to show that the Louisville fiasco—if such it was—did not weigh heavily on Wilson, for he made no mention of it two weeks later. He seemed in good enough spirits, and full of determination; and although he made an irate comment or two, he did not overflow with the Trollope-like malice emphasized by Ord's excerpts.

Presumably, then, Ord was capable of altering not only Wilson's letters but his diary also, either in substance or spirit, to suit his purpose; but what does that purpose appear to be? Not initially to attack Audubon, for in 1814 Audubon's work was virtually unknown and offered no threat to Wilson's reputation. In 1824, however, Audubon had come to Philadelphia seeking a publisher. Ord had seen his paintings, and no doubt recognized that they threatened both Wilson's eminence and the new edition he himself was then preparing. Yet in the absence of direct evidence, Ord's intent has to be inferred from his writing. He appears to have been concerned with more than assembling and preparing for publication the remnants of Wilson's work; he was interested also in standing forth both as Wilson's champion and defender, and as his corrector and successor. He conveys the impression that Wilson was a man appreciated by few but Ord himself, one whose way was beset by such fools and knaves as the people of Louisville. This feeling could be merely the outgrowth of a warm friendship; but this explanation is too simple. Malvina Lawson, daughter of the engraver, in a memoir has indicated that Ord was an unbearably opinionated man with no gift for friendship. Certainly Ord's high-handed editorial methods and his comments correcting Wilson smack more of the irascible dominie than the devoted friend.

Whether this minor ornithologist and editor wrought well or ill would be quite unimportant, were it not for the fact that a great deal of writing about Wilson has depended on Ord's opinions and Ord's "documents," and so has gone awry. A good case in point is the concern felt over Ord's charge that Thomas Jefferson treated Wilson in an inexcusably shabby way. Ord's story, buttressed by his own versions of letters passed between William Bartram, Wilson, and Jefferson, is that Jefferson apparently showed "contemptuous neglect" of Wilson's request that he be allowed to accompany Pike's expedition to the Arkansas and Red rivers (1806), even though he knew from Bartram's recommendation and Wilson's earlier gifts of drawings that the ornithologist was well qualified. Jefferson, according to Ord, was "either so scandalized at the informal application of our ornithologist, or so occupied in the great concerns of his exalted station, that no answer was returned to the overture." Ord published his charges in his biographical account of Wilson, and they came to the attention of the former President in 1818.

The aging Jefferson, distressed by this attack, searched unsuccessfully among his own records and correspondence to discover the truth of the matter. He then wrote to General James Wilkinson, the officer who had been in charge of arranging the Pike expedition, noting that he himself could find "not a scrip of the pen on the subject of that expedition," and suggesting that the enterprise was primarily a military scouting and exploring one, ordered by Wilkinson under a general commission, and "too rapid to be accommodated to the pursuits of scientific men." Wilkinson's answer confirmed Jefferson's recollections of the matter, and noted that Pike's own account of the expedition demonstrated "its utter inaptitude to the deliberate investigations of the naturalist." * Precisely why the Wilson-Bartram petition went unanswered is still not explained, but it is clear that Jefferson's direct authority over the Pike expedition was remote, and in no way comparable to his personal concern with the expedition of Lewis and Clark. It therefore seems probable that he referred Wilson's letter to a subordinate, who failed to take proper action.

Whatever the anger felt by George Ord in this affair, it is evident that Wilson by no means lost his affection for Jefferson, since he was happy to include the President's remarks on the song of the wood thrush in *American Ornithology*. This he did with the remark that he was quoting "a letter from a distinguished American gentleman . . . whose name, were I at liberty to give it, would do honor to my humble performance, and render any further observations on the subject from me unnecessary." The letter was written by Jefferson in April 1805, primarily to thank Wilson for "elegant drawings" he had sent

* The matter of the Pike expedition is fully discussed in James S. Wilson, *Alexander Wilson* (New York, 1906), pp. 78–91.

to the President. In the manner of amateur ornithologists of every station of life, Jefferson then went on to describe a mysterious bird he had encountered. The description he offered was confusing, properly pertaining to no North American bird; but Wilson, perhaps disingenuously, extracted Jefferson's remarks on the bird's song and applied them to the wood thrush.

That relations betwen the two men continued to be cordial is indicated by the fact that Jefferson was one of Wilson's first subscribers, offering his support as early as October 1807, on the basis of the prospectus. In December 1808 Jefferson received Wilson in Washington — "very kindly," according to Wilson himself. In short, it seems plain that Wilson never lost his early admiration for Jefferson, and did not break with him because of the "contemptuous neglect" erroneously inferred by Ord.

But if Ord was hasty and unjust in indicting Jefferson, he was on firm ground when in 1840 he accused Audubon of copying bird figures from Wilson. Ord made his charges before the American Philosophical Society, of which he had been secretary, vice-president, and councilor. He directed the attention of the society to a passage in *Ornithological Biography* in which Audubon charged that Wilson had copied the figure of the "Small-headed Flycatcher" from Audubon's "already large collection of drawings," without acknowledging the source. Ord denied this, asserting that Wilson's diary disproved the charge, and that he himself had been with Wilson earlier, when the bird was first collected. But Ord was not content with refutation; he went on to say that Audubon's figures for the female red-winged blackbird and the female Mississippi kite were "copied from the American Ornithology, without the least acknowledgment of the source from whence they had been derived."

How much Wilson derived from Audubon's drawings and observations during their short association in Louisville is impossible to say; but no bird figure executed in Audubon's distinctive later manner can be found in Wilson, and certainly there is little resemblance between Wilson's "Small-headed Flycatcher" and Audubon's. But on the other hand, three of Wilson's figures are to be found in Audubon: the two given by Ord, and the "female" cerulean warbler (Plate 48 in Audubon, Plate 17 in Wilson). In Audubon the kite is reversed, deprived of a toe, and designated "female" (although the sexes are not readily distinguishable). The blackbird is similar in every important respect. The cerulean warbler is partially obscured by leaves, and is called "female" – incorrectly, Wilson's bird being plainly a male. In addition to these unmistakable plagiarisms, Audubon drew a flicker (Figure 1, Plate 37) which duplicates Wilson's in all but details of plumage, and an orchard oriole and a tufted titmouse in attitudes strongly reminiscent of those found in Wilson.

Three explanations suggest themselves. The first is that Wilson's figures were copied from early Audubon drawings, when the two ornithologists met in March 1810. This notion, however, may be dismissed. Wilson's cerulean warbler was already drawn, engraved, and printed; it was to be found in one of the volumes which were opened for inspection on Audubon's counter. Furthermore, both the blackbird and the kite were executed in the forthright Wilson manner, not in the more active style of Audubon. Finally, it is inconceivable that Wilson could have copied Audubon's kite so minutely (and Lawson engraved it so exactly) that the two birds should superimpose perfectly, as they do when Wilson's figure is reversed and placed over Audubon's. It is far more likely that the Audubon figure was copied from Lawson's final engraving.

The second explanation is that these three birds, admittedly cribbed, were the work of a subordinate, not of Audubon himself. Herrick, the best of Audubon's biographers, takes this view, asserting that Robert Havell (Audubon's engraver) or one of his assistants may have placed the kite on the plate without Audubon's sanction. (Herrick dismisses, for reasons not clear, the charge of plagiarism of the blackbird, and appears not to be aware that the cerulean warbler is also copied.) This idea is difficult to accept. Audubon was nothing if not an artist, and he scarcely would have drawn only the top figure of the kite plate without realizing that the resulting composition greatly lacked weight in the center (where the Wilson bird was placed). It also seems unlikely that even under the pressure of great tasks, Audubon would have countenanced such meddling by subordinates. The magnificent elephant folio edition of *The Birds of America* was no mere commercial venture; it was Audubon's creation, the work of his life, and scarcely to be left to the discretion of engravers. But even if we assume Herrick's unlikely notion — must we not also assume that Audubon, upon seeing the alterations made, would ask whence the figures came? And, being told, would either acknowledge his debt or rework the plate?

The third explanation seems the most straightforward and plausible one. It is that Audubon copied three birds from Wilson, without apology, explanation, or acknowledgment. The fact that such pirating, with or without admission of the source, was fairly common at the time does not absolve Audubon, especially when it is recalled that he accused Wilson of this offense. Nor does it appear fruitful to postulate subtle motives or invent exculpatory excuses. Audubon's achievements are magnificent, needing no justification — but he himself is not immaculate. He was a man not wholly honest, wholly reliable, wholly pure; he was a mixture, and in his special way a genius, and certainly not bound by a foolish consistency. So much the student must know if he would understand Audubon.

The student may also discover that Audubon was ultimately untouched by such affairs as this controversy with the partisans of Wilson, and careless of the outcome. Thus the extraordinary inconsistency of his statements about helping Wilson; for after saying in his first volume of text that he obtained for Wilson "birds which he had never before seen," Audubon in the third volume denied his own assertion: "But alas! WILSON was with me only a few times, and then *nothing* worthy of his attention was procured."

Walt Whitman wrote, "Do I contradict myself? Very well then, I contradict myself. (I am large, I contain multitudes.)" Audubon's answer at last would have been the same.

5 *Fulfilling Genius: John James Audubon*

If it were possible to find a single key to the personality of the extraordinary man who was John James Audubon, that key would be the word *artist*; and not merely artist as manipulator of phrases or of pencil and paint, but artist as devotee of the creative, communicative act. Stephen Benét said Audubon lived to look at birds, which is part of the truth; but more fundamentally, he lived to impart his vision. For all his abundance and complexity, Audubon was a singularly dedicated man. In his own words, he was "a devoted and enthusiastic lover of Nature's beauteous and wondrous works . . . from the earliest period," and at length he knew that his love could not go uncelebrated. No less than William Lloyd Garrison, Audubon would be heard.

Audubon was born in 1785, at the seaport town of Aux Cayes near the southwest tip of the Caribbean island called Hispaniola by Columbus, and known to its French rulers as Saint Domingue. He was, it appears, the bastard son of the French naval officer Jean Audubon and a French Creole woman; but his father acknowledged him, educated him in France, and sent him at eighteen to America to live on one of the Audubon properties, Mill Grove near Norristown, Pennsylvania. Early known as Jean Rabin, Audubon appears to have received (at age fifteen) the baptismal name of Jean Jacques Fougère. Later he styled himself Jean Jacques Laforest Audubon; but in America he soon shortened and anglicized the name, and the title page of his first great folio read: *The Birds of America* . . . by John James Audubon.

Of course it is greatly important to the biographer of Audubon to know that he was justly and even indulgently treated by his father, and that his youth was generally a happy one. In the narrow sense, however, the special importance to be attached to his earlier years in France arises from his training in art, at the school of Jacques-Louis David in Paris. Audubon himself claimed that his hand was first guided by this famous classicist painter. Nevertheless it is difficult to detect any immediate effect of Audubon's art study in the paintings of birds he did as a youth in France and America. Perhaps it was hard for the fledgling painter to incorporate David's classical rules with so minor a discipline as bird painting. Yet he was later to achieve just such a union, producing in his mature years bird pictures combining the greatest fidelity and animation with as rigid a sense of classical composition as ever was shown by David.

If the early bird drawings (surviving examples are dated 1805 and 1806, France, and 1807, America) scarcely hint at the great paintings Audubon was to produce in a decade or two, they indicate that this gifted French youth was interested in birds from the start, and did not, as did Wilson, begin his study in middle life. They also provide a hint that Audubon had yet to find himself, both artistically and in other ways. These drawings were the casual and at times careless work of an insouciant young man, an international vacationer who was devoted to nature but not ruled by her. Shortly, however, Audubon was to change both his geographical position and his way of living. Mill Grove, the paternal estate where the young Audubon played at being lord of the manor, was not to produce the work which the world would acclaim. Not the placid valley of the Perkiomen, not the towns and fields and woodlots of this long-settled region, but the forests and brakes and swamps of the Ohio and Mississippi valleys largely engendered *The Birds of America.* In 1807 Audubon set out for Kentucky, avowedly to make his fortune as a merchant, actually to develop his life work with birds. His bride, Lucy Bakewell, was soon with him, and for twelve years the frontier was their home.

"Frontier" may be an ambiguous term. Audubon was not going off to barter his goods with the Indians, or to establish a wilderness trading post. Kentucky's Blue Grass region had been discovered by Daniel Boone nearly forty years earlier, and in 1776 Boone laid out the Wilderness Trail which brought settlers through the Cumberland Gap to this favored country. By the end of the Revolution there were twenty-five thousand settlers here and in other sections of the trans-Allegheny west. George Rogers Clarke founded Louisville in 1778; by the time the Audubons arrived, the town had a thousand people. The Indians of the region had been pacified or driven out, and Negro slavery had come. Therefore Kentucky was no longer a howling wilderness, and its population no longer the "cutting edge" of the frontier.

Yet wilderness there was, huge stretches of it, and it was Audubon's somber privilege to be witness and recorder of its decline, from the day he first saw "the grandeur and beauty of those almost uninhabited shores" to the time when the river valley would be "more or less covered with villages, farms, and towns, where the din of hammers and machinery is constantly heard." And as to the inhabitants: if they were no longer pioneers in buckskin, they were yet far from being gentry in buckles and lace. Alexander Wilson's trenchant descriptions of the people are borne out again and again by Audubon, who was himself nearly the victim of lawlessness, and who has much to say about the river folk, the squatters, the backwoodsmen, and that part of the population "derived from the refuse of every other country." The cities of the river valley, especially those of the Deep South, were civilized enough; but elsewhere life was lived much as it must be on all frontiers.

Audubon, in contrast to Wilson, has been celebrated in many books, both sentimental and scholarly. There is no need here to recount his comings and goings in detail, nor to discuss his personal life, always interesting but usually given a disproportionate amount of space. Our concern is with his career as an ornithologist, and the unadorned facts are enough as a start.

Hardly cut out for mercantile pursuits, Audubon spent much time observing, collecting, and drawing birds when he should properly have been attending to business — which was one cause for the failure of the Audubon-Rosier partnership, dissolved in 1811. Living in the little town of Henderson, Kentucky, from 1811 to 1819, Audubon continued his studies, while trying and failing at several commercial enterprises. Adjudged bankrupt in 1819, he left Henderson for Cincinnati, where he spent nearly a year employed in the private natural history museum organized by Dr. Daniel Drake. Here he learned much of "closet" ornithology — chiefly taxidermy and taxonomy. Late in 1820 he set out from Cincinnati for a journey of observation and collection down the rivers to New Orleans, taking with him Joseph Mason, a young botanist who had much to do with the beautiful floral backgrounds that grace *The Birds of America.* Working in and near New Orleans, Audubon by 1824 had so far advanced his collection of paintings that he returned to the East to find a publisher. (Years later Audubon stated that only upon meeting Charles Lucien Bonaparte during his 1824 journey did he receive the idea "of presenting the fruits of [his] labors to the world"; but this assertion was part of his case vis-à-vis Wilson, and can be ignored.)

Philadelphia, the capital of American natural science, was of course his first objective. It would seem only fitting that the city which had nurtured Wilson's excellent work should also serve Audubon. But it was not to be. There were particular reasons why Audubon was refused: he was thought by some to be flamboyant and unscientific, by others to embody a threat to the city's own Wilson, by still others to be overambitious (his proposed work was to cost not $120 a set, but $1,000). Ord and Lawson, involved in a new edition of *American Ornithology*, were hostile; Titian Peale, himself something of a bird painter, was collaborating with Bonaparte in a supplement to Wilson's work, and was uncoöperative. Yet there was more to the Philadelphia rebuff than mere financial considerations. The city was changing; the big "original" men no longer flourished; those who remained to set the tone of art and learning were of the second order, with vested interests in what had gone before. Barton, the inspired amateur, was long gone, the aged William Bartram had died the previous year, and of course Alexander Wilson was dead. Charles Willson Peale, like his friend Thomas Jefferson, had reached his eighties, and was soon to die. His museum had already become a stock company, losing its earlier, more personal character. Peale's sons, though artists of remarkable competence and craftsmanship, were lesser persons. In ornithology there was only George Ord and Thomas Say, the latter primarily an entomologist. Bonaparte was but a visitor. To be sure, the Philosophical Society still functioned—Ord was then serving as secretary—and the Academy of Natural Sciences (with Ord as vice-president) was in the process of building up its bird collection. But the institutions were greater than the men. Philadelphia was not as it had been.

New York received Audubon more cordially, but could not offer a publisher for his work. Perhaps the project was too grandiose for any American house to undertake. Doubtless Bonaparte had been right in advising Audubon to seek a publisher in Europe; but Audubon lacked the money to make the voyage, and so for a time nothing could be done. He returned to his wife in Louisiana, continued his bird work, gave lessons in dancing, fencing, drawing, and French, and saved money for passage. On May 17, 1826, he set sail for Liverpool on the schooner *Delos*.

✢ ✢ ✢

In Great Britain there came to Audubon fame and notoriety, praise and abuse, the friendship of many powerful persons and the enmity of a few. At times he was close to bankruptcy; again, he was relatively affluent. But his great and crucial achievement was securing the publication of *The Birds of America*, begun by W. H. Lizars of Edinburgh late in 1826, soon taken over by the Havells of London, and completed by Robert Havell in 1838. In Audubon's own words, "This work, comprising four hundred and thirty-five plates, and one thousand and sixty-five figures, was finished on the 20th of June 1838, without the continuity of its execution having been broken for a single day, and the numbers having been delivered with exemplary regularity; for all which I am indebted to my friend and Engraver, Mr. Robert Havell."

This plain recital of fact conceals the years of struggle, during which Audubon collected and painted many new birds, supervised the vast work of engraving and coloring, solicited most of the subscriptions, and personally supervised the financing of the entire $100,000 publishing project. Yet Audubon's words convey the one fact which is finally significant: *The Birds of America* appeared, the work which was (in the words of Baron Cuvier) "le monument le plus magnifique qui ait encore été élevé à l'ornithologie" saw the light of day.

Cuvier's words apply now as they applied then. *The Birds of America* remains "the most magnificent monument yet raised to ornithology"; no subsequent work has been projected on so heroic a scale, nor executed with such immense bravura. Audubon's achievement retains its vigor and force; and because this is true, it is possible today to understand, on much the same terms as applied then, the impact of Audubon's work upon his own time. The work seems quintessentially American in its sheer physical size (the untrimmed pages measured nearly twenty-seven by forty inches), in its exuberant color, its complexity and variety, its unbounded vitality. And so it appeared at the time. "Imagine," said the French critic Philarète-Chasles, "a landscape wholly American, trees, flowers, grass, even the tints of the sky and waters, quickened with a life that is real, peculiar, trans-Atlantic. . . It is a real and palpable vision of the New World, with its atmosphere, its imposing vegetation, and its tribes which know not the yoke of man." The British ornithologist William Swainson, viewing Audubon's work, declared that the mantle of great bird art, long unclaimed, had "at length been recovered in the forests of America."

These comments suggest that much of Audubon's appeal was based on the vast, undefiled wilderness he seemed to represent. The American Woodsman, as he was called, was a romantic figure in an age of Romanticism. He knew, and in his work celebrated, Wordsworth's "impulse from a vernal wood"; he had trod the banks of the Susquehanna, where Southey and Coleridge had planned to found their ideal pantisocratic society; with Byron's Manfred, his joy was in the wilderness; with Keats, he had seen beauty in "the mid-forest brake, Rich with a sprinkling of fair musk-rose blooms." To a society increasingly concerned with the urban ugliness of industrialism, and turning to nature for refuge, Audubon brought a vision of the New World, beautiful, unspoiled, free.

Even more explicitly than did his paintings, his writings expressed the optimism, the color and fullness—and even the danger—which for many Europeans marked the American venture in the new land. Between 1831 and 1839, Audubon published (in Edinburgh) his *Ornithological Biography*, five volumes of text on the birds figured in his *Birds of America*. Many passages on the birds themselves were celebrations of the American wilderness; but Audubon was not content with the topical limits imposed by bird accounts, and interspersed among them sixty "Delineations of American Scenery and Manners." In most of the "Scenery" pieces we find Audubon in the familiar role of devotee of the wilds. In the "Manners" sections we discover, as in Wilson's letters, the social commentator, keen, witty, occasionally sentimental, now and again cruel. Like Wilson, Audubon was a patriot, and reacted to various aspects of American society with the true patriot's critical discrimination. Yet whatever his strictures, the over-all impression he conveys is one of love for his adopted land, and of hope, of acceptance, even of wonder. One could never call Audubon a jingo, but certainly he must be called an enthusiast in the American cause.

"The Squatters of the Mississippi" is perhaps the most typical of his reports on life as he had seen it lived on the frontier. A colorful and sturdily optimistic tale, it describes how a self-reliant yeoman family moves from worn-out fields in Virginia to an unclaimed tract on the west bank of the Mississippi; how together they clear the land, build a house, secure food by hunting the ever-abundant game, plant crops, fell timber, and find a market for their raft of logs; and how the area receives new immigrants, until at length "where a single cabin once stood, a neat village is now to be seen." Audubon concludes:

> Thus are the vast frontiers of our country peopled, and thus does cultivation, year after year, extend over the western wilds. Time will no doubt be, when the great valley of the Mississippi, still covered with primeval forests, interspersed with swamps, will smile with corn-fields and orchards, and enlightened nations will rejoice in the bounties of Providence.

Even more idyllic is his description of life in the Great Pine Swamp, a tract of timber in Northumberland County, Pennsylvania. Going there to obtain new birds, Audubon stayed at the house of the lumberman Jedediah Irish, deep in the forest. Describing his host, Audubon says:

> Reader, to describe to you the qualities of that excellent man were vain; you should know him, as I do, to estimate the value of such men in our sequestered forests . . . The long walks and long talks we had together I never can forget, or the many beautiful birds which we pursued, shot, and admired. The juicy venison, excellent bear flesh, and delightful trout that daily formed our food, methinks I can still enjoy. And then, what pleasure I had in listening to him as he read his favourite poems of BURNS, while my pencil was occupied in smoothing and softening the drawing of the bird before me! Was not this enough to recall to my mind the early impression that had been made upon it by the description of the golden age, which I here found realised?

It is not difficult to imagine the effect of such writing on an age still looking back to Rousseau.

But Audubon was not inclined to pass over the more violent and somber aspects of frontier life. If "The Squatters of the Mississippi" is a backwoods idyll, "The Regulators" is a grim tale of a horse thief who is caught by self-appointed vigilantes, killed, and decapitated, his head being stuck on a sharpened tree limb as a warning to others. If Audubon at one place acclaims "Hospitality in the Woods," elsewhere he tells how he narrowly missed being murdered in his sleep by vicious settlers in whose cabin he had taken refuge for the night. Audubon hastens to assure his readers that such an event is exceedingly rare in his "abundant and free country," but the grimness of the story remains. Again, if Audubon (himself a slaveholder) can indicate acceptance of the practice of Negro slavery (as in "Scipio and the Bear"), in "The Runaway" he gives a touching account of the effects of separating Negro families by selling husband, wife, and children to different masters.

There are many other aspects to Audubon's "Delineations," some of which will be mentioned in later chapters. Because it concerns the impression Audubon made on his own time, however, one further aspect should be noted here—that is, the extraordinary personal warmth and perceptiveness which many of these accounts show. Several of the "Delineations" concern neither scenery nor manners, but are character sketches of people Audubon had known. In his account of Thomas Bewick, Audubon is at his most genial, showing how keenly he reacted to the personality of this unusual man, and how quick he was to appreciate grace and kindliness. But there is no hero-worship here; Audubon responds to Bewick as an equal, with warmth, gaety, and humor. At one point he writes:

> Now and then he would start and exclaim, "Oh, that I were young again! I would go to America too. Hey! what a country it will be, Mr. AUDUBON." I retorted by exclaiming, "Hey! what a country it is already, Mr. BEWICK!"

In two sketches dealing with the strange genius Rafinesque, Audubon is at his most satirical. "The Traveller and the Polecat" shows the hapless "Mr. D. T." (elsewhere "Mr. deT.") being encouraged by Audubon to approach a skunk, while innocently exclaiming, "Mr. Audubon, is that not a beautiful squirrel?" Gleefully the ornithologist relates the inevitable outcome of such an encounter. "The Eccentric Naturalist" is a similarly cruel lampoon, detailing the various hoaxes which Audubon visited upon his odd companion. These accounts reflect little credit on their author, but they serve to remind us that he was a colorful and complex individual.

Indeed, everything which Audubon did seems to direct our attention to the man himself. In a manner rare among scientists, the personality of this ornithologist permeates and even dominates his work. Audubon the painter, Audubon the observer and investigator, Audubon the bird biographer, Audubon the woodsman and teller of tales—all these are manifestations of the larger whole, the Audubon personality; and this fact helps explain the impression the man made beyond the circles of his special pursuits. Sir Walter Scott was scarcely an expert critic of either science or bird art, but he had no need to be; he responded to Audubon the man. After meeting the ornithologist, he wrote in his journal:

> He is an American by naturalization, a Frenchman by birth; but less of a Frenchman than I have ever seen—no dash, or glimmer, or shine about him, but great simplicity of manners and behavior; slight in person, and plainly dressed; wears long hair, which time has not yet tinged; his countenance acute, handsome, and interesting, but still simplicity is the predominant characteristic.

Another view of Audubon is given by an anonymous writer in the London *Athenaeum*:

> We can remember when his portfolio excited delight in Edinburgh, London, and Paris, rivalling in smaller circles a new Waverley novel. The man also was not a man to be seen and forgotten, or passed on the pavement without glances of surprise and scrutiny. The tall and somewhat stooping form, the clothes not made by a West-end but by a Far West tailor, the steady, rapid, springing step, the long hair, the aquiline features, and the glowing angry eyes, — the expression of a handsome man conscious of ceasing to be young, and an air and manner which told you that whoever you might be he was John Audubon, will never be forgotten by anyone who knew or saw him.*

Two rather diverse pictures, yes — but alike in emphasizing the personal impact which Audubon made. There come to mind descriptions of another notable visiting American, also a scientist of international reputation, also a person of apparent simplicity, with long hair and home-made clothes, also a self-made man of humble origins, also a writer, a cosmopolitan, a man of grace and charm, and a friend of the great and powerful. That man is of course Benjamin Franklin; and for all the differences of time, station, and attainments, the comparison is just. In the eighteenth century, no American scientist impressed Europe as did Benjamin Franklin; in the nineteenth, none as did John James Audubon. And in the homeland at least, the fame of both endures. Franklin is immortal; and as for Audubon, such were his achievements and such was his personality that today he is the best remembered scientist of nineteenth-century America.

Audubon's great initial success was in Europe, as the foregoing would indicate and as his subscription records show. In 1831 he listed one hundred and eighty subscribers to *The Birds of America,* all but eighteen of them British (twenty-nine from the Manchester area alone) and only seven of them American. But recognition in America was quick in coming, once Audubon had achieved fame abroad. Among many indications of his growing American reputation, his

* Both these comments on Audubon are quoted by Francis Hobart Herrick, *Audubon the Naturalist* (2 vols.; New York: Appleton-Century-Crofts, 1917), I, 367, 200.

subscription list is only the most obvious and mensurable. Nearly all of the sixty-three new subscriptions given in 1834 were from the United States, several of them taken out by institutions. A financial crisis in Britain in 1837 helped reduce the list of British subscribers sharply, and two years later the Manchester group, for example, was down to nine. The final list, given in the fifth volume of *Ornithological Biography,* showed eighty-two American subscribers to seventy-nine European.

The distribution of Audubon's American support provides food for thought. Immediately a contrast to Wilson's experience suggests itself, for Audubon procured only five Pennsylvania subscriptions (all from Philadelphia, two from institutions) while on the other hand Boston and its environs treated him handsomely. To Audubon Philadelphia was "this icy city," Boston "this fair city"—and the epithets indicate the treatment he received. One of his early New England champions had been Edward Everett, congressman from Massachusetts and later governor of the commonwealth, who was instrumental in obtaining a subscription on behalf of the Congressional Library, and who sponsored legislation to admit *The Birds of America* duty free. The Boston Athenaeum, through Thomas H. Perkins, had appeared among the few American subscribers on the first list, and on the second was "Harvard University, Cambridge, Massachusetts, Josiah Quincey, President."

Several prominent New Englanders were praised by Audubon for assisting him in his tasks—perhaps the most unexpected of these persons being "the Honourable DANIEL WEBSTER," who sent the two Labrador ducks appearing on Audubon's plate, having killed them off "the Vineyard Islands." In all, the Boston area had seventeen subscribers on the final list, and the rest of New England six more. Thus Audubon's experience here was precisely the reverse of Wilson's. Pennsylvania contributed more than a quarter of Wilson's subscriptions, while New England did the same for Audubon; and New England's six per cent for Wilson had its counterpart in Pennsylvania's six per cent for Audubon. Clearly, both regions had changed, and here was one of the signs. In the support which New England offered Audubon was mirrored not merely the changes wrought by rum and cotton, textiles and whaling and the China trade, but also the shift of America's cultural center from Philadelphia to Boston.

New York City, where Wilson ultimately did rather well, was quite as generous as Boston in subscribing to Audubon (although on the basis of population, the metropolis should have done three times as well). "Columbia College of New York" subscribed, as seventeen individuals did also. Southern cities gave Audubon a mixed reception; the two largest, Baltimore and New Orleans, taking only six subscriptions between them, no more than the total for Savannah, the smallest of the major seaboard towns. Charleston, center of natural science in the South, subscribed for four copies, three for institutions. (John Bachman, the famous Charleston naturalist, did not subscribe, but received from Audubon a gift copy of *The Birds of America*, handsomely bound in Russian leather.) The remainder of Audubon's subscriptions were scattered: several from state governments, plus a few others, as widely distributed as Albany, Louisville, and Mobile.

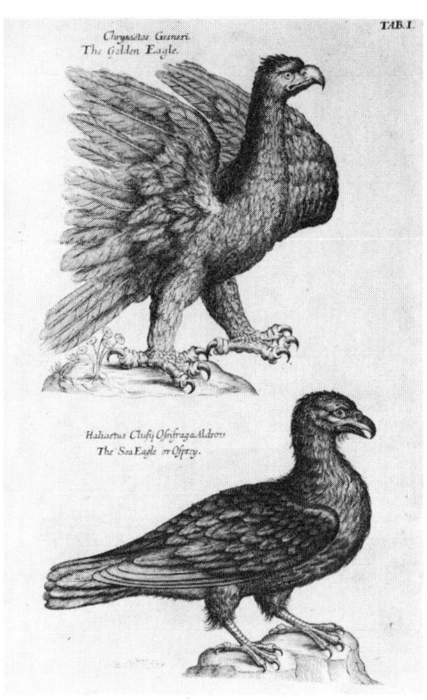

13. Plate 1 is entirely in the medieval manner; the eagle balances precariously on dragon-like claws, his right wing short and ragged, his left one impossibly distorted, his neck elongated, his eye fiercely staring. The osprey, anatomically more plausible, has no plumage pattern; its feathers are scaly on the back, furry on the neck and breast.

PROGRESS IN BIRD ART from medieval grotesquerie to accurate drawing may be seen in three plates from a single work, Ray's edition of "The Ornithology of Francis Willughby" (1678).

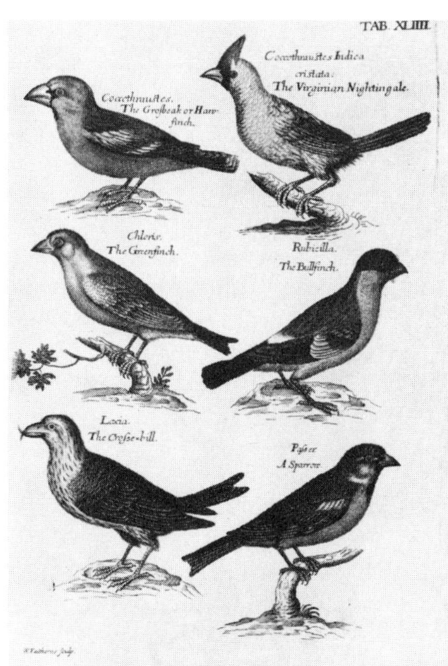

14. Plate 44 contains six recognizable birds (one, the "Virginian Nightingale," is the American cardinal). But there is little life in them, and they are arranged without regard for artistic effect.

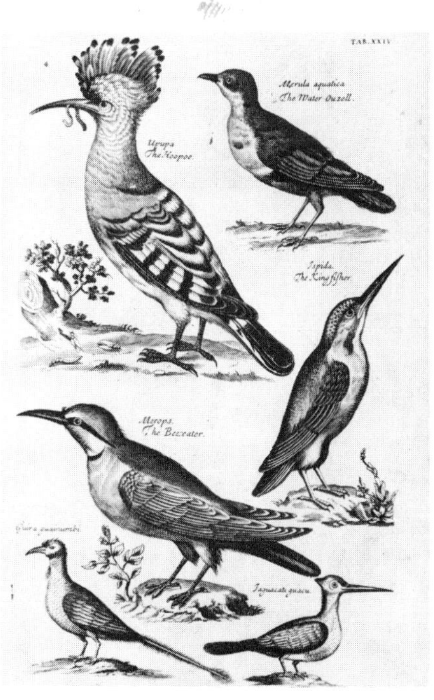

15. Plate 24 shows three birds rendered accurately and with lifelike stance. (The kingfisher pose may not be characteristic, but the drawing is well managed.) The ouzel (uppermost) is also convincing; only the bottom figures of exotic birds are poor. The plate as a whole is well composed.

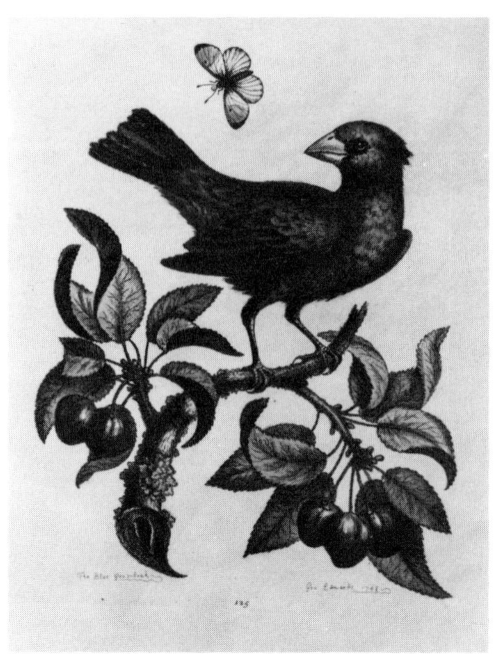

16. The blue grosbeak appears on a branch laden with bright cherries and intensely green leaves, and turns to look at a yellow butterfly.

FURTHER ADVANCE in British bird drawing is shown in Edwards' "Natural History of Birds," completed in 1751. Especially notable is the use of flowers, fruits, and greenery as decorative features.

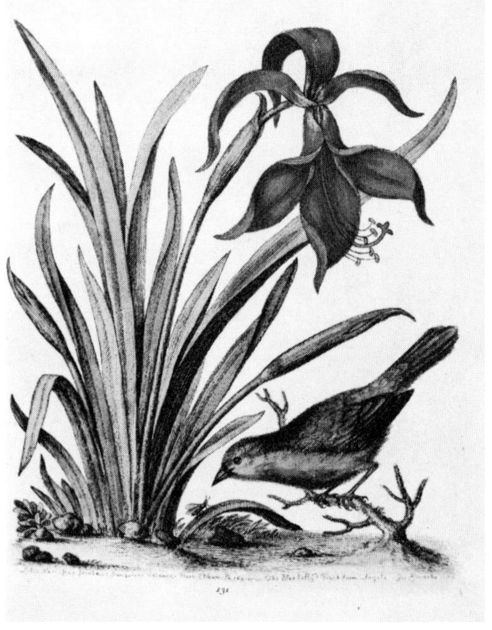

17. The "Blue belly'd Finch from Angola" reaches for an insect beneath the imposing foliage and large orange flower of the lily.

CONTINENTAL WORKS of the latter eighteenth century (Figures 18–20) show a good deal of diversity.

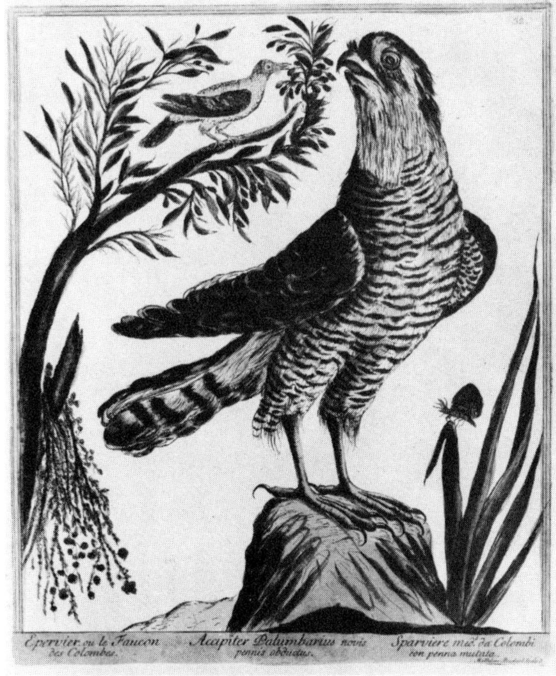

18. A distraught and bedraggled pigeon hawk (from *Recueil de cent-trente-trois oiseaux*, 1784) stares at a small bird with yellow body and pink wings (which may be either intended victim or assailant); a five-legged butterfly looks on.

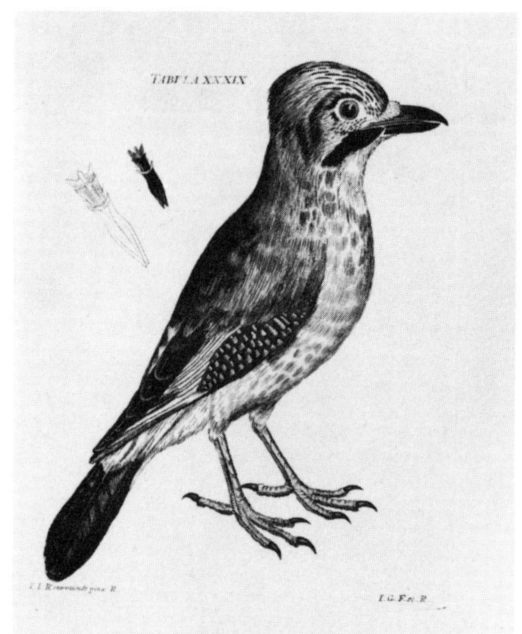

19. A jay, drawn by Rotermundt for *Elementa Ornithologica* (1774), stands stiffly and stares fixedly; yet its plumage is carefully rendered.

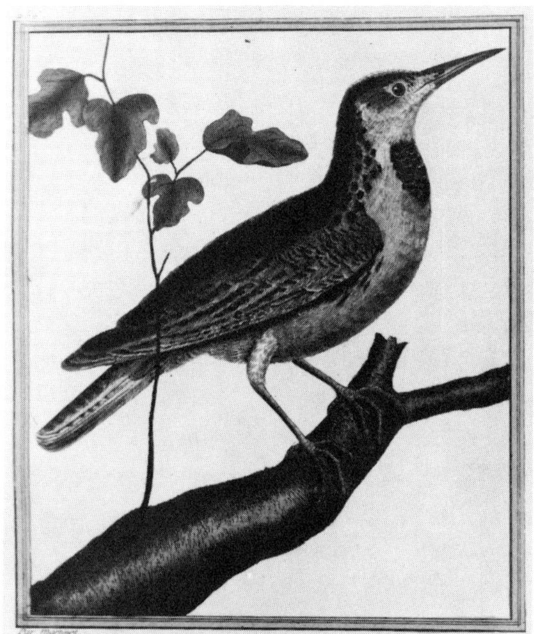

20. An American meadowlark, drawn by Martinet for Buffon's folio edition, is well managed, but the shriveled feet reveal a stuffed specimen as a model, and the massive perch shoots out an implausible twig with a few hastily drawn leaves.

6 *Bird Art and Audubon*

The comment in the London *Athenaeum*, it may be recalled, stressed Audubon's portfolio rather than his *Ornithological Biography* as the main source of his public reputation. Audubon's volumes of letterpress were considerable achievements, not merely as works of science but even as literary efforts; no less rigorous and discriminating a writer than Henry Thoreau spoke of reading Audubon with delight. Yet words were not Audubon's most effective medium; they might convey something of his exuberant love for nature, they were necessary for transmitting certain facts about birds, but they were not his primary means of communication. Furthermore, English was not his native tongue, nor was the pursuit of scientific data his main interest. Both in achieving an acceptable prose style, and in gathering and correlating ornithological notes (especially with regard to anatomy), Audubon owed a great deal to the British ornithologist William MacGillivray. The *Ornithological Biography* was to some degree at least a collaborative effort.

Audubon's portfolio, on the other hand, was quintessentially his own. Quite properly, the magnificent colored engravings made from his watercolor originals have been and remain the principal basis of his renown. Audubon was not a scientist with a talent for drawing birds, as was Wilson; he was instead a great painter of bird life, with a talent for ornithology. No Occidental bird art preceding Audubon can properly be compared with his *Birds of America,* and it is doubtful that his achievement has been matched since, although it has been approached in Britain by John Gould and his associates, and in the United States by Louis Agassiz Fuertes.

It may be that Audubon stands out so prominently because he has so few serious competitors. A person investigating the general subject of bird painting is bound to discover that the rendering of birds has never been a central motive in the art of any so-called Western country; and he will realize that here the contrast with the Middle and Far East is very great. At least as early as the third millennium before Christ, falcons, geese, and owls appeared as important features on Egyptian frescoes; and elsewhere in the Middle East bird art developed very early also. In China, bird painting reached a high level of achievement in the Sung Dynasty (960–1279) or even earlier, in the work of Huang Ch'uan and Hsü Hsi. The Chinese manner, which combined remarkable fidelity with extraordinary swiftness and grace of expression, was carried virtually unchanged into modern times, and was transmitted with many other features of Chinese culture to the Japanese. In the eleventh century, there was Ts'ui Po, in the twelfth Li An-chung, in the fourteenth Wang Yuan; Lin Liang in the Ming Dynasty (1368–1644) and other painters in the succeeding Ching Dynasty carried on the tradition.

A full understanding of any art demands a knowledge of the culture from which it grows, and no such knowledge is pretended here. Nevertheless certain comments may be hazarded. Even a casual inspection of Chinese bird painting makes one aware of its subtlety and sophistication. The painter's vocabulary is often elliptical and suggestive, his brushwork thin and swift, his patterns beautifully formalized and controlled. Yet it is part of the magic that his birds are fully alive, located naturally within the pattern, and existing neither as symbols nor as miniature human beings, but as the creatures they are. The mynah, the magpie, the gyrfalcon, the swan, the egret, the dove, the finch, the sparrow — we recognize them all, we can assign them a genus and perhaps a species name. Is Chinese bird art then simply representational? Far from it, indeed. Not only is it highly mannered in technique, in selection of detail, in compositional theory; there is something in it which for want of better words one might call mood or spirit. No doubt this springs from the Chinese attitude toward nature, itself a part of a broader outlook based on religion and philosophy. To Western eyes at least, the Chinese painter sees birds with sympathy and affection, as creatures neither inferior to the human being, nor bound up with human preoccupations, but rather as distinctive inhabitants of a larger world which takes in all natural things, grass and flowers and trees, beetles and locusts, tigers and mountains, clouds, climate, life and death. It further appears that such a world is less apart from human existence than coextensive with it.

Again, this is but speculation. But even the most obvious features of Chinese bird art — its technical virtuosity, its fidelity to nature, its stylistic maturity — provide a contrast to the bird art of the West, and emphasize how profound the gap between the two cultures has been, over a period of many centuries. Not until relatively recent times did there appear an Occidental counterpart to the work of the great Oriental masters.

Whatever there was of Greek and Roman bird art has survived only in fragments — a bird motive on an urn, a fowl or some other domesticated bird on a fresco, an eagle to represent kingliness and military might — and there seems to be no evidence that such art carried over into later European painting. Medieval bird painting is presumably too sparse to permit a safe generalization. The art of the so-called Italian primitives, dating from the thirteenth century, provides the earliest body of work from which to draw general ideas. Here we have birds represented in two ways, as winged beings in more or less human shape (angels) or as symbolic accessories, recognizable as birds in outward form but denoting a religious idea. The notion that birds may represent the human soul (or the transfigured body) in its flight to heaven is said to trace back to Egypt. Certainly the notion that heavenly creatures, whether souls or messengers of God, fly about on the wings of birds is plainly shown in Italian primitive painting, which of course was very largely religious in inspiration. Then as to the use of birds for symbolic purposes: a certain amount of superstitious belief concerning birds had grown within the Christian dogma during the Middle Ages, and was reflected in early devotional pictures.

A fairly late work, "Madonna and Child" by the fifteenth-century Florentine painter Benozzo Gozzoli, provides an example of both bird conventions. Mary holds the infant Jesus, who carries in his left hand a goldfinch, recognizably drawn and in proper scale; while the background of the painting is taken up by angels who have not only bird wings, but even feathered bodies (or bird-feather cloaks which cover all but neck, head, and halo). An odd feature of these angels is their apparent lack of arms, but otherwise they represent the usual conception of heavenly creatures endowed with a bird's equipment and powers of flight. The goldfinch here is one of several birds which might have been used in association with Christ. According to the legend, this bird in the infant's hand would eventually render him a service *in extremis*; for when the crown of thorns would be pressed down upon the Saviour's brow, a goldfinch would fly down and pull the thorns away, thereby staining its plumage forever with Christ's blood. In the case of the goldfinch, only the "face" region around the bill was so reddened; but the same deed performed by a robin stained its breast, and by a crossbill, its plumage generally. An allied notion is that the crossed mandibles of the latter bird became so when it attempted to rescue Jesus by pulling the nails from the cross. Again, the color of the robin's breast was also attributed to the bird's habit of bringing a drop of water each day to cool the tongues of men in hell, the heat of the infernal fires scorching the breast red.

Such ideas gave birds their minor place in early Western art. Nearly five hundred devotional paintings featuring the goldfinch alone have been discovered; but this scarcely constitutes a notable body of bird art. Even considering the legends mentioned, plus the story of St. Francis' preaching to the birds, and the symbolic use of the pelican for Christ, the dove for the Holy Ghost, and the eagle for John the Evangelist, one finds relatively little that concerns birds in Christian dogma; and therefore it is not surprising that there should be few birds – except of course for angels – in religious painting.

To a degree, the Renaissance turned artists away from devotional art toward portraiture and landscape; but in neither type did birds appear in an important way. Occasionally a portrait of a courtier would show a falcon on the wrist, as in "Man with a Falcon" by Titian and "The King's Falconer" (Portrait of Robert Cheseman) by Hans Holbein the Younger, both with accurately rendered peregrines. Landscapes, especially those by Dutch and Flemish artists, might feature a bird or two, generally put in for mere decorative effect, and of uncertain species. Such chance appearances certainly do not indicate a school of bird painting, or even a minor preoccupation with birds as subjects.

But painting of birds in and for themselves was not entirely lacking. Pisanello (1395–1455) was recognized as an expert bird and animal painter by Vasari, who characterized as "most beautiful" certain "small animals and birds scattered through the work, as accurate and lifelike as it is possible to imagine." Pisanello's notebooks, containing many bird sketches and studies, also reveal his interest. In the sixteenth and seventeenth centuries, the German etcher and painter Albrecht Dürer, the Flemish artists Roeland Savery, Frans Snyders, and Jan Fyt, and the Dutch painter Melchior Hondecoeter, were noted for depictions of birds — although frequently the subjects were dead game birds, composed for still-life studies, and of no interest as living wild creatures.

One of Savery's pictures, however, is a special case. It is "Landscape with Birds," a remarkable small oil into which are crowded dozens of European and exotic species, nearly every one of them readily identifiable. The scene is a highly artificial one, showing a pond in the center, with high banks of greenery on either side; and the birds are everywhere, perched, flying, floating, wading, or walking. There can be no doubt that Savery used live specimens for his work; his creatures, for all their unlikely juxtapositions, are shown in convincing and often animated attitudes. The explanation seems to be that he employed as subjects birds confined in menageries, especially those established by Maximilian II at Ebersdorf and by Rudolf II at Prague. It is thought that Rubens and Breughel, whose joint picture "The Garden of Paradise" also shows many birds, similarly used these menageries.

One other "landscape with birds" deserves mention, the bizarre and haunting dream-world of Hieronymus Bosch's "Garden of Delights." Many of the winged creatures shown here are not birds of any assignable variety, but are fanciful or allegorical figures of bird-like form. The center panel, on the other hand, contains several species (the tawny owl, kingfisher, green woodpecker, hoopoe, goldfinch, robin, and mallard) depicted in quite an accurate manner; but these birds are of monstrous size — for example, a human being is shown resting among the crest feathers of the hoopoe. The use of birds in such a special, symbolical way never became an important feature of Western art, but something of the same idea is represented in Winslow Homer's black corvines circling over a red fox, and in the strange avian creatures painted by the twentieth-century artist Morris Graves.

What emerges, however, from the foregoing is the fact that birds as such meant little to the painters of the late Middle Ages or the Renaissance. When they used them at all, it was nearly always in terms either anthropomorphic or anthropocentric: birds in human form, or birds as accessories to human religion, human sport, or human diet. To discover bird art devoted to the bird itself, one has to turn to the developing science of ornithology.

The rendering of birds for ornithological illustration during the Middle Ages was done entirely by hand, just as the manuscripts they accompanied were manually reproduced. Not enough such work survives to allow a valid generalization; but the samples provided by *De Arte Venandi cum Avibus* by Frederick II of Naples suggest that medieval bird drawing was poor in every respect, with grotesque disproportions, uncertain stance, awkward flight attitudes, unconvincing plumage and odd expressions. These same criticisms apply to the earliest illustrations made from woodcuts, a method of reproduction which came into use about 1400. Even such relatively superior works as Pierre Belon's *L'Histoire de la nature des oyseaux* (Paris, 1555) or Conrad Gesner's *Historiae Animalium, Liber III, qui est de avium natura* (Zurich, 1555) were not well served by their woodcut illustrations. As the ornithologist C. J. Temminck said, "Belon and Gesner have given us roughly drawn pictures of certain birds, but they are no more than crude efforts."

It should not be supposed, however, that the medium itself was at fault. Although woodcuts scarcely allowed the minute detail possible in the later-developed method of engraving on metal, they were nevertheless found entirely adequate for rendering the fine articulations and subtleties of line demanded by early botanical works. For example, John Gerard's famous *Herball* (1597) was beautifully illustrated by woodcut, and two centuries later Thomas Bewick was to show how well the woodcut could be employed in ornithology, given both the scientific learning and the artistic skill to permit proper use of the medium. Botany, or more properly the study of herbs, was an ancient pursuit, associated for centuries with medicine; bird science was relatively new and seemingly far less useful. Not until ornithology became fairly mature did illustrations become artistically acceptable and scientifically valid.

The introduction of engraving on metal apparently served to make illustrating somewhat less laborious, and also tended to enlarge the size of the pictures. The Frankfurt edition of Aldrovandus' *Ornithologiae* (1610–1613) contained fifty folio plates, many demonstrating considerable advance over earlier woodcut prints. Individual engravings of raptores, parrots, corvines, gallinaceous birds, herons, and bitterns are often rather accurate; except in a few cases, however, illustrations of smaller species are far less successful, and none of the plates is pictorially interesting.

The illustrations for John Ray's edition of *The Ornithology of Francis Willughby* (1678) had many figures copied from Aldrovandus. The first plate, showing the latter's golden eagle and ossifrage, augurs ill for the rest. All the medieval mannerisms are here: the staring eye and fierce expression, the clumsy and reptilian claws, the scaly or furry plumage, the inadequate topography and pattern, the doubtful anatomy and uncertain stance. Yet other plates, containing original work or adapting better figures from Aldrovandus, show real advance in nearly all respects. Perhaps the best of them is Plate 24, in which the three central figures, the hoopoe, the kingfisher, and the bee-eater, are notably well done. Accurate representation, the first demand of scientific illustration, is achieved; these birds are instantly recognizable, their proportions are true, their plumage patterns are correct. There is an attempt to convey different color tones and feather textures; and what is even more remarkable, there is a suggestion of animation in some of these figures, achieved not with grotesque distortions and strained attitudes, but by means of stance and poise, implying both a knowledge of anatomy and a familiarity with the attitude of the living bird. To a lesser degree, the same virtues are to be found in other of Ray's plates.

Yet each advance implies further objectives to be attained. Having reached the stage of adequate representation, the illustrator is faced with additional requirements. Superficial accuracy is not enough; if science is satisfied, art still waits to be served. Ray's forty-fourth plate suggests this fact. For mere identification the six birds here are proper enough, but they are stiffly arranged and monotonously similar in attitude. Ray, in short, had reached the level of illustration but not of art—and indeed, these two would not really be joined until a century and a half had passed.

The work of Mark Catesby (*The Natural History of Carolina,* 1731–1748) has been discussed earlier. Briefly, Catesby represents advance in the total conception of bird painting, combining as he did large leaf and floral patterns, fruits, berries, and even insects with his birds. In addition, his plates were of folio size and hand-colored, and included only one species of bird per plate. Catesby's birds, strictly considered, were generally poor, but in the pictorial sense his work was greatly superior to what had gone before. Catesby inaugurated a style of bird painting which would be perfected a hundred years later by Audubon, who knew of his work.

Eleazar Albin's illustrations for *A Natural History of Birds* (1731–1740) were, in the words of the subtitle, "Curiously Engraven from the Life . . . and carefully colour'd . . . from the Originals, drawn from the live Birds"—a fact which should have given the plates a quality of life which regrettably they do not possess. Apparently Albin was not enough the artist to profit from his idea; his birds show little of the animation one might expect, they are nearly always drawn in the conventional profile attitude, and they are not particularly well colored. The plates for George Edwards' *Natural History of Birds* (1743–1751), on the other hand, seem to combine many virtues and to be free of the older, less desirable mannerisms. His engravings have pleasing designs; he employs greenery, flowers, fruits, and insects in his patterns and locates his birds well within them. The birds themselves are carefully drawn, and show animation. His color is good, if somewhat garish. Yet in a sense Edwards' very achievements reveal what is lacking. No longer distracted by medieval grotesquerie or the rigor mortis of mounted specimens, one is free to discuss the total artistic effect; and here Edwards fails. His pictures are simply pretty. Precisely why is difficult to say. The matter is perhaps covered, but scarcely illuminated, by the assertion that Edwards' plates, however carefully conceived and faithfully executed, still have no vigor, no tension, no style, and therefore fail as art.

Yet Edwards was the best of British illustrators until the work of Thomas Bewick appeared at the end of the eighteenth century. Meanwhile, F. N. Martinet was becoming the foremost bird painter of France. His illustrations for Brisson's six-volume *Ornithologie* (1760) were few but expert, showing close attention to expression and feather texture and pattern, plus a certain animation. The effect of his engravings was often vitiated, however, by surrealistic rock outcrops, distant scraps of scenery, and decorative but nonessential flowers and leaves. Martinet was also the principal illustrator for the ten sumptuous folio volumes of Buffon's *Histoire naturelle des oiseaux* (1771–1786), but in them showed little advance in technique beyond his work for Brisson. Martinet was at his best with such large species as hawks, parrots, and macaws—nearly all, no doubt, drawn from living birds. His smaller birds, done from mounted specimens, were usually not so successful. From the merely formal nature of the decorative accessories used in many of the illustrations, and from the repetition of design and pose, one receives the strong impression that Martinet's work for Buffon was in the nature of a mass-production business. In any event, Martinet was a skilled illustrator who drew birds with great exactitude, but achieved little by way of decorative effect.

Buffon's work was issued in several sizes, and the quarto edition (1775) was largely illustrated by de Seve, who was Martinet's equal regarding feather texture, stance, and the sense of life, and his superior in composing artistic patterns. De Seve's rocks, like Martinet's, were often geometrical, and his trees unnaturally massive and gnarled, with the result that his scenery may be repetitious and conventional. Nevertheless it is plain that de Seve made an effort to design his pictures as artistic wholes, and to avoid cluttering them with incidental bric-a-brac.

Three other continental works of about this time would tend to indicate that the skill and accuracy attained by de Seve, Martinet, and Edwards was not the general rule. The illustrations for *Naturgeschichte der Vögel aus den besten Schriftstellern mit Merianischen und neuen Kupfern* (Heilbronn, 1774–1782) were scarcely modern in any sense, but provide an excellent epitome of all the earlier mannerisms in bird art—ungainly pose, staring eye, awkward and anatomically doubtful animation, scaly plumage, poorly articulated legs and feet, odd expressions, and badly managed accessories. Another German work, *Elementa Ornithologica Iconibus Vivis Coloribus Expressis Illustrata* by Jacob Schaeffer (Ratisbon, 1774), was transitional; the illustrator, I. I. Rotermundt, still employed the stiff attitudes of medieval art, but exhibited also a close attention to feather texture and pattern and even to individual "facial" expressions. The color also was quite good. An odd folio called *Recueil de cent-trente-trois oiseaux de plus belles espèces, gravés sur 87 planches et colorés d'après nature par d'habiles maîtres*, published in Rome in 1784, belied its title at several points. These "most beautiful species" were consistently mismanaged by the "skilled masters" who drew them, and seemed to have been colored not "from nature" but from an overactive imagination. A certain crude vigor and involvement is all that saves these creations from being preposterous.

The final years of the eighteenth century saw the publication of several British works containing bird art of considerable merit: Thomas Pennant's *Arctic Zoology*, illustrated by Moses Griffiths and perhaps others; James Bolton's *Harmonia Ruralis, or . . . A Natural History of British Song Birds . . . with Figures the Size of Life . . . by the Author*; William Lewin's *The Birds of Great Britain*; and especially Thomas Bewick's *History of British Birds*. Bewick was an artist limited to modest achievement by his medium, the woodcut. It is a matter of conjecture how well he might have done with watercolor or oil; but the skill and understanding which inform his woodcuts are such that one wishes Bewick had found a more flexible medium for his exceptional talents.

In general, by the end of the eighteenth century European bird drawing had shaken itself free of grotesquerie and had reached the level of representational accuracy. Certain illustrators had attempted to rise above this level by the use of natural accessories or scenery, or by giving animated poses to the birds themselves. None, however, had notably succeeded. Of competent and even talented illustrators there were several; true artists of bird life there were none.

America's Alexander Wilson represents no real advance, although the large, crowded, colorful plates of the nine-volume *American Ornithology* are skillfully done and often quite pleasing in general effect. The fact that Wilson was forced by limited means to crowd three hundred and twenty figures into seventy-six plates suggests one reason for his comparative failure. Very seldom could he devote a single plate to a single species; but one of these plates, the seventy-sixth, showing the peregrine, indicates how well he might have done had he used such a method more often. An original watercolor in the collection of the Museum of Comparative Zoölogy at Harvard indicates that the peregrine was supposed to appear on the seventy-fifth plate, along with a raven and two vultures. Wilson's editor or engraver transferred the peregrine to a separate plate, where it appears in an appropriate setting of grassy tundra. The result goes much beyond mere illustration; this is bird art of a sort which had not been achieved before.

But the great bulk of Wilson's work was far less impressive; most of his birds were thrown together with little regard for relationship or artistic effect. It is a revelation to study the original paintings—Wilson worked in dry watercolor augmented with pencil and perhaps chalk or crayon—and discover how often separate bird drawings were scissored out and patched with others to make up a plate for the engraver. The most blatant example, perhaps, occurred on Plate 39, where two purple martins, a Connecticut warbler, and a chimney swift were pasted together on a hastily drawn, conventional tree branch (rendered all the more dubious by the fact that the swift does not perch on trees). Again, the sculptural strength and dignity of his life-sized hawk paintings (those of the red-tail, rough-leg, and broad-wing, for example) were greatly vitiated by reduction and crowding.

Wilson may not have died, as Audubon alleged, "under the lash of a bookseller," but his art suffered greatly under the lash of economic necessity. The artist he was or might have been is suggested by his original paintings; but he is known to the world through his engraved plates, and all but a few of them are poor art.

❧ ❧ ❧

Perhaps Audubon learned from Wilson's failures; but perhaps also he would have needed no such lesson. Audubon was cast in the heroic mold, and when he projected his *Birds of America* in elephant folio size, one species to each plate and every figure as large as in life—and the complete set to cost one thousand dollars—he reflected nothing so much as the grandiose personality of John James Audubon. Here was the man who would make great art of ornithological illustration, and provide the Western world with the first such work to stand beside the bird painting of the Orient.

Audubon was truly an innovator in one way only, in drawing from freshly killed birds rather than from mounted specimens or from skins. (Still-life artists had of course used unmounted birds, but not to illustrate the creature in the state of nature.) Others had drawn birds life-size, or had devoted single plates to single species, or had used backgrounds of flowers, greenery, or scenes. No doubt Audubon learned from many predecessors, but he imitated none. He took what had been given, and made of it something new.

Donald Culross Peattie, one of our best-known writers on Audubon, has spoken of three phrases into which *The Birds of America* falls: the first, to about Plate 150, full of exuberance which may be excessive but is always informed by genius; the second, to about Plate 370, with the artist in full command of his mature techniques; and the third, showing a decline signalized by crowding of numerous figures into a single plate, by repetition of backgrounds and artificiality of scenes. Peattie also notes that Joseph Mason contributed numerous paintings of flowers and greenery to the first phase, and that an artist named Lehman was responsible for some of the scenes to be found in the second.

There is considerable justice to this estimate. It is certainly true that the last group of plates, featuring western birds lately procured from Townsend, shows both haste and crowding. Audubon himself complained that in order to complete his work in something like the originally proposed four hundred plates, he was "obliged to introduce, and in some instances to crowd, a number of species into one and the same plate, in order to try to meet the wishes of those who had by their subscriptions in some measure assisted . . . in the publication of that work." As to the supposedly poor scenic effects of the third phase: while it is true that many of the plates showing groups of smaller birds were executed with little regard for appropriate scenery or foliage, the shore and water birds continued to be given much the same kind of setting as was used earlier. Two plates, 409 and 421, contain scenes very much like the minute views of farms and seaside towns attributed to the Swiss artist George Lehman; and it is an open question whether numerous backgrounds of this sort were necessarily a desirable thing. In the first phase Audubon had been content with swiftly suggested backgrounds (Plates 31, 51, 81, 106, 121, and 141, for example) or had used none at all. Because so many of the species shown between Plate 200 and Plate 435 are shore or water birds, a certain monotony of setting was inevitable; but it is doubtful if a proliferation of vistas of seaside towns would have greatly improved the situation.

The problem of self-imitation comes up quite early in Audubon, and is not confined to the final phase. (All references here are to the elephant folio edition, limited to four hundred and thirty-five plates; the New York edition of 1840 was increased to five hundred plates, many of the added ones clearly cribbed in pattern or detail from earlier work.) One spray of flowers shown first on Plate 70 is imitated on Plates 109 and 130; another from Plate 70 appears on Plate 109 also. There are numerous similarities in the poses of birds, for example on Plates 3 and 20, 82 and 147, and 9, 19, and 85. The bluebird on Plate 36 was simply copied for Plate 113. In addition, three birds were copied directly from Alexander Wilson.

Peattie's mention of the work of Joseph Mason brings up another question, reflecting not so much on Audubon's artistic judgment as on his good faith. Peattie asserts that Mason painted scores of floral and foliage details for the plates of the first phase. The critic John Neal went even further, charging that Mason also painted parts of the birds themselves and got no credit from Audubon. The artist never deigned to answer Neal with a point-by-point refutation, and it appears that the exact truth will never be known. However, a glance at Audubon's apprentice bird paintings, done long before he met Mason in 1820, shows that he had both the idea of floral compositions and the ability to draw them, almost from the beginning. Precisely when Audubon began to paint birds is not established, but work dated as early as 1805 reveals the use of fruits and greenery as compositional features. The "Sedge Bird femelle of Albin" (1805) has a stalk of heavy grass as a perch, and a redstart from the same year is placed on a branch of blackberries. A wood thrush painted at Mill Grove "14 Aout 1806" perches on a nearly vertical spray of chokecherries; a Kentucky warbler dated 1809 rests on a leaf of a yellow lady's slipper; a "Red Winged Starling" done in June 1810 is placed on a carefully depicted stalk of milkweed; a white-throated sparrow of April 1812 perches on a truncated but very well drawn spray of pokeberries.*

The interesting feature of nearly all these paintings is the general accuracy and finish of the plant life, which often contrasts with poorly drawn or implausibly located birds. The truth of the matter is of course that flowers and foliage and grass, being static and relatively uncomplicated subjects, are easier to paint than birds. Audubon in this period had by no means mastered the look of a bird, but in the simpler work of rendering plants he had come far. It may be true that he employed Mason to do his floral painting; but it is certainly true that much earlier he himself had done considerable work of this kind, and had worked out his compositional theories.

It appears that Audubon did not acknowledge whatever contributions were made by Mason, one reason perhaps being the falling-out which occurred between the two after a year or so of association. However, Audubon was more generous on another occasion, when in discussing new birds obtained from Townsend and appearing from about Plate 350 on, he admitted that "the plants, branches of trees, and flowers which accompany these figures" were largely drawn by

* These Audubon originals are in the collection of the Houghton Library, Harvard University.

John Bachman's sister-in-law, Miss Maria Martin. Of course personal reasons may have prompted this admission. Audubon's close ties with the Bachman family were further cemented by the marriage of his son John to Maria Bachman in 1837, and of his son Victor to Mary Eliza in 1839.

"Did Shakespeare write Shakespeare?" "Did Audubon paint the Audubons?" These questions appear equally fruitless, and at last equally irrelevant. Not the man but the work is ultimately important. It is time to examine it.

Decorative pattern is what first impresses a person casually inspecting *The Birds of America.* As the critic Lloyd Goodrich says, "Audubon had a superb decorative sense. The patterns of plumage and markings, the rich profusion of foliage, flowers, blossoms and fruit in which he placed his creatures, were composed into stunning decorative designs." * Audubon's designs are essentially managed in planes, most frequently, indeed, in a single plane of birds and plants. This is not to say that his paintings lack a third dimension; within the plane given, his subjects are treated in the round, but he does not use the "peep-hole" foreground frame, and employs the middle distance and background vistas only in painting ground, shore, and water birds, and then by no means always. When he does use two planes (as in the case of the turkey cock and hen, the pied-billed grebe, the rails and bitterns) or three planes (as with the long-billed curlew, snowy egret, Wilson's snipe, little blue heron, and many others) he clearly separates the planes in a manner reflecting his early training at the school of the great classicist David. But in every case the foreground plane contains the principal subject, the bird, and generally all other important decorative motives. It is perhaps this use of essentially flat, close-up patterns which gives his paintings much of their impact and sense of immediacy. Audubon knew better than to dissipate his effects with extraneous depth; he virtually never gets lost amidst the greenery. His work, for all its abundance and detail, is under rigid, almost classical control.

Point of view is another means Audubon manipulates to achieve his effects. A Wilson plate seldom has any point of view at all; com-

* *American Watercolor and Winslow Homer* (Minneapolis: Walker Art Center, 1945), p. 15.

monly the birds appear at whatever position and angle the engraver chanced to put them, and impart no sense of the position of the observer. With Audubon the observer knows quite clearly where he is situated; that is, always close up and at eye level with the bird, whether it be on the ground, in low briers, perched among flowers, high in a tree, or flying far over the earth. In effect, the bird is not moved into place for the observer, but the other way around, for this world is not anthropocentric but ornithocentric. We are at ground level to see two black vultures squabbling over the head of a deer; we peer through blackberry brambles to see the towhee; we rise no higher than the cleome flower to watch the rufous hummingbird. We find ourselves far up in a black walnut tree to look at a crow, and we fly hundreds of feet above earth and water with the golden eagle and the osprey. Again there is a sense of immediacy, of identification, of intimacy and understanding.

Audubon's compositional ideas, his use of line and mass, no doubt could be the subject of extended and minute study. Some of his effects are based on simple rules; others are more complex in their origins. The classic triangle, either simple or reinforced, is the compositional basis for his paintings of the black vulture, the cerulean warbler (Plate 49), the belted kingfisher, the bluebird, the pine siskin, the Canada goose, and others. Similarly, the triangle is the basis for nearly all of Audubon's "miniature garden" plates (as of the house wren, pipit, and many of the sparrows) which are ground-level views showing the bird in the midst of rocks, moss, berries, and small flowers.

But beyond this relatively obvious convention, Audubon's compositions grow increasingly more complicated, and quickly transcend glib analysis. His famous paroquet plate, for example, seems to depend more upon intricate line relationships and distribution of masses than upon any single compositional principle. The same applies to his wonderfully successful view of towhees in the midst of brambles, and of savannah sparrows seen low in sedge grass. The plates of the two cuckoos, the Key West dove and the black-crowned night heron, drawn on the longer axis of a rectangle and crowded with flowers and foliage, present another kind of problem. And then what of the plates of the short-billed marsh wren, the barn swallow, the black-throated blue warbler (Plate 148), the rough-legged hawk (Plate 166), the

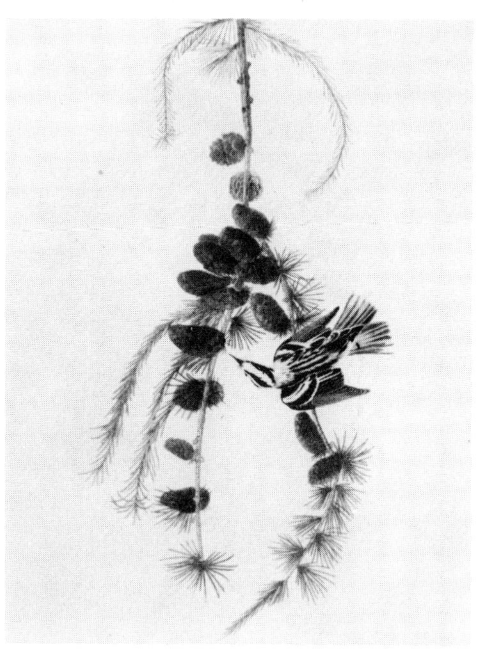

21. Close to Oriental bird painting in swiftness and delicacy of handling is this plate of the black and white warbler — but with this crucial difference, that with Audubon each feather, each tamarack needle, each cone scale, is worked out minutely, not artfully suggested.

THE FLEXIBILITY AND RANGE of Audubon's artistic theory is indicated by Figures 21–24 — paintings so diverse as to suggest a different artist for each of them.

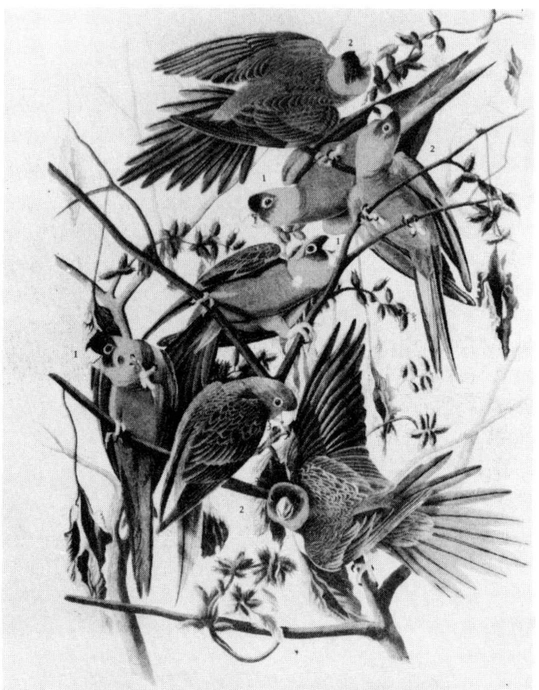

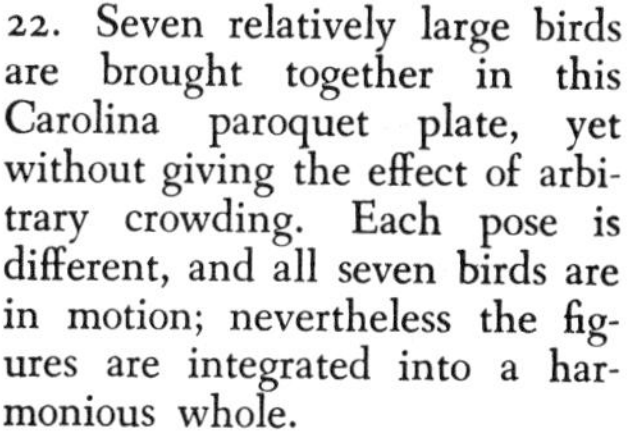

22. Seven relatively large birds are brought together in this Carolina paroquet plate, yet without giving the effect of arbitrary crowding. Each pose is different, and all seven birds are in motion; nevertheless the figures are integrated into a harmonious whole.

23. A family of house wrens, their home an old felt hat stuck on a twig, demonstrate not merely Audubon's virtuoso composing abilities, but also his sense of humor. When this plate was reproduced in Warren's *The Birds of Pennsylvania* (1888) the excrement had disappeared from the hat.

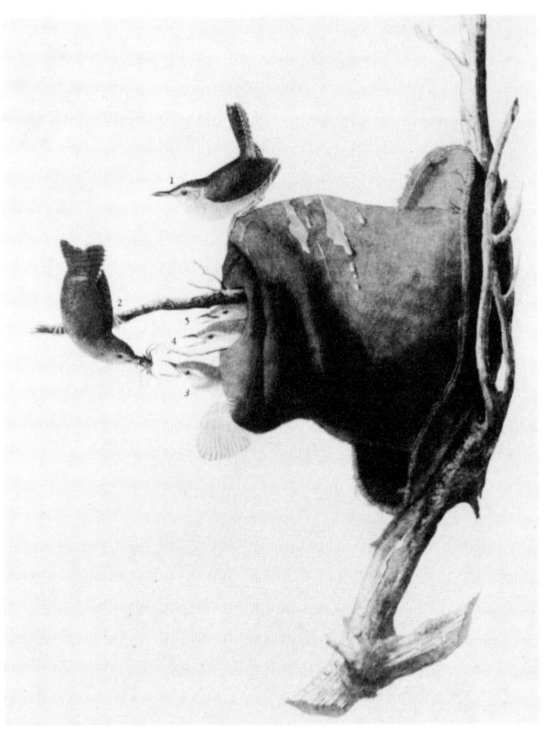

24. One of several stark renderings of powerful birds was Audubon's painting of the rough-legged hawk. No compositional accessories beyond a bare limb and the hawk's victim are used; the plate depends for its success on the feeling it conveys of wild strength and vigor.

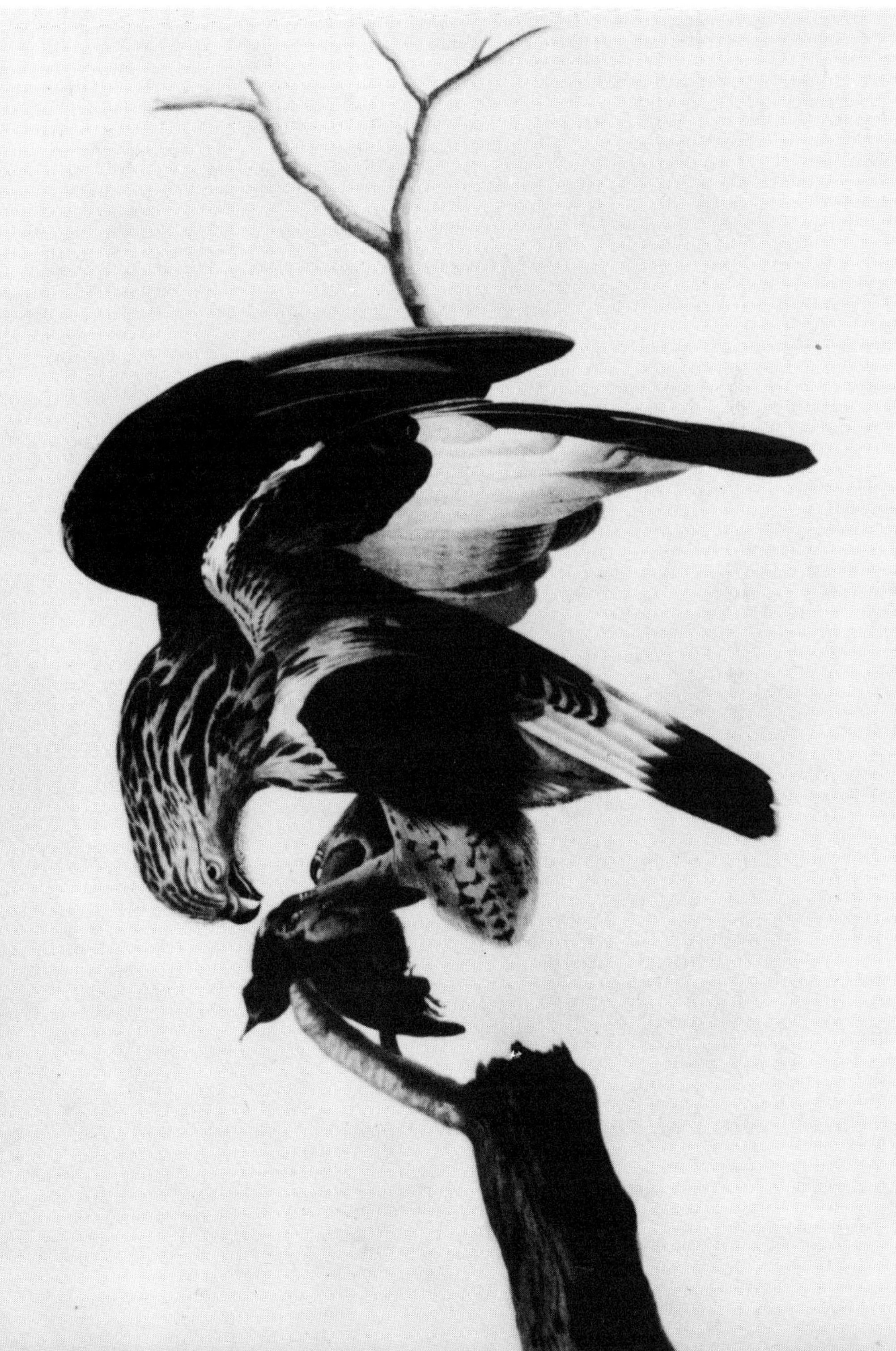

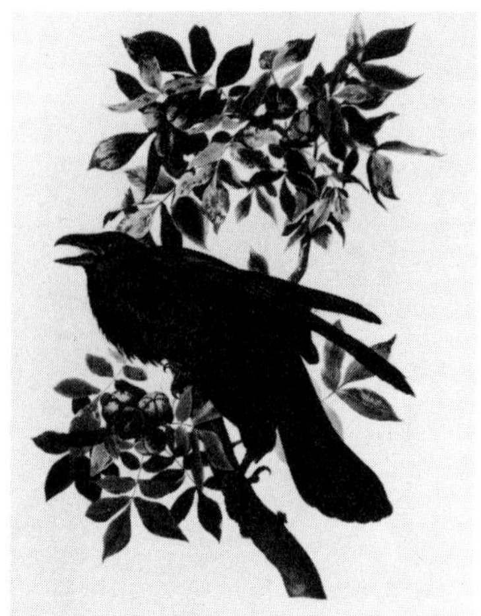

25. The raven utters its hoarse note from a perch in a hickory tree.

POINT OF VIEW in Audubon's paintings is always close up and at eye level with the bird, even though (as with the osprey and others) the subject may be flying far over earth or water. Figures 25–30 show his versatile handling of this aspect of bird art.

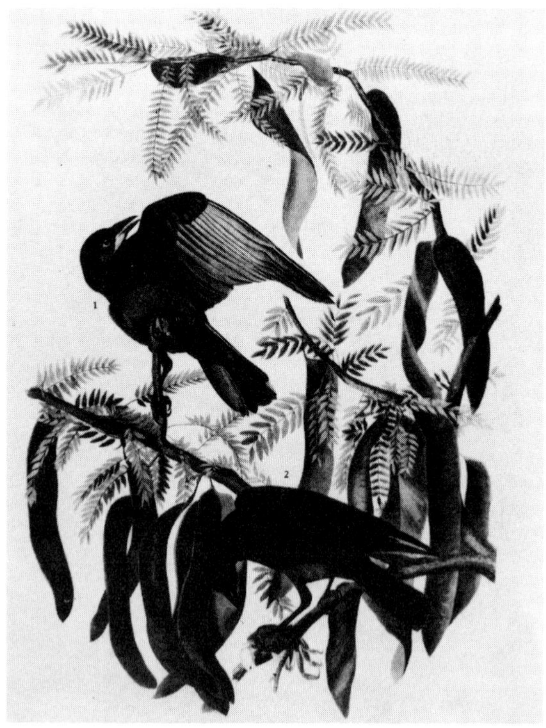

26. Fish crows preen or consume prey high among the brownish, twisted pods and pale foliage of the honey locust.

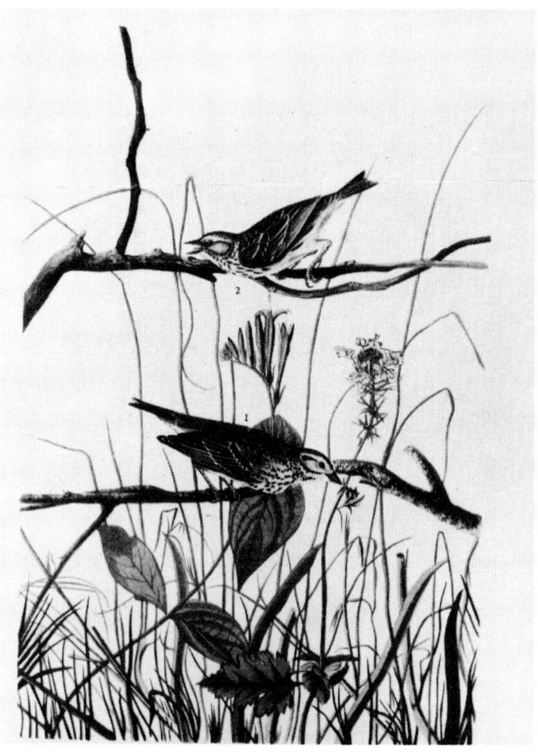

27. Savannah sparrows perch among low flowers and sedge grass.

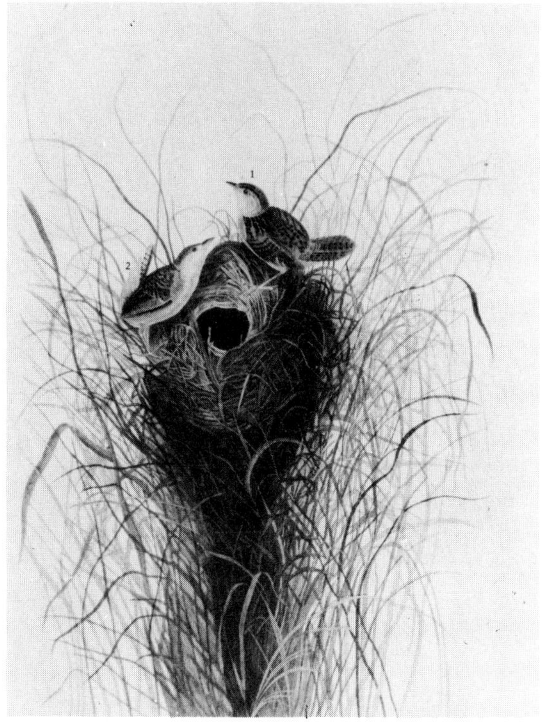

28. Short-billed marsh wrens are shown by the entrance of their nest, woven of tall grass.

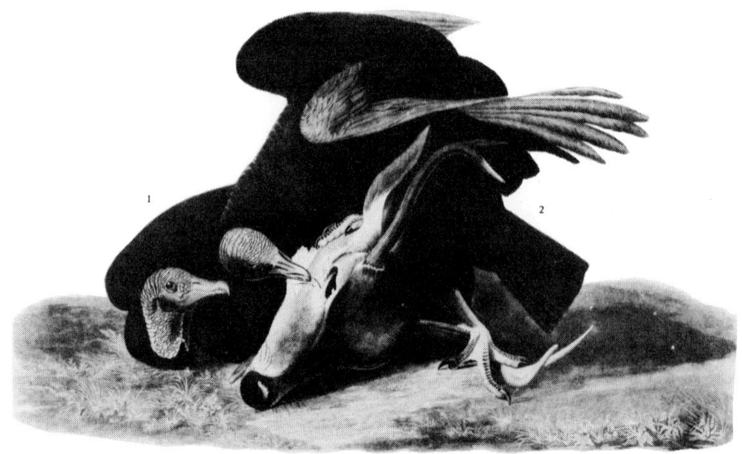

29. Two black vultures crouch on the ground, one reaching for the eye of a dead buck deer.

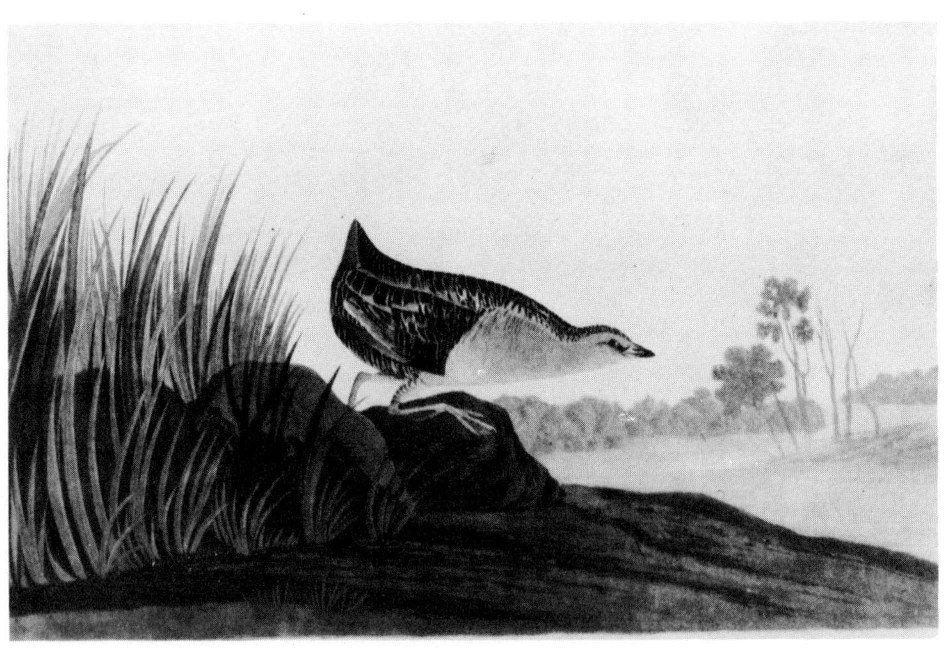

30. A yellow rail darts from the reeds at the edge of a swamp.

31. One of Audubon's more successful attempts was this well-integrated "mob scene" of western woodpeckers. The plate is well composed, and the birds (except for figure 10) are shown in convincing and animated attitudes.

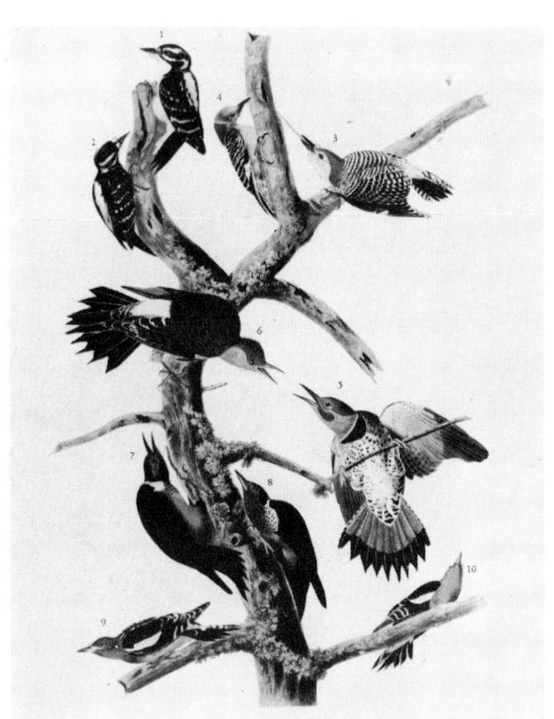

CROWDING SEVERAL SPECIES into one plate was something which Audubon, perhaps learning from Wilson, wished to avoid. As his "Birds of America" neared completion, however, he was forced to adopt this method in order to include numerous western species lately procured from Townsend.

32. This unlikely conclave of owls may be criticized on several counts. It is too crowded with plumage of similar textures and tones; figures 2 and 4 are awkwardly done; the perches are implausible, and the scene is artificial and arbitrary.

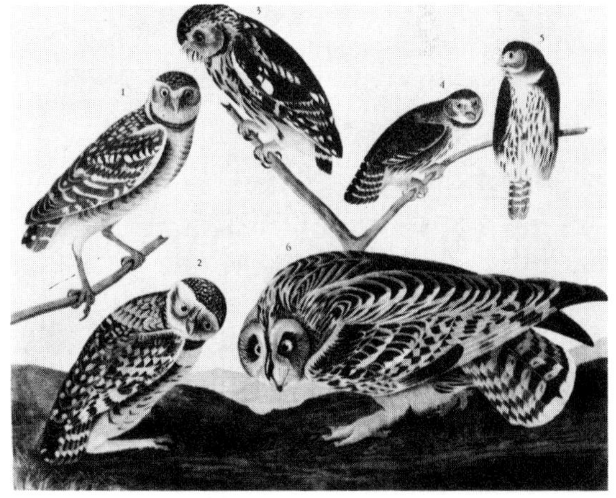

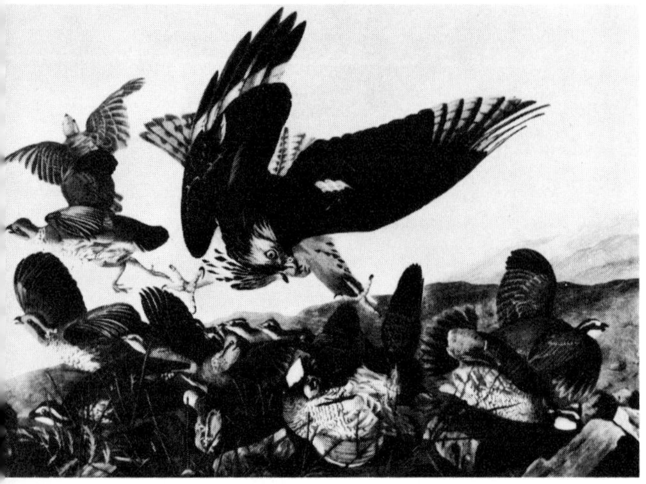

33. One of the soaring hawks – apparently a red-shoulder – produces a virtual explosion of action as it swoops down on a covey of quail; but however valid the original idea, the conception has gotten out of hand. Confusion is too absolute, and both the hawk and his intended victims are excessively distorted. In addition, this hawk is a poor choice as a predator attacking quail; rodents and insects make up most of its diet, with poultry and game birds far down on the list.

VIOLENT ANIMATION, such as often appears in Chinese bird painting, was used frequently by Audubon to achieve dramatic effect. Here, in two studies of hawks attacking prey (a favorite Oriental subject), may be seen both success and failure.

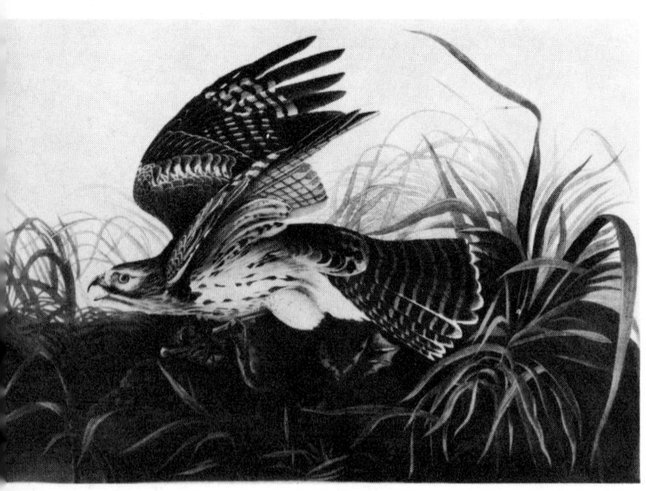

34. A painting of another red-shoulder, this one preying on a bullfrog, is a masterpiece of its kind, rivaling the best of Chinese work. Tightly composed and under full artistic control, the plate nevertheless imparts a keen sense of wild and vigorous life.

Canada warbler, or the loggerhead shrike, in which the weight of the composition is placed above the center? It would seem that such paintings must appear top-heavy and out of balance — but they are actually among Audubon's most arresting achievements. (It should not be forgotten, by the way, that Audubon was designing each painting to be printed on a folio page measuring 39½ by 26½ inches, and of course knew that all but his largest designs would have, in effect, a wide mat of white paper.)

Concerning Audubon's use of color Goodrich comments, "He was a magnificent colorist, never afraid to use the most brilliant hues of plumage or flower, but always preserving an impeccable sense of harmony, and that clarity that only watercolor can give." * Like his compositional designs, Audubon's color harmonies are of considerable variety. One thinks first of the brightest and most vivid of his paintings — the orange, yellow, and black oriole amidst the orange, yellow, and deep green of the tulip poplar, or the golden yellow of the blue-winged warbler with the bright pink and green of the mallow, or the glowing blues of the jay set off by red and yellow trumpet flowers. Yet in Audubon there are many other approaches to color. The seven paroquets on his plate, with their bright yellow and iridescent green plumage, are contrasted with the pale browns and grays of the cocklebur branches and fruits on which they feed. The roseate spoonbill displays its magnificent hues against a background of grays and dull greens. The oriental plumage of the wood duck has only the green of sycamore leaves as a setting, and the flashing pattern of the ivory-billed woodpecker is emphasized by contrast with the gray tree stub on which the bird perches. Or the contrast may be reversed, as when the soft gray of the Canada jay is set amidst autumn-tinted oak leaves, or the gray kingbird is placed among the vivid pink spurs of *Agati grandiflora.*

Again, Audubon may employ a color harmony that approaches monochrome. The reddish browns and fawns of the hermit thrush are reflected in the berries and twigs of its perch — and there is no other color on the plate. The gray and white of the phoebe are largely duplicated in the dry cotton bolls which complete the composition. The slate-colored junco perches on a dry twig from which hang a few gray

* *American Watercolor and Winslow Homer*, p. 17.

ash berries. Similarly, many of the shore and water birds, with patterns predominantly white, black, gray, or beige, are shown in settings equally low-keyed and severe.

Special note should be taken of Audubon's handling of large birds of dark plumage, especially black corvines. Beginning with the raven and continuing through the black vulture, the fish crow, the turkey vulture, the common crow, the boat-tailed grackle, the great gray owl, and the California condor, Audubon produced works of extraordinary strength and control. In the case of the corvines and the grackle, foliage of gray and green is used (plus brown on the fish crow plate), but with notable severity, as though to augment the somberness of the plumage. The vultures and the owl are allowed no foliage at all, but perch on stark limbs or crouch over the almost colorless head and horns of a deer. There seems no reason to doubt that Audubon appreciated the dramatic value of such low-keyed renderings of dark and powerful birds.

Audubon's usual method of achieving dramatic effect was by animated poses and occasionally by exciting situations. For this he has been criticized, often justly. The most valid part of such criticism concerns the strained attitudes he often imparts to his birds, especially when they are shown fighting or stretching for food. His use of limp dead birds permitted Audubon certain poses which in the live bird would be doubtful, and such depictions often produce an unhappy grotesquerie. For example, a catbird with tail raised to show the under tail coverts reaches with drooping wings and humped back for a blackberry; a bluebird with limply closed wings and dangling feet hangs in midair, supposedly soaring upward; a mockingbird all too plainly dead makes ready to peck at the rattles of a timber rattler; a golden plover patently laid out for drawing is shown speeding through the air. Such mistakes, however, are less the outcome of a false theory than the occasional penalty for a bold and valid idea. When Audubon is in full control, he produces plates such as those of the black-crowned night heron, the red-shouldered hawk (Plate 71), the prairie chicken, the pied-billed grebe, the turkey hen, the duck hawk — work which rivals the best of Chinese bird painting in animation and the sense of life.

A word should be said concerning Audubon's drawing and brush technique. Like Wilson, he painted his birds in dry watercolor, seldom if ever employing washes, and augmented his work with pencil and perhaps chalk or crayon. No less than Wilson, he was a representational painter, achieving his artistic effects on the basis of realism, not impressionism or willful exaggeration. The original paintings show an astonishing attention to detail; the smallest feathers are worked out exactly, yet without giving the impression of scaliness which such attention produced in earlier bird drawing. Audubon's command of feather texture was extraordinary; from the minutely mottled, soft and owl-like plumage of the night hawk to the bronze sheen of the turkey, his renditions were unfailingly expert.

In the larger sense, Audubon depicted birds in all their aspects so very well because he apprehended them so fully and deeply. His was not a mere affectionate interest, but something much more pervasive. It was a passion, an emphatic devotion, which enabled him to produce such works as he did. Without this he might have been merely a greatly talented illustrator; with it, he became the only great bird artist yet to appear in the Western world.*

The success of Audubon's work both culminated and concluded, as Wilson's achievement had begun, the era of what might be called "public ornithology" in the United States for the nineteenth century. America had produced two notable birdmen, each in his own way a remarkable person. Their great ornithological works were finished, and nothing like them would appear again. Why this should be true is not easily discovered, but certain suggestions may be hazarded. The great initial task, that of finding, naming, describing, and figuring the species of the vast new country, was largely finished. Very many birds, particularly of the West, were yet to be found, and many of the species already discovered were to be reconsidered; but such tasks would be the work of several individuals, none of them approaching either Audubon or Wilson as a personage, a public figure, a man to be reckoned with. A determinist might say that the times called for these

* An index to the continuing popularity of Audubon's paintings may be found in the number of reprints which have appeared since the original folio edition. The most complete of the recent editions is that issued by The Macmillan Company in 1946; the Audubon illustrations for the present work were taken from that edition.

two ornithologists, and they appeared; on the other hand, Carlyle might have said that American ornithology was engendered and established by two great personalities, Wilson the pioneer and prophet, Audubon the fulfilling genius. Wherever the truth may lie, this much is plainly the fact: their like would not be seen again.

It may well be that the need for such figures was past, and another sort of ornithologist was called for. Wilson and Audubon provided natural science with a vast amount of material for subsequent extension, refinement, and correction. There were many mistakes concerning classification, habits, and occurrence in *American Ornithology*, and Audubon's work was riddled with errors. Ord, Peale, and Bonaparte began the correcting process for Wilson, and Audubon attempted his own emendation with a long appendix to the fifth volume of *Ornithological Biography*, in which he admitted numerous "errors relative to the species," and with *A Synopsis of the Birds of North America*, a handbook to serve as "a systematic index, in which the nomenclature should be corrected, and the species arranged agreeably to my present views." But such work was only a beginning. The entire problem of classification, for example, would engage taxonomists for the rest of the century, with no end in sight; and this was but one aspect of the technical work of making ornithology an increasingly exact science. The work was there, and had to be done; but the penalty was a multiplicity of effort, a tendency toward specialization, a decline in creativity—and consequently the disappearance of the sort of birdman whose impact on American culture was immediate and direct.

In eloquent words and frequently beautiful paintings, these two men had shown America her own birds. In so doing they had obliterated Buffon's insulting notions of "degeneration," and had made a place for themselves not only among American scientists, but among the best of the Western world. In the American wilds they had found a plethora of riches; they had looked to nature, seeking beauty, and had found it in abundance. Audubon had celebrated his devotion in the greatest bird paintings ever to appear outside the Orient; Wilson had done the same in engaging prose and lyrical verse. In their work was the joy of discovery, the eloquence of love, to which others with the calling not of scientist but of writer were soon to respond.

7 *Literary Birdman: Henry David Thoreau*

> Books of natural history make the most cheerful winter reading. I read in Audubon with a thrill of delight, when the snow covers the ground, of the magnolia, and the Florida keys, and their warm sea-breezes; of the fence-rail, and the cotton tree, and the migrations of the rice bird; of the breaking up of winter in Labrador, and the melting of the snow on the forks of the Missouri; and owe an accession of health to these reminiscences of luxuriant nature.
>
> *Henry D. Thoreau, in* The Dial, *1842*

These were the opening sentences of the first important essay by Thoreau to appear in print. Ostensibly a review of natural history reports compiled under a commission of the Massachusetts legislature, Thoreau's article was actually a long philosophical essay on nature, largely adapted from the author's journal for the years 1837 to 1842. That Thoreau should begin with a tribute to Audubon was no accident; books on the science of living things had long interested him, and of these none could impart a greater "thrill of delight" than the volumes of *Ornithological Biography*. Years earlier, in letters to his brother John, Thoreau had shown a keen interest not only in birds but also in bird science; and his journals almost from beginning to end contained numerous references to ornithology.

In reading over the passages on birds in Thoreau's journal, one notes that very often the content is neither emotional nor philosophical, but technical. This journal, drawn upon by Thoreau for much of

A Week on the Concord and Merrimack Rivers and *Walden*, and by subsequent editors for several posthumous volumes, is full of exact observations of birds. In a manner appropriate to the professional naturalist, Thoreau makes notes on spring and fall migrants, nesting species, winter visitors, and stragglers or accidentals; on mating and nesting habits, and the care of young; on food and the methods of acquiring it; on field marks, mannerisms, and distinctive behavior; on songs and call notes. With comments on birds in relation to a particular habitat, he enters the field presently called ecology; with notes expressing concern over the growing scarcity of certain species, the field of conservation. Even the birds shot and brought to him have their uses; he may express his regret at the useless sacrifice of harmless life, but if the bird is new or rare, he will also describe it minutely and record its measurements.

Considering his time and the field equipment at his disposal, the bird notes which Thoreau gathered are remarkably free from errors. One reason is of course that Thoreau was an exceptionally interested, painstaking, and intelligent observer, a man of real aptitude for seeing clearly and recording accurately. The other reason quickly emerges from his notes: he was acquainted with the best American ornithologists, and turned to them often. The time was past when even so well-educated an American as Thomas Jefferson had only the antique Catesby or the misguided Buffon to show him American birds; Thoreau had Wilson and his editor, Thomas M. Brewer, Audubon and his friend Spencer F. Baird, and Thomas Nuttall, W. B. O. Peabody, and J. P. Giraud, Jr. These ornithologists are frequently cited (Wilson, Nuttall, and Audubon most of all) and in at least one passage Thoreau refers to all seven of them.

A casual reading of Thoreau's formal works fails to indicate the extent of his dependence on such authority. His freedom from error would suggest the use of accurate references, but in general the ornithological data in his journal provided him with raw material for elaboration and extension, especially in passages of a reflective or emotional kind in which the citing of authorities was scarcely appropriate. Such writing, the end product of his long study of nature, gave Thoreau the distinctive place he holds in American literature, as our first great nature writer. Only a study of his journal, certain of his letters, and the testimony of associates demonstrates how much of his work depended not on nebulous "appreciation" of nature, but on close and rigorous study.

Consider this picture of Thoreau the observer, given by Ralph Waldo Emerson in his journal for May 21, 1856:

> Yesterday to the Sawmill Brook with Henry. He was in search of yellow violet (*pubescens*) and *menyanthes* which he waded into the water for; and which he concluded, on examination, to have been out five days. Having found his flowers, he drew out of his breast pocket his diary and read the names of all the plants that should bloom this day, May 20; whereof he keeps account as a banker when his notes fall due; *Rubus triflora, Quercus, Vaccinium,* etc. The *Cypripedium* not due till to-morrow. Then we diverged to the brook, where was *Viburnum dentatum,* Arrow-wood. But his attention was drawn to the redstart which flew about with its *cheap, cheap chevet,* and presently to two fine grosbeaks, rose-breasted, whose brilliant scarlet "bids the rash gazer wipe his eye," and which he brought nearer with his spyglass, and whose fine, clear note he compares to that of a "tanager who has got rid of his hoarseness." Then he heard a note which he calls that of the night-warbler, a bird he has never identified, has been in search of for twelve years, which, always, when he sees it, is in the act of diving down into a tree or bush, and which 't is vain to seek; the only bird that sings indifferently by night and by day . . . There came Henry with music book under his arm, to press flowers in; with telescope in his pocket, to see the birds, and microscope to count stamens; with a diary, jack-knife, and twine; in stout shoes, and strong grey trousers, ready to brave the shrub-oaks and smilax, and to climb the tree for a hawk's nest. His strong legs, when he wades, were no insignificant part of his armour.

No American knew Thoreau as did Emerson, and no better picture of Thoreau the naturalist has come down to us than this brief, suggestive passage. Here is the devoted student, still seeking the identity of a bird after twelve years of searching; the initiate to the mysteries, a bit proud perhaps of the authority with which he reads the floral lesson for the day; the unwearied lover, his eye still caught by the beauty of the redstart or the rose-breasted grosbeak, his ear still attuned to its song; and here too is the plain and practical Yankee, going forth dressed not for a nature walk, but for a walk in nature, ready to wade the river or climb the hawk-tree or push through the greenbrier — ready, in short, to meet nature as much as possible on her own terms. He knew, as Wilson and Audubon also knew, that to discover the facts you must go and look for them. Discover he would, and go he did, whatever the hour, the weather, or the season.

But why bother with discovery at all? If mere facts were his only concern, the ornithologists could supply them in abundance. Certainly Thoreau had no professional interest in the matter, and no ambition to contribute to natural science as such; the bird list appended to his writings on the Maine woods comprised his only systematic ornithological effort. Neverthless he wished to see for himself, depending neither on the testimony of others nor on his own emotional responses, but on the facts as found.

One who seeks to analyze this outlook had best recall immediately that Thoreau was by tendency and often by vocation a handy man with a talent for many trades, who took pride in knowing what he was about. At one time or another he was a pencil-maker, a carpenter, a mason, a plasterer, a small farmer, a surveyor. "Yankee ingenuity," a parochial term which may be broadened to apply to the multiple skills born of necessity anywhere in rural or frontier America, was his by inheritance and personal bent. Thoreau was not shy about letting his readers know that he commanded such skills, nor that he was an expert fisherman, camper, mountain-climber, and explorer. Carried over into nature study, this kind of outlook produced a man who examined his flora and fauna until he knew what he was talking about; who learned by seeing and hearing, not by mere book-reading; who apprenticed himself to such masters as Audubon and Wilson but who checked the facts until they squared with his own experience — and if the masters needed correcting, correct them he would.

❧ ❧ ❧

Thoreau had little respect for closet ornithology, that aspect of science which forgets the living bird. He did not wish, he said, to know the length of the eagle's entrails, or obtain "petty knowledge" of a hawk's plumage by killing the bird; he found little grace in stuffed specimens, and once or twice he went so far as to disavow bird science altogether. But his more characteristic outlook was that indicated in the passage quoted from *The Dial*: ornithology at its best was a window opened wide to nature. Furthermore, in Thoreau's opinion, reading the great naturalists was no less worthy an occupation than reading the masters of literature, for both may teach us truth. This attitude is clearly implied in an entry he made in his journal in 1852 — especially in the last few words:

> I have been to the libraries (yesterday) at Cambridge and Boston. It would seem as if all things compelled us to originality. How happens it that I find not in the country, in the fields and woods, the *works* even of like-minded naturalists and poets. Those who have expressed the purest and deepest love of nature have not recorded it on the bark of trees with the lichens; they have left no memento of it there; but if I would read their books I must go to the city, — so strange and repulsive both to them and to me, — and deal with men and institutions with whom I have no sympathy. When I have just been there on this errand, it seems too great a price to pay for access even to the works of Homer, or Chaucer, or Linnaeus.

The juxtaposition of Homer, Chaucer, and Linnaeus will seem strange only to those who fail to understand Thoreau's catholic range of interests. Linnaeus, the great "original," the pioneer explorer and systematizer, was a guide to one aspect of nature as Homer and Chaucer were guides to another; and Thoreau was not a man who necessarily elevated the poet above the scientist. More especially, he was not one who believed that to know birds and flowers was less meaningful than to know men. All were to him creatures of the greater entity, nature; and if Chaucer could illuminate one part of nature, Linnaeus could reveal another.

That nature is a vast interrelationship embracing men no less than birds and lichens was for Thoreau fundamental doctrine. In the words of the critic Joseph Wood Krutch:

> Perhaps no man before him had ever taken quite so literally the term "fellow creatures," and perhaps that is one of the most significant things about him. When he spoke of having "a little fishy friend in the pond"; when he held interviews with a woodchuck, or hoped that one of his games had taught the fox something, he was expressing in his own special, humorous way a sense of intimacy and of fellowship to some degree novel. Insofar as it was simply an outpouring of love, the banal analogy would be, of course, St. Francis. But there is an intellectual difference which is of some importance.

> Thoreau could feel as he did, not so much because he was tender toward inferior creatures as because he did not think of them as inferior; because he had none of that sense of superiority or even separateness which is the inevitable result of any philosophy or any religion which attributes to man a qualitative uniqueness, and therefore inevitably suggests that all other living things exist for him. St. Francis preached to the birds; many moderns have hoped, on the contrary, that the birds would preach to them.*

Again and again Thoreau's references to birds corroborate this attitude. He says of the hawk:

> The same thing which keeps the hen-hawk in the woods, away from the cities, keeps me here. That bird settles with confidence on the white pine top and not upon your weathercock. That bird will not be poultry of yours, lays no eggs for you, forever hides its nest. Though willed, or *wild*, it is not willful in its wildness. The unsympathizing man regards the wildness of some animals, their strangeness to him, as a sin; as if all their virtue consisted in their tamableness. He has always a charge in his gun ready for their extermination. What we call wildness is a civilization other than our own.

Of the great blue heron:

> John Garfield brought me this morning (September 6th) a young great heron . . . It measured four feet, nine inches, from bill to toe and six feet in alar extent, and belongs to a different race from myself and Mr. Frost [a minister of Concord]. I am glad to recognize him for a native of America, – why not an American citizen?

Of the great horned owl:

> The hooting of the owl! That is a sound which my red predecessors heard here more than a thousand years ago. It rings far and wide, occupying the spaces rightfully, – grand, primeval, aboriginal sound. There is no whisper in it of the Buckleys, the Flints, the Hosmers who recently squatted here, nor of the first parish, nor of Concord Fight, nor of the last town meeting.

Of the nighthawk:

> Wonderful creature, which sits motionless on its eggs on the barest, most exposed hills, through pelting storms of rain or hail, as if it were a rock or part of the earth itself, the outside of the globe, with its eyes shut and its wings folded, and, after the two days' storm, when you think it has become a fit symbol of rheumatism, it sud-

* Joseph Wood Krutch, ed., *Great American Nature Writing* (New York: Sloane, 1950), pp. 5–6.

denly rises into the air a bird, one of the most aerial, supple, and graceful of creatures, without stiffness in its wings or joints! It was a fit prelude to meeting Prometheus bound to his rock on Caucasus.

Of the chickadee:

> We are left with the chickadee's familiar notes, and the jay for trumpeter . . . The fields are bleak, and they are, as it were, vacated. The very earth is like a house shut up for the winter, and I go knocking about it in vain. But just then I heard a chickadee on a hemlock, and was inexpressibly cheered to find that an old acquaintance was yet stirring about the premises, and was, I was assured, to be there all winter. All that is evergreen in me revived at once.

And of birds generally:

> Their Maker gave them [winter birds] the last touch and launched them forth the day of the Great Snow. He made this bitter, imprisoning cold before which man quails, but He made at the same time these warm and glowing creatures to twitter and be at home in it . . . The traveller is frozen on his way. But under the edge of yonder birch wood will be a little flock of crimson-breasted lesser redpolls, busily feeding on the seeds of the birch and shaking down the powdery snow! As if a flower were created to be now in bloom, a peach to be now first fully ripe on its stem. I am struck by the perfect confidence and success of nature. There is no question about the existence of these delicate creatures, their adaptedness to their circumstances.

Thus in his journal Thoreau repeatedly expressed a characteristic conviction about nature and man's place in it. The hawk is civilized in its own way, not in man's; the heron is of a different race of Americans, but may also be called a citizen; the horned owl was an aborigine in the land long before the white squatters came; the chickadee is not simply a pretty little bird, but an old acquaintance, cheery in the harshest weather; the nighthawk and the redpoll and the rest are perfectly adapted to natural conditions from which men may shrink. In such passages Thoreau celebrates "the perfect confidence and success of nature," a nature in whose eyes all creatures are equal, and in which man is by no means lord of creation, but may indeed be at times an interloper and misfit. What is here forthrightly stated, in notes for the day, Thoreau expressed more implicitly in his formal prose.

❧ ❧ ❧

Before looking closely at Thoreau's principal books, it may be useful to consider the general tradition of prose nature writing upon which he could draw. Immediately it becomes plain that the word "tradition" is open to question, simply because the body of work is so sparse and scattered. Few works (other than natural histories of one sort or another) suggest themselves; one looks in vain for creative prose commensurate with Aristophanes' *The Birds*, Chaucer's *The Parliament of Fowles* and "The Nonnes Preestes Tale of the Cok and Hen, Chauntecleer and Pertelote," John Skelton's *The Armonye of Byrdes*, or such Elizabethan lyrics as Robert Greene's "Menaphons Roundelay." Even in later times, there appeared no obvious prose counterparts to the bird poems of Keats, Shelley, Wordsworth, or Bryant. Most of the nonscientific prose concerning birds written before the middle of the nineteenth century must be sought for in odd corners of literature, and when found is seldom impressive.

A work of quite early origins, however, provides an immediate exception to this general rule of scarcity. The fables of Aesop, many of them about birds, were intended to serve neither "science" nor religious dogma, but rather to amuse and instruct—and they were early influential in Western Europe and Great Britain. It is thought that King Alfred in the ninth century may have rendered Aesop into English prose; in the fourteenth century John Lydgate selected certain of the fables for translation into verse; and in 1484 the pioneer English printer William Caxton issued a prose version "translated out of Frensshe in to Englysshe." By such renditions there came into the language the tales of the wolf and the crane, the fox and the crane, the nightingale and the sparrow hawk, the kite and the pigeons, the eagle, raven, and tortoise, and Juno and the peacock. Each tale characterized a bird or two—in human terms, of course, but with a sense of avian individuality. Thus the crane used its long neck and bill to take a bone from the wolf's throat, or to eat food served in a tall, narrow jar; the pigeon was shown as a nimble flier, the kite as a bird of prey; the nightingale was required to sing its sweetest song to save its fledglings; and the peacock was told to be content with its beauty, as the nightingale with its song and the raven with its wisdom.

In a sense the term Aesopian is a generic one, signifying composite authorship. Aesop himself lived from about 620 to 560 B.C., but his tales, presumably never written down by him, were later adapted by the Latin fabulist Phaedrus, who in turn was employed as a source by others. There is no need here to trace the history of these animal fables, but it is pertinent to suggest that such tales were only one manifestation of a common interest in living creatures, and are related to the animal epic (e.g., Reynard the Fox), the use of birds and other creatures as symbols (the owl for wisdom, the eagle for valor, the kite for gluttony, and so on), and to vulgar belief and superstition (as in the bizzare notion concerning the origin of the barnacle goose, or the idea that the raven's croak portends death). In short, Aesop's winsome stories represent written examples of a larger entity, common animal lore; and although such lore generally remains obscure, or emerges only in verse or song or in verbal relation, it is present in all cultures, and is a source of subject matter to any writer who will seek it out. The tenth-century Saxon did not need to consult a manuscript to learn that there was a small brownish bird which sang very beautifully in his woodlands, a bird he called "nightegale." Similarly, the farmers of Concord and the Indians of Maine with whom Thoreau talked had their own names and their own notions of birds, independent of formal learning. Common bird lore is ever present, and may be of use; but more often than not it is both too special and too fabulous and inaccurate to serve the ends of the serious writer.

Falconry was of course one of the major outdoor sports of the Middle Ages and the Renaissance, and called forth such works as *De Arte Venandi cum Avibus* by Frederick II and *The Booke of Faulconrie or Hauking* (1575) by George Turbervile. Although both these works contained some material of general interest, they were essentially treatises on a special use to which nature might be put, and were not intended to interpret or celebrate nature generally. The same may be said of Izaak Walton's *The Compleat Angler* (1653; fifth edition 1676), which is full of special lore in regard to fishing (and in some degree to hunting), but which has only passing references to other aspects of the enjoyment of nature. However, the character Auceps in the first chapter speaks in complimentary terms of certain birds which cannot be trained for hunting, but instead are both useful for food and "pleasant to mankind"—the lark, the blackbird, the throstle, the linnet, the robin, the nightingale, and so on.

Elsewhere, birds appear principally as "enemies of fish," those mentioned being the cormorant, bittern, osprey, gull, kingfisher, heron, and (mistakenly) the swan, goose, and duck. Yet it must be noted to Walton's credit that he does not recommend the killing of such birds, and this fact verifies a general impression made by *The Compleat Angler*: that Walton knew there is more to nature than the quarry it provides, and more to fishing than merely landing fish.

In 1789 there appeared *The Natural History of Selborne*, by Gilbert White, curate of the Selborne parish in Hampshire. The author characterized it as "his idea of *parochial history*, which, he thinks, ought to consist of natural productions and occurrences as well as antiquities." It is a curious work, difficult to assign to any particular genre of literature. Consisting almost entirely of letters, it is related superficially to the Earl of Chesterfield's *Letters to his Son* (1774) and more closely to Crèvecoeur's *Letters from an American Farmer* (1782). It may also reflect to a slight degree the eighteenth-century vogue of the epistolary novel. Furthermore, as Krutch has shown, in subject matter *The Natural History of Selborne* was less a distinctive and original production than it was a manifestation of the widespread interest in natural history to be found among the gentry of the time. (Alexander Wilson's many references to ornithological data received from various gentlemen would indicate a similar interest in America.) Finally, although over a third of the letters were addressed to Thomas Pennant and usually concern birds, the work is not properly an ornithology; and despite the author's stated aim to write "parochial history," the book is not to any important extent historical.

If *The Natural History of Selborne* must be characterized, let it be called a biological miscellany. Doubtless birds receive the most attention, but White's interests range over much of the field of biology, from plants through insects, arachnids, and mollusks to the vertebrates, both cold- and warm-blooded. Of course White devotes passages to many other aspects of his parish — its economy, its population, its geology, topography, weather, and so on — and originally included a section of "Antiquities" (almost entirely devoted to the ecclesiastical history of the parish) in his book. Nevertheless the work in the main is a collection of notes, comments, and speculations on living things of the Selborne area, given in the form of letters addressed to Pennant or to Daines Barrington, Recorder of Bristol.

As such, *Selborne* is scarcely "nature writing" in the creative sense. That the letters were written in a consciously literary style is quite plain; but the subject matter consists almost entirely of diversified data, and the work as a whole has no unity except a superficial one imposed by the epistolary form. Yet there are aspects of the book which attracted as critical a reader as Thoreau, and which assure its survival in our own day. In his matter-of-fact way, Gilbert White parades before us a varied pageant of living creatures, and offers a restrained commentary on the procession. He is casual but not detached, catholic but not haphazard, precise but not niggling; and perhaps best of all, he has an engaging affection toward his creatures, but abjures both moralizing and sentimentality. He very evidently enjoys what he is doing, and without raising his voice, he communicates his pleasure to the reader. Indeed, one of the most enduring impressions made by the book is of the personality of Gilbert White himself, an elderly English cleric quite content with a life spent observing and recording the "natural productions and occurrences" of his native parish.

If Thoreau found much to interest him in *The Natural History of Selborne,* he eventually wearied of the work of another Anglican clergyman writing of nature at about the same time as White. William Gilpin, prebendary of Salisbury and vicar of Boldre, published his best known work, *Remarks on Forest Scenery and Other Woodland Views*, in London in 1791. Here again is a work not easily classified under any one of the rubrics of literature. Aesthetics is the discipline to which it is most clearly related, and Thoreau was mistaken if he expected Gilpin to say anything particularly interesting or important about nature apart from painting or landscape art. The words "forest" and "woodland" in the title signified to Gilpin only raw materials for pictures. To the accompaniment of numerous classical references and much historical lore, he discussed the aesthetics of various English trees as they appear (or should appear) in special English scenes—forests, parks, copses, groves, glens, and so on. But for all his greenery and his minute detail in pictorial matters, Gilpin mentioned any sort of wildlife but rarely and birds scarcely at all. In the artificiality of his approach to nature Gilpin looked back to the calculated picturesqueness of Alexander Pope's garden, and in his determination to establish pictorial rules for outdoor scenes, he anticipated the shrill aesthetics of John Ruskin. But in any case, he took a view of nature far different from that of Thoreau, as the latter soon realized.

The noted British author Oliver Goldsmith is mentioned by Thoreau in an unexpected way. "The booming of the bittern, described by Goldsmith and Nuttall, is frequently heard in our fens"—so wrote Thoreau in *The Dial.* Perhaps he referred to the forty-fourth line of *The Deserted Village*, "The hollow sounding bittern guards its nest"; but on the other hand, he may well have been thinking of the passage on the bittern in Goldsmith's *An History of the Earth and Animated Nature*, an eight-volume work first published in 1774. The fifth and sixth volumes of this encyclopedic effort concern birds, and comprise one of the most curious works of ornithology ever put together. In his range of authorities, Goldsmith was encyclopedic indeed; he quoted or cited Pliny, Galen, Gesner, Aldrovandus, Catesby, Linnaeus, Brisson, Buffon, Réaumur, Edwards, Albin, Pennant, and especially Willughby. Such uncritical inclusiveness hints at the truth about the entire work, that it was a piece of hack-writing turned out by Goldsmith to make money. Yet it is far from a worthless production. Not merely were these volumes illuminated by Goldsmith's intelligence and literary grace; very often his factual matter was sound enough, and if at times he was willing to accept dubious data (for example, concerning the Andean condor), elsewhere he showed a commendable spirit of scientific skepticism, refusing to endorse tales contradicted by reason or personal observation.

Two British ornithologies, William Yarrell's *A History of British Birds* (1839–1843) and William MacGillivray's *History of British Birds* (1837–1852), were cited by Thoreau, and should be mentioned in passing. Both were works of science, not of literature, but the distinction is seldom absolute, and especially in MacGillivray (who had greatly helped Audubon in editing *Ornithological Biography* for style) Thoreau found a scientist who possessed not only facts but also warmth and a gift for words.

* * *

American prose concerning birds begins with the early travelers and chroniclers, some of whose work has been considered in the first chapter. Often such writers were short on facts and long on imagination, and seldom did they achieve creative expression; but because they were first on the scene and observed or were told of American wildlife in its pristine state, they could be useful to later writers. Thoreau cites Captain John Smith at least once and John Josselyn several times — not, however, for bird data, but for notes concerning fish and mammals.

Excluding scientific works and the accounts of such foreign visitors as Peter Kalm, the first full-length prose work on the subject of American nature was William Bartram's *Travels through North and South Carolina, Georgia, East and West Florida* (1791). In the formal sense a piece of travel literature, Bartram's book was really an account of "the various works of Nature" which he encountered on his excursions through the states of the southern seaboard. Bartram could not undertake his journeys primarily as original explorations, since by the 1770's the area he traversed was fairly well known, for all the wilderness that remained. Yet in a broad sense he was indeed exploring; with only Mark Catesby and his own father as major predecessors, he was seeking out the plants and animals and natural resources of these states, and this search provided the narrative framework of his book. In addition, he was interested to learn all he could of the Indian tribes of the area, and his data comprise a broad anthropological study, one of the earliest of its kind.

How accurate such data were, or how dependable his botany, ichthyology, herpetology, and so forth, is not to be decided here. It is quickly apparent, however, that his accuracy in bird matters is often open to question. A case in point is the following:

> Here [on the islands off the town of Sunbury] are also a great variety of birds, throughout the seasons, inhabiting both sea and land. First I shall name the eagle, of which there are three species. The great grey eagle is the largest, of great strength and high flight; he chiefly preys on fawns and other young quadrupeds.
>
> The bald eagle is likewise a large, strong, and very active bird, but an execrable tyrant: he supports his assumed dignity and grandeur by rapine and violence, extorting unreasonable tribute and subsidy from all the feathered nations.

> The last of this race I shall mention is the falco-piscatorius, or fishing-hawk: this is a large bird, of high and rapid flight; his wings are very long and pointed, and he spreads a vast sail, in proportion to the volume of his body. This princely bird subsists entirely on fish which he takes himself, scorning to live and grow fat on the dear-earned labours of another; he also contributes liberally to the support of the bald eagle.

This passage contains several errors. There are not three species of eagle in this area, but one only, the bald eagle; the "great grey eagle" is an unknown bird, and the "fishing-hawk" or osprey (which has, by the way, neither a rapid flight nor pointed wings) had not been classed with the eagles since Catesby at the latest. From Catesby, Bartram might also have learned that the bald eagle "supports his assumed dignity and grandeur" in part by eating carrion; and he would have discovered from closer observation on his own part that the eagle extorts no more "tribute and subsidy from all the feathered nations" than any of the large raptores—and much less than some of them.

A basic difficulty and no mere factual error is the attitude implied by such expressions as "execrable tyrant," "unreasonable tribute and subsidy," and "scorning to live and grow fat on the dear-earned labours of another." It is perhaps legitimate to speak of the eagle's appropriating the osprey's fish as "execrable," so long as we recognize that this kind of moral judgment has no relevancy to the actions of wild creatures. But the terms "tyrant," "unreasonable," and "scorning" clearly imply avian motives analogous to human ones: the eagle is a willful oppressor who maintains his station in bird society with extortionary demands, whereas the osprey turns his back on such evil actions and earns his living honestly.

It is possible to attribute a good deal of such anthropomorphism to Bartram's weakness for rhetoric. What Carlyle called "a wondrous kind of floundering eloquence" appears to the dispassionate reader of the *Travels* simply an outlook and a prose style more suited to the romancer than the scientist. Bartram tended to dramatize both himself and his subjects; he presented himself to the reader as the dauntless adventurer of the primeval wilderness, risking his life again and again amidst the snakes and alligators and wolves whose precincts he invaded. At times he could be forthright and factual; but characteristically Bartram was romantic, rhetorical, and even declamatory. For all his gentleness and modesty, Bartram had a good deal of the Byronic in his makeup. It is not surprising that Wordsworth and Coleridge found much to interest them in Bartram's tales of wild and exotic nature; nor that both of them, and Coleridge especially, drew upon him for their own work. It is also scarcely remarkable that Thoreau should have reproved Bartram for his exoticism, and should have manifested little or nothing of Bartram's attitude and manner when he came to write *A Week* or *Walden*.

John James Audubon shared much of Bartram's approach to nature, and there are many passages from *Ornithological Biography* which might be inserted in the *Travels* and pass unnoticed. Dissimilar as they were in many ways, the Quaker Naturalist and the American Woodsman had certain traits in common. Basic in both their temperaments was an enthusiasm for nature which approached religious awe, and which was expressed without emotional or literary reticence. Such words as "lovely," "glorious," "majestic," "sublime," "magnificent," and so forth, constantly recur in the writing of both men, as do words with a different but equally romantic connotation, "awful," "gloomy," "fearful," "tempestuous," and the like. The emotionalism implied by terms of this sort leads quite easily into the pathetic fallacy regarding nature generally, and encourages an anthropomorphic view of individual creatures—faults to be detected more in Bartram than in Audubon, but present in both. In addition, these two men shared Rousseau's view of man's relation to wild nature; the section quoted earlier from Audubon's "The Great Pine Swamp" echoes several passages in the *Travels*. Innocence and joy are to be found in the naturalist's simple life; and when in later years worldly experience comes, and "shades of the prison house" close upon the man, it is a matter of great regret. "Ah! where are the moments which I have passed, in the fulness of ecstasy, contemplating the progress of these amiable creatures [white breasted nuthatches]! Alas! they are gone, those summer days of hope and joy are fled, and the clouds of life's winter are mustering in their gloomy array"—so exclaimed Audubon, voicing a sentiment which is implicit in nearly every chapter of Bartram's *Travels*.

* * *

Carlyle wrote to Emerson that the *Travels* had "grown immeasurably *old*." Presumably he was thinking not merely of the distance in years, but in outlook and style also, which separated Bartram from the middle period of the nineteenth century. Bartram and even Audubon were pioneers who celebrated an era which was gone and would not return. Their times were past; they could not speak for this later day. Neither Thoreau nor any other writer could look to them for models. Bartram could be read for his antique charm, but his scientific information and his literary style had become outmoded. Audubon still evoked "a thrill of delight" for his spirited tales of "luxuriant nature," and his ornithological data still commanded respect; but his ingenuous enthusiasm, his fervor, his flamboyance both in outlook and vocabulary, were scarcely appropriate to Thoreau's needs. And so with other writers to whom he might turn; at separate points each might be useful, but when it came to the final, personal resolution, the new approach, the original synthesis that is art, Thoreau would be his own man.

It is important to consider Thoreau's principal nature writings in order of composition, inasmuch as they show a development in treatment of birds which is obscured by the arbitrary order of publication. "Excursion to Canada," for example, was published in part as an article in 1853, a year before *Walden* appeared; but *Walden* was largely written by the end of 1847, whereas the article was written five years later. It is important also to consider only those works which were actually prepared by the author for publication; several volumes were gathered from Thoreau's journal and issued posthumously, but these are too diverse and inconclusive to serve the purposes of the present study.

Thoreau's first nature essay, "Natural History of Massachusetts," was the work of a recent initiate into nature's mysteries, an enthusiast, a celebrant who had not yet found his own vocabulary of homage.

> Those [birds] which spend the winter with us have obtained our warmest sympathy. The nuthatch and chickadee flitting in company through the dells of the wood, the one harshly scolding at the intruder, the other with a faint lisping note enticing him on; the jay screaming in the orchard; the crow cawing in unison with the storm; the partridge, like a russet link extended over from autumn to spring, preserving unbroken the chain of summers; the hawk with warrior-

> like firmness abiding the blasts of winter; the robin and lark lurking by warm springs in the wood; the familiar snow-bird culling a few seeds in the garden, or a few crumbs in the yard; and occasionally the shrike, with heedless and unfrozen melody bringing back summer again: —
>
> His steady sails he never furls
> At any time o' year,
> And perching now on Winter's curls
> He whistles in his ear.

There is little in this passage to suggest Thoreau as its author. The observations are correct but unremarkable; the diction is facile but not distinguished; and the general attitude toward birds is one of affection tinged with patronizing amusement. Here and elsewhere in the essay birds are characterized in traditional and rather bombastic figures of speech — "warrior-like firmness," "ship of the line," "national bird," "tyranny of Jove in its claws," "new dynasty," and the like. Thoreau had not yet learned to accept the bird on its own terms, nor had he achieved the insights which later so distinguished his writing.

"A Walk to Wachusett," a narrative piece written in 1842 or 1843, was more restricted in scope than his first essay, and plainer in diction. Here the birds are observed directly and treated simply, as sprightly, companionable, musical creatures whose presence enhanced the pleasure of walking to the mountain and camping on its top. If they inspired no philosophical conclusions, at least they were presented in a clear and forthright way, in prose uncluttered by allusive banalities.

"A Winter Walk" (1843), perhaps the most evocative and lyrical short prose work Thoreau ever wrote, hints at new directions. Thoreau was beginning to transcend commonplace observations of bird life, and to look more deeply and react more subtly.

> The deep, impenetrable marsh, where the heron waded, and bittern squatted, is made pervious [by its freezing] to our swift shoes, as if a thousand railroads had been made into it. With one impulse we are carried to the cabin of the musk-rat, that earliest settler, and see him dart away under the transparent ice, like a furred fish, to his hole in the bank; and we glide rapidly over meadows where lately "the mower whet his scythe," through beds of frozen cranberries mixed with meadow grass. We skate near to where the blackbird, the peewee, and the kingbird hung their nests over the water, and the hornets builded from the maple in the swamp. How many gay

> warblers, following the sun, have radiated from this nest of silver-birch and thistledown. On the swamp's outer edge was hung the supermarine village, where no foot penetrated. In this hollow tree the wood-duck reared her brood, and slid away each day to forage in yonder fen.

Here is the type of intimate and empathetic look into nature for which Thoreau is famous. He does not condescend, he does not go too far in personalizing his creatures, he does not moralize; instead he finds his way into their lives as far as his knowledge and understanding will permit. This passage, with its altered quotation from Milton and its lapses into conventional literary diction, is by no means the best example of his writing in this vein, but it shows him making a new and fruitful approach to birds and wildlife generally.

One other important attitude is implicit at many points in "A Winter Walk," and stands forth clearly in this passage:

> Standing quite alone, far in the forest, while the wind is shaking down snow from the trees, and leaving the only human tracks behind us, we find our reflections of a richer variety than the life of cities. The chickadee and nuthatch are more inspiring society than statesmen and philosophers, and we shall return to these last as to more vulgar companions.

To find refuge from the common life of men by turning to nature is a desire as old as urban society. Certainly Thoreau was saying nothing new; but he was foreshadowing in this early passage both the alienation from his time, and the compensating rapport with things of the wild, which would make *Walden* at once so somber and so heartening a book.

A Week on the Concord and Merrimack Rivers is a work which fits into no narrow system which might be devised to schematize Thoreau's development. The river journey it describes was experienced in 1839, and the two voyageurs were Thoreau and his brother John; but the book was written eight years later, at Walden Pond, when the beloved brother was dead. When Thoreau himself characterized *A Week* as "a hypaethral or unroofed book, lying open under the ether," he spoke part of the truth. If Thoreau ever composed a Song of Innocence, it was here—but the innocence was tinged by bereavement and the experience of intervening years.

Perhaps because of this ambivalent approach, *A Week* demonstrates several essential aspects of Thoreau's attitude toward birds. His earliest interest in birds was that of the hunter, and in 1839 he had not yet outgrown it: "We obtained one of these handsome birds [passenger pigeons] which lingered too long upon its perch, and plucked and broiled it here with some other game, to be carried along for our supper; for, beside the provisions which we carried with us, we depended mainly on the river and forest for our supply." So much pertains to his outlook at the time of the river trip; but the sentence which immediately follows reflects a later view of things: "It is true, it did not seem to be putting this bird to its right use to pluck off its feathers, and extract its entrails, and broil its carcass on the coals; but we heroically persevered, nevertheless, waiting for further information."

The "further information" on better uses for birds is to be found in the same volume. Perhaps, as on Wachusett, birds may serve as companions, sharing the adventure of the journey; or they may enhance the beauty of the sunset on the last day on the river; or they may help express the antiquity of the American earth, substituting for tales of Greece and Rome their own more ancient reminders; or they may recall to the naturalist the great age of life itself, and all the ages that have passed beneath the eye of so ancient a bird as the bittern, "which may have trodden the earth while it was yet in a slimy and imperfect state." Or, finally, in the world of birds and trees we may find a refuge from the life of towns:

> There is something indescribably inspiriting and beautiful in the aspect of the forest skirting and occasionally jutting into the midst of new towns, which, like the sand-heaps of fresh fox-burrows, have sprung up in their midst. The very uprightness of the pines and maples asserts the ancient rectitude and vigor of nature. Our lives need the relief of such a background, where the pine flourishes and the jay still screams.

* * *

Walden was among other things the chronicle of twice four seasons spent by Thoreau at a small pond near Concord, where a century later the pines still flourish and the bluejays scream. But it was very much else besides. It was a great and complex work of social criticism and philosophy, scarcely to be reduced to easy formulas for quick apprehension. In *Walden* Thoreau achieved both his most profound statements of radical doubt and his most poignant and lyrical confessions of faith. The doubt concerned human life as he had seen it lived; the faith, human life as it should or might be lived. Presumably we shall never know all the things which made him speak as he did, whether yea or nay. Yet it is altogether plain that one deep source of affirmation for Thoreau was his knowledge of nature and love for her works. To divide such a love into its separate manifestations is of course an artificial procedure. Birds may have claimed Thoreau's deepest affection; nevertheless they were but part of the larger entity he celebrated. To single out for study only the birds in *Walden*—as indeed in any worthwhile work treating of nature—is admittedly to make the part represent the whole; but fortunately Thoreau mentioned birds explicitly and often, and wrote of them with an affection seldom vouchsafed any other class of living creatures.

Quoting the Harivansa, Thoreau early in the book wrote, "An abode without birds is like meat without seasoning." But such, he said, was not his abode at Walden Pond.

> I was not only nearer to some of those [birds] which commonly frequent the garden and the orchard, but to those wilder and more thrilling songsters of the forest which never, or rarely, serenade a villager,—the wood-thrush, the veery, the scarlet tanager, the field-sparrow, the whippoorwill, and many others.

Here was a subtle shift of position and emphasis. "I found myself suddenly neighbor to the birds; not by having imprisoned one, but having caged myself near them." Thoreau had not merely taken a nature walk, nor made a temporary retreat to the wilds in order to seek out the birds; instead, he had taken up residence where the birds were, and where, indeed, they might seek out him. Soon a phoebe built in his shed, a robin made her nest in the pine against the cabin, a ruffed grouse led her brood into his clearing. Thoreau had not so much fled the town as he had returned to live within an older order of things, where the brute creatures were his neighbors.

The sense of being among friends appears again and again in

Walden. Thoreau planted his beanfield to the cheerful song of the brown thrasher, and found it "a cheap sort of top dressing in which I had entire faith." In the notable passage beginning "It was no longer beans that I hoed, nor I that hoed beans," he told how his work was transformed by the presence in the sky overhead of the nighthawk, the "hen hawk," and the wild pigeon. Elsewhere he noted how the summer night was enhanced by the calling of owls and whippoorwills, and the winter day brightened by visits from jays and chickadees.

Then in his penultimate chapter, "Spring," Thoreau composed a rhapsody to the returning birds, whose song made all things new again.

> The first sparrow of spring! The year beginning with younger hope than ever! The faint silvery warblings heard over the partially bare and moist fields from the blue-bird, the song-sparrow, and the red-wing, as if the last flakes of winter tinkled as they fell! What at such a time are histories, chronologies, traditions, and all written revelations?

A few pages later appeared an even more lyrical celebration of a migrant bird, a pigeon hawk, transfigured by Thoreau's words into a symbol of all feathered creatures whose wings make a home of air.

> On the 29th of April, as I was fishing from the bank of the river . . . I heard a singular rattling sound, somewhat like that of the sticks which boys play with their fingers, when, looking up, I observed a very slight and graceful hawk, like a night-hawk, alternately soaring like a ripple and tumbling a rod or two over and over, showing the underside of its wings, which gleamed like a satin ribbon in the sun, or like the pearly inside of a shell. This sight reminded me of falconry and what noblesse and poetry are associated with that sport. The Merlin it seemed to me it might be called: but I care not for its name. It was the most ethereal flight I had ever witnessed. It did not simply flutter like a butterfly, nor soar like the larger hawks, but it sported with proud reliance in the fields of air; mounting again and again with its strange chuckle, it repeated its free and beautiful fall, turning over and over like a kite, and then recovering from its lofty tumbling, as if it had never set its foot on *terra firma*. It appeared to have no companion in the universe, — sporting there alone, — and to need none but the morning and the ether with which it played. It was not lonely, but made all the earth lonely beneath it. Where was the parent which hatched it, its kindred, and its father in the heavens? The tenant of the air, it seemed related to the earth

> but by an egg hatched some time in the crevice of a crag; — or was its native nest made in the angle of a cloud, woven of the rainbow's trimmings and the sunset sky, and lined with some soft midsummer haze caught up from earth? Its eyry now some cliffy cloud.

Here is perhaps the most ecstatic passage to a bird ever written in English prose. Only a few short sections of Audubon's work approach it; we must look to poetry to find its equal. Yet for all its intensity, this passage does not give Thoreau's last word. *Walden* praises nature not merely for her beauty, as here, but for her truth also. From the life of birds we turn to consider the life of men, and see where we have failed.

> Hither [to White and Walden ponds] the clean wild ducks come. Nature has no human inhabitant who appreciates her. The birds with their plumage and their notes are in harmony with the flowers, but what youth or maiden conspires with the wild luxuriant beauty of Nature? She flourishes most alone, far from the towns where they reside. Talk of heaven! ye disgrace earth.

❧ ❧ ❧

Thoreau wrote nothing further in book form. All his prose subsequent to *Walden* consisted of shorter pieces, most of them accounts of his travels to Maine, Canada, and Cape Cod. Written to be sold to magazines, they were shaped at least in part by the special requirements of the magazine article. The travel pieces, "Ktaadn and the Maine Woods," "Excursion to Canada," the chapters which make up *Cape Cod*, and "Chesuncook" (all of them written and largely published between 1848 and 1858), in general hewed to the narrative line, and offered few reflective comments except in passing. Only in "Walking," "Autumnal Tints," "Wild Apples," and "Night and Moonlight," essays prepared for publication not long before the author's death in May 1862, did Thoreau attempt a return to the outlook and style of *Walden*.

In the travel articles especially a marked change from earlier work is to be found. A new interest in human characterization appears, while the old devotion to wild creatures is little in evidence. Thoreau's fellow human beings, not his brute neighbors, take the stage, and speak their parts in a way which shows Thoreau to have been a sharp and even sardonic judge of character. Such birds as do appear are treated hastily, and often identified by vernacular names and general attributes. It almost seems that Thoreau had abandoned the interpretation of nature and had found refuge in considering the common life of men. A dubious refuge it was at best, if we may judge by the dryness and brittleness of the later travel pieces, especially *Cape Cod.* The human comedy was not Thoreau's province. He was too rigorous, too moralistic, too special a person to vibrate in kind with common humanity. It is with relief that we find him reverting to his proper métier, nature, in his final essays. Here, as in *Walden,* he could speak with authority. He began the essay "Walking" with this characteristic passage:

> I wish to speak a word for Nature, for absolute freedom and wildness, as contrasted with a freedom and culture merely civil, — to regard man as an inhabitant, or a part and parcel of Nature, rather than a member of society. I wish to make an extreme statement, if so I may make an emphatic one, for there are enough champions of civilization: the minister and the school-committee and every one of you will take care of that.

But the birds which had disappeared did not return to Thoreau's pages, except as hurried visitors. To be sure, two of the four final essays explicitly concerned trees — but Thoreau had not allowed narrow limits of subject matter to inhibit him earlier. In any case, one would expect to find birds under such ample titles as "Walking" and "Night and Moonlight," but they scarcely appear. Had Thoreau abandoned the study of birds? Had he ceased to love them, or to find in them beauty and meaning? Yes, if we may judge by these essays alone. But the truth is that he had done nothing of the sort, as his journal very convincingly shows. Indeed, by the testimony of the journal, Thoreau had not merely continued his devoted pursuit of birds, he had intensified it. During the 1850's, the average length of his bird entries, and the number of species mentioned, greatly increased over the previous decade; yet this was the period when his formal writing relegated birds to minor notices.

The solution to the paradox appears when we compare not the number of species mentioned or entries made in the two decades, but the different attitudes they reflect. In this connection the critic Norman Foerster correctly discerned "the constant increase in the proportion of fact to comment as the *Journal* proceeds." * Not that Thoreau had abandoned his love of birds for mere ornithology — far from it. He was more unwilling than ever to "collect" birds for information; in 1854 he wrote, "In Boston yesterday an ornithologist said significantly, 'If you held the bird in your hand — ;' but I would rather hold it in my affections." But collecting field notes of the living bird became more and more an end in itself, until it seems to the reader that Thoreau has gotten lost amid his facts, scarcely knowing what to do with them. The love remains, but it is sublimated into data, not released into praise, as earlier. Even where the bird sets in motion a typically Thoreauvian train of thought, a philosophical response to the bird's challenge, the element of celebration is nearly always missing. Birds were still objects of loving attention; but they no longer afforded Thoreau the same kind of joyous release which had burst forth in *Walden*.

Perhaps it was no longer possible for Thoreau to write of birds as he once had, because he no longer believed as he once did. *Walden*, despite its rejection of vulgar standards of human life, was an affirmative book in that it proposed other standards — broadly, accord with the verities of nature, and more narrowly, the study of birds as special vessels of nature's truth and beauty, her "perfect confidence and success." Such a study was Thoreau's own refuge still — but not his credo in public discourse. If Thoreau had once been nature's priest, now his faith was clouded by doubt. Thus toward the end he spoke of trees, and called for "absolute freedom and wildness," but said little or nothing of the sporting hawk or the warbling bluebird, icons of an earlier time.

Thornton Wilder has said of Thoreau, "through his long inquiry he heard the closing of three doors . . . the doors to Love, Friendship, and Nature." † Nature's door, which concerns us here, did not close swiftly, but it came nearly shut at last. Its swing was hastened in the final years by incongruous political activity, confining shop

* Norman Foerster, *Nature in American Literature* (New York: Macmillan, 1923), pp. 92–93.

† Thornton Wilder, "The American Loneliness," *The Atlantic Monthly*, August 1952, p. 66.

work and consequent failing health, and perhaps most of all by the general public apathy toward his crucial writings. He had been the prophet of nature, but his prophecy had gone unheeded, his ministry had failed. The birds he loved still, but they could not help him, for the weight which bore upon him would not be lifted by their wings.

8 *Emerson and Other Worthies*

Any notion that Ralph Waldo Emerson was, in his outlook on nature, merely an elder counterpart of Thoreau should be unsettled by the paragraph already quoted from Emerson, and should disappear entirely upon examination of his treatment of birds. No great acumen is needed to discover the gentle mockery of Emerson's words, especially in the section beginning, "There came Henry with music book under his arm, to press flowers. . ." But Emerson was not a man to chide another gratuitously; if he registered in this journal entry his disapproval of Thoreau's pursuit of fact, it was because he supposed Henry to be misguided. Elsewhere he warned Thoreau never to find out the true name of his "night warbler," lest the charm of the mysterious bird disappear in the light of mere identity. For Emerson, in short, the fact was of no benefit (and might even be of harm) unless it could be made to flower into a truth. Concerning scientific taxonomy he said:

> The true classification will not present itself to us in a catalogue of a hundred classes, but as an idea of which the flying wasp and the grazing ox are developments. Natural History is to be studied, not with any pretension that its classification is permanent, but merely as full of tendency . . . The pre-eminent claim of natural science

> is that it seeks directly that which all sciences, arts, and trades seek indirectly, – knowledge of the universe we live in. It shows man in the centre, with a ray of relation passing from him to every created thing. But to gain this advantage we must not lose ourselves in nomenclature.

Two central ideas which dominated Emerson's outlook on nature may be found in this brief excerpt. The first is the notion of natural creatures as "developments" of "an idea" – elsewhere more specifically denominated Oversoul or God. However complex and even contradictory Emerson's many statements on the natural order, his belief in its divine origin and beneficent character is unmistakable. To this belief he could refer all doubts – as Thoreau, for all his celebration of nature's truth and beauty, could not. Increasingly Thoreau was unable to find the flower of divine truth in the facts he garnered and deposited in his journal; but Emerson saw the workings of God everywhere, and rather deplored the idea that anything so peripheral as ornithological or botanical data could be reckoned of central use to the poet or philosopher. Again from his journal: after telling a story of a dull boy learning his alphabet, he asks, "Is it not exquisite ridicule upon our learned Linnaean classifications? 'What shell is this?' 'It is a *strombus.*' 'The devil! is that a *strombus?*' would be the appropriate reply."

A second Emersonian attitude emerges in the passage declaring that natural science "seeks . . . knowledge of the universe we live in [and] shows man in the centre, with a ray of relation passing from him to every created thing." A dual meaning may be inferred from these words, both aspects of which are important in Emerson's outlook. Natural science is a means by which men seek reality, and being only one of many similar human endeavors, is both fallible and incomplete. But whatever its limitations, it does show "man in the centre"; the human being, highest and best of earthly beings, is central in God's creation. By discrete quotation Emerson may be made to deny this point of view; nevertheless it was for him basic and enduring doctrine. How far it is from Thoreau's characteristic attitude toward his fellow-creatures, his brute neighbors!

Another of Emerson's journal entries makes an arresting contrast with Thoreau's passage on the sporting pigeon hawk, or even with his remarks on the hen-hawk with its "civilization other than our own."

> I saw a hawk to-day wheeling up to heaven in a spiral flight, and every circle becoming less to the eye till he vanished into the atmosphere. What could be more in unison with all pure and brilliant images. Yet is the creature an unclean greedy eater, and all his geography from that grand observatory was a watching of barn-yards, or an inspection of moles and field-mice. So with the pelican, crane, and the tribes of sea-fowl — disgusting gluttons all. Yet observe how finely in nature all disagreeable individuals integrate themselves into a cleanly and pleasing whole.

The pattern here is a familiar one in Emerson's thought — the integration of separately disturbing facts into an ultimately optimistic conclusion. But the details he assembles are, to say the least, open to question. By what standard does he judge the hawk to be "unclean" or "greedy"? On what basis can the pelican or the crane or "the tribes of sea-fowl" be considered "disgusting gluttons"? These are epithets of a person who, first, has his facts wrong, and second, applies merely human standards to life quite outside our own. "Unclean" is an incongruous word to apply to a hawk — or, if the hawk is unclean, then so is every bird, each in its own way. The sparrow eats dry and bloodless seeds, but bathes in the roadside dust; the swift is a denizen of the pure air, but makes his nest in a sooty chimney by gluing twigs together with saliva; the ruby-throat is a tiny jewel of a bird which feeds its young by vomiting up flower nectar. These observations are valid enough as mere facts; as judgments in the Emersonian manner they are meaningless. Then as to greediness and gluttony: wild creatures eat to live, bound as they are by an intricate ecological situation; what or how much they eat is scarcely a matter of choice or reflective thought. Only the human being knows and can systematically follow the unnatural custom of eating far more than he requires to live and reproduce.

At the risk of beating a dead horse, one may inquire further into this passage to discover just where Emerson made a wrong turning. There is, to be sure, very often an element of willfullness in Emerson's moralizing; the man who could find God emergent in a load of bricks or a barbershop is capable of nearly any wrench of logic. But there is no mystery about his difficulty in this passage on birds. He simply had little or no first-hand knowledge of either hawks or pelicans or cranes or sea-fowl. Almost certainly, he had never investigated the everyday life of any hawk living in the Concord woods; had he done so, he would not have assumed that high soaring is an act of hunting – nor indeed that any of the soaring hawks is commonly a raider of barnyards. Moreover, it is quite unlikely that Emerson had ever seen either a crane or a pelican in the wild; and he knew so little of "sea-fowl" that he did not indicate whether he meant ducks or cormorants, gulls or petrels, phalaropes or gannets. All "the tribes," perhaps – but such lumping together of diverse species is an absurdity.

Yet Emerson may not properly be taxed for his paucity of factual data. Not merely did he tend to think of wild creatures in literary and philosophical terms; he specifically abjured close study, which to him jeopardized the divine mystery and beauty of nature. Under "Beauty," in *The Conduct of Life*, he said:

> We should go to the ornithologist with a new feeling if he could teach us what the social birds say when they sit in the autumn council, talking together in the trees. The want of sympathy makes his record a dull dictionary. His result is a dead bird. The bird is not in its ounces and inches, but in its relations to Nature, and the skin or skeleton you show me is no more a heron, than a heap of ashes or a bottle of gases into which his body has been reduced, is Dante or Washington. The naturalist is led *from* the road by the whole distance of his fancied advance. The boy had juster views when he gazed at the shells on the beach or the flowers in the meadow, unable to call them by their names, than the man in the pride of his nomenclature. Astrology interested us, for it tied man to the system . . . Alchemy, which sought to transmute one element into another, to prolong life, to arm with power, – that was in the right direction.

This seems deliberate obscurantism; yet it is not. Rather it is a statement of profound and positive faith. Note that the naturalist by his studies "is led *from* the road" – that is, diverted from the way of truth, which for Emerson was the apprehension of God through the wonder of His natural works. Let scientists, then, but change the direction and intent of their pursuits. Let the ornithologist interpret the message of the birds, the astronomer read the lesson of the stars, and the chemist unlock the mystery of life, and they will be admitted to the company of the wise; but until then, pursuing mere science, they strain for trifles.

⁂

Because Emerson never really learned his birds, the references to them in his journal are relatively few and likely to be imprecise. Similarly, his formal prose has little to do with birds. He belongs in this book mainly because he directly influenced later bird writers—notably John Burroughs—and because his general outlook on nature, widely accepted in nineteenth-century America, both complemented and competed with Thoreau's.

"I expand and live in the warm day like corn and melons" is one of the most memorable sentences from the first of Emerson's two essays entitled *Nature*. On its face it seems an assertion of intimate identity with growing things, very much in the manner of Thoreau. In fact, however, Emerson uses it only to illustrate the childish (or mistaken) view that the world of the senses is real; whereas, he goes on to say, nature actually represents only the outer dress of the Idea in God's mind. "Idealism sees the world in God"—and so Emerson would have us see it. A similar progression of thought occurs in the passage beginning, "Standing on the bare ground,—my head bathed by the blithe air, and uplifted into infinite space,—all mean egotism vanishes. I become a transparent eye-ball; I am nothing; I see all"—up to this point a celebration of exquisite sense perception. But the passage ends, "the currents of the Universal Being circulate through me; I am part or parcel of God." In *Walden*, the chapter "Solitude" begins much as Emerson's passage does: "This is a delicious evening, when the whole body is one sense, and imbibes delight through every pore." But where Emerson invokes the deity, Thoreau then speaks of bullfrogs and alder trees, into whose world his senses have translated him. Emerson talked much of God; Thoreau, little.

Many passages from both the earlier and later *Nature* essays testify to Emerson's belief in the primary importance of man in nature's scheme, and to his conviction of the subsidiary and auxiliary function of the lower orders of being. In the first, discussing nature as commodity, he acclaims "the steady and prodigal provision that has been made for [man's] support and delight on this green ball which floats through the heavens. . . Beasts, fire, water, stones, and corn serve him. . . Nature, in its ministry to man, is not only the material, but is also the process and result. All the parts incessantly work into each other's hands for the profit of man." In the second essay, while chiding mankind for being unworthy and unaware, he again and again states the same hierarchy: God, man, and nature, in descending order. In the divine mind all things are of one stuff, but in the world as it appears to us there is a gradation from higher to lower.

> We are escorted on every hand through life by spiritual agents, and a beneficent purpose lies in wait for us. We cannot bandy words with Nature, or deal with her as we deal with persons. If we measure our individual forces against hers we might easily feel as if we were the sport of an insuperable destiny. But if, instead of identifying ourselves with the work, we feel that the soul of the workman streams through us, we shall find the peace of the morning dwelling first in our hearts, and the fathomless powers of gravity and chemistry, and, over them, of life, pre-existing within us in their highest form.

Thoreau, on the other hand, was not nearly so sure of the beneficent character of nature, and was by no means convinced of man's special importance in the scheme of things. The skepticism implicit in so much of his writing comes out clearly, almost harshly, in this passage from *Walden*:

> But the most luxuriously housed [person] has little to boast of [regarding shelter against the cold], nor need we trouble ourselves to speculate how the human race may be at last destroyed. It would be easy to cut their threads any time with a little sharper blast from the north. We go on dating from Cold Fridays and Great Snows; but a little colder Friday, or greater snow, would put a period to man's existence on the globe.

The differences, then, were deep—so deep indeed that one is tempted to think of the philosophical similarities between these two Concord Yankees as fortuitous and superficial. Yet both looked to nature for truth and beauty; both found in it a resource for the spirit; and perhaps most important of all to the present inquiry, both apprehended nature sensuously, emotionally, and with mystical joy. The insights thus achieved were resolved in different ways, but they sprang from similar feelings. Moreover, both Emerson and Thoreau used their insights to illuminate the human predicament. The love of nature was for neither man an end in itself, but was a means toward a better life. In short, both were moralists who found criteria for human conduct by contemplating nature.

In terms of literature, Emerson and Thoreau were unquestionably the two most influential nature writers to appear in nineteenth-century America. Between them they established canons of prose nature writing which dominated the century, and which are yet to be entirely supplanted. None of the later bird essayists to be taken up here could claim independence from their influence. Thoreau speaks through those writers who stress close observation and intimate knowledge of wild creatures; who feel a kinship with them that transcends mere affection; who draw from them chastening lessons and sobering analogies; who love them for their own special virtues and attributes, and refuse to judge them in human terms. Emerson is echoed by those who find in nature an easy bridge to God; who observe wild creatures primarily in generic, not specific terms, in order to provide themselves with convenient moral illustrations; who endow those creatures with human motives and characteristics, and measure them by human standards of conduct; and who place them beneath man in the hierarchy of creation. For general outlook, later writers might turn to Thoreau for a philosophical skepticism and humility, or to Emerson for an optimism, almost an innocence, unshaken by momentary doubts.

The minor Transcendentalists who looked to Emerson for intellectual leadership, and who could claim Thoreau as a sort of *ex officio* member of their group, produced some poetry but very little noteworthy prose on the subject of birds. Margaret Fuller, in her travel book *Summer on the Lakes, in 1843*, showed considerable knowledge of wild flowers but made little mention of birds. Despite the affection she shows for nature, there is not much evidence that it was an important preoccupation of hers. Nature was to her as to Emerson, something to be apprehended in a general way for philosophical insights. Thomas Wentworth Higginson quotes her as saying that "Nature will not be stared at" — an attitude verified by her flower fable, "The Magnolia of Lake Ponchartrain," which asserts (in impeccably Emersonian terms) that the quest for nature's secret drives the seeker "back upon the centre of [his] being," to find there "all being."

Higginson himself was the one nature writer who might be called an associate of the Transcendental movement — and then only because he had a personal acquaintance with authors of the group, not because he was of their persuasion. His essays remind one of Thoreau—but a Thoreau domesticated, urbanized, tamed. Higginson knew Thoreau, and had gone walking with him, and often mentioned him with approval; he did not, however, share with him the desire to crow like Chanticleer, to wake his neighbors up.

Outdoor Studies [*and*] *Poems* (1890) suggests by its title an important fact about Higginson's nature essays, that they were exercises in a particular genre by a man who had yet other studies which engaged his attention. He is in fact far better known as an abolitionist, a soldier, an editor, a literary critic and a friend of Emily Dickinson than as a writer on nature. The eleven essays which compose *Outdoor Studies* were published in the *Atlantic* over a period of twenty-two years, 1858–1880; but even this meager list is deceiving, since two of the pieces are narratives of travel, another is a discussion of maternal love, and a fourth—"Saints, and their Bodies"—is a plea for the sort of physical exercise that produces "rosy female faces and noble manly figures."

Most of the remaining essays stress flowers, and only one wholly concerns birds. "The Life of Birds," first published in 1862, shows how well Higginson had learned Thoreau's lesson of accurate observation without absorbing his rigorous social outlook. This is a familiar essay on the subject of birds, executed by a man who could discover the pertinent facts and cite the proper authorities (he mentions MacGillivray, Audubon, Brewer, Wilson) while abstaining from social comment. His joy in nature is conveyed to the reader quietly and with restraint. His diction is felicitous and bland; his humor is mild; his sympathies are many, his crotchets few. Higginson was not an important writer on nature, but he was an able and ingratiating one; and he was an early representative of a significant group of essayists—Flagg, Burroughs, Torrey, Bolles—whose writings on birds helped to extend and popularize the work begun by Thoreau.

In the original version of "The Life of Birds," Higginson complained that American bird study, so magnificently begun by Audubon and Wilson and expertly carried on by Brewer and Nuttall, had lately tended to disappear from public concern; but he listed in a footnote four articles which had recently appeared in the *Atlantic*, indicating that the tide was turning. The first, "Our Birds, and Their Ways," by J. Elliot Cabot, was less an essay than a series of personal observations of winter birds, casually strung together, and presented without philosophical interpretations. The other three were by Wilson Flagg: "The Singing-Birds and Their Songs," "The Birds of the Garden and Orchard," and "The Birds of the Pasture and Forest."

Early in the first essay, Flagg says: "The value of such pleasures [of nature study] consists not so much in their cheapness as in their favorable moral influences . . . The quiet emotions, half musical and half poetical, which are awakened by listening to the songs of birds, belong to this class of refined enjoyments." This strain of moralizing, mildly Emersonian in tone, runs through these essays and later ones, and appears in many places in his book *A Year with the Birds* (1881). But Flagg's most pervasive interest was in bird songs; he goes much beyond Thoreau and Emerson in attempting to render songs in verbal form, and appends several pages of musical notation to the essays, in which songs are approximated by the use of scales.

Wilson Flagg was a writer with a great deal of charm, superficially factual in presenting his data and working out his song notations, but with an approach more literary than scientific, and a style more useful in imparting feelings than in describing particulars. Perhaps the most significant thing about him is the assumption which underlay much of his work – that the reader knew beforehand the bird in question, and that the author's duty therefore was not to identify or describe it, but to add something new concerning its song. In this way Flagg clearly implied that readers of *The Atlantic Monthly* in the sixth decade of the nineteenth century had a fairly wide acquaintance with birds, and would understand without elaboration references to the chipping sparrow or the nighthawk or the veery.

Higginson's mention of these *Atlantic* articles suggests a noteworthy fact about the editorial policy of that magazine. Articles on nature were from the beginning an important feature; the Cabot essay came out in the second issue (December 1857), Thoreau's "Chesuncook" was begun in serial form some months later, and the list of nature authors in succeeding years was to include not only Flagg and Higginson, but also John Burroughs, Clarence King, John Muir, Bradford Torrey, and Frank Bolles.

9 *"John o' Birds": John Burroughs*

John Burroughs' first important article appeared in the *Atlantic* for November 1860, but it was not about birds, and it concerned general nature only in an indirect way. It was an essay entitled "Expression," and began:

> The law of expression is the law of degrees, — of much, more, and most.
>
> Nature exists to the mind not as an absolute realization, but as a condition, as something constantly becoming . . . The landscape has a pleasure for us, because in the mind it is canopied by the ideal, as it is here canopied by the sky.

With these words setting the tone for the entire essay, it is scarcely remarkable that James Russell Lowell, then the magazine's editor, held up its publication until he had checked Emerson's writings to make sure Burroughs was not plagiarizing. From beginning to end, "Expression" is Emersonian, not merely in thought but also very largely in diction. Burroughs was here suggesting (by the flattery of imitation) what he later stated explicitly, that reading Emerson at the age of nineteen was a crucial and formative experience: "I read him in a sort of ecstasy. I got him in my blood, and he colored my whole intellectual outlook. He appealed to my spiritual side; his boldness and unconventionality took a deep hold upon me." * Yet when Burroughs achieved his own characteristic idiom, he almost completely abandoned both Emerson's literary mannerisms and his attitude toward nature. Therefore it is well to look rather narrowly at Burroughs' words, and to consider in what particular way Emerson was influential.

John Burroughs, born in 1837 on a farm in Delaware County, New York, came of Old School Baptist stock. Later in life he recalled the rigorous Calvinist atmosphere of his home, and the theological disputes his father engaged in; and it is entirely plain that he reacted strongly against the harshness and intolerance to which he was witness. Burroughs became, indeed, something of an agnostic, Emerson serving him as a sort of halfway house on his journey. "His boldness and unconventionality took a deep hold upon me" – in other words, Emerson helped Burroughs escape the religiosity of his home, by telling him to rely on his own impulses, especially those of awe and reverence toward nature. Both men reacted against formal theology; but Emerson reconstituted his beliefs in terms of the Oversoul, whereas Burroughs could not and did not do so. There persisted in Burroughs much of the pantheistic emotionalism of his liberator, but he fought shy of committing himself too forthrightly on the issue of God; and at times, particularly in his earlier books, he explicitly denied the divinely benevolent character of nature by avowing a type of Darwinism.

Burroughs' first bird article, "With the Birds," appeared in the *Atlantic* for May 1865. It suggests that he was moving away from Emersonianism, but had not fully achieved his own characteristic outlook. Working at his dull tasks in an office of the Treasury Department in Washington, Burroughs is cheered by recollections of birds he has seen in the free outdoors: "With these angels and ministers of grace thus to attend me, even in the seclusion of my closet, I am led more than ever to expressions of love and admiration. I understand the enthusiasm of Wilson and Audubon, and see how one might forsake house and home and go and live with them the free life of the woods."

* Quoted by Clara Barrus, *The Life and Letters of John Burroughs* (2 vols.; Boston: Houghton Mifflin Company, 1925), I, 41.

A few paragraphs later, relating that he shot a thrush for identification purposes, he writes, "I turn this Thrush in my hand, — I remember its strange ways, the curious look it gave me, its ineffable music, its freedom, its ecstasy, — and I tremble lest I have slain a being diviner than myself."

These passages are neither good Burroughs nor good Emerson, but in style or in attitude they echo both men. The religious overtones and much of the diction suggest Emerson; yet the act of shooting a bird, and the enthusiasm for ornithological study implied by the references to Wilson and Audubon, foreshadow the later Burroughs. No doubt recognizing that neither passage properly represented him, Burroughs dropped both when he revised the essay for publication in *Wake Robin* (1871).

Between "Expression" and "With the Birds," John Burroughs made a discovery equal in its immediate effect to his coming upon Emerson, and even more lasting in its influence on his career as an author. In the spring of 1863, while visiting the library of the Military Academy at West Point, he encountered the work of a man he later called "one of the most striking figures in our history" — John James Audubon. A biographer of Burroughs, Dr. Clara Barrus, has called this one of the most significant events of his life. Burroughs had always been interested in the outdoors, but Audubon's magnificent work gave his interest the particular orientation which dominated his life. From that time on, Burroughs was to be a writer on birds before anything else.

"With the Birds" indicates that Burroughs was an exceedingly apt pupil in his newly discovered study. The bulk of the article is given over to characterizations of the author's favorite birds, and there is no questioning the accuracy of most of what he has to say. Only three major errors appear. Burroughs confused the European with the American cuckoo when he said the latter "deposits his eggs in the nests of other birds, having no heart for work or domestic care." He was mistaken in saying that Thoreau could not have heard a wood thrush in northern Maine; the bird is a regular nesting species in certain areas of the state, and accidental elsewhere. In the third instance, Burroughs was on shaky ground when he gave ragged-looking tail feathers as the reason a particular wood thrush refused to migrate until late in the fall — "the sylvan prince could not think of returning to court in this plight."

The first two errors were corrected by Burroughs before this essay was reprinted in *Wake Robin,* but the other was allowed to stand. In two cases the reasons are not far to seek. The statement about the cuckoo was en error regarding the nesting habits of a well-known bird, and the comment on Thoreau was not merely a misguided attempt to correct a respected authority, but also a denial of an established fact of distribution. In both cases, Burroughs had only to be shown the proper references to see that he was wrong. The third case, however, was not so simple. It would be quite impossible to prove that a thrush lingered about in the fall because it felt ashamed of ragged feathers; but disproving the idea is equally out of the question. Nevertheless the rigorous student of birds tend to abjure such easy anthropomorphism as Burroughs invokes, and to look askance upon a phrase like "the sylvan prince" or "returning to court." That Burroughs elected to retain this passage suggests the fact that he did not shrink from personalizing birds. Analogous passages are to be found in almost all his bird essays. They may appear to the scientist highly dubious and to the literary critic regrettably sentimental; but they tended to appeal to the common reader, and must be recognized as an important reason for the great popular vogue which Burroughs enjoyed.

⁂

Darwinism and anthropomorphism may seem too antithetical to be incorporated in a single book; yet Burroughs in *Wake Robin* achieved the union, or at least the juxtaposition, of the two. At one point he may treat a bird sentimentally, as a miniature human being; elsewhere he may simply shoot it, ending its life as easily and as impersonally as nature herself does. At the very start, in the Preface, he dismisses Emerson's (misquoted) query, "Have you named all the birds without the gun?" as inapplicable to his study. He describes how he himself goes about collecting specimens, and he gives this advice to beginning bird students: "First, find your bird; observe its ways, its song, it calls, its flight, its haunts; then shoot it (not ogle it with a glass), and compare with Audubon."

Such passages, whatever their harsh implications, may be put down to their author's enthusiastic pursuit of ornithology. Not so the following, which describes the fate of a cowbird fledgling Burroughs discovered in the nest of a Canada warbler: "Taking the interloper by the nape of the neck, I deliberately drop it into the water, but not without a pang, as I see its naked form, convulsed with chills, float down stream. Cruel? So is Nature cruel." Here the heartlessness implied in the shooting of specimens is given a rationale: human cruelty toward lesser creatures is simply a manifestation of the cruelty which Darwin had shown to exist everywhere in nature. In *Birds and Poets* (1877) Burroughs made his position even plainer:

> The boy is part of Nature; he is as indifferent, as careless, as vagrant as she. He browses, he digs, he hunts, he climbs, he halloes, he feeds on roots and greens and mast. He uses things roughly and without sentiment. The coolness with which boys will drown dogs or cats, or hang them to trees, or murder young birds, or torture frogs or squirrels, is like Nature's own mercilessness.

Alfred Tennyson, deeply shaken by evolutionary ideas even before Darwin's work appeared, cried out against "Nature . . . so careless of the single life"; Burroughs accepted her thus with scarcely a tremor. Again from *Birds and Poets*: "Nature does not care whether the hunter slay the beast or the beast the hunter; she will make good compost of them both, and her ends are prospered whichever succeeds."

In Burroughs' view, nature's indifference toward her separate creatures encompasses man, himself part of the natural order. Tennyson, unable to deny this fact, nevertheless deplored it. "Let the ape and tiger die," he wrote; let man work out the beast from his nature, and move "from darkness up to God," taking his intended place as heir to all the ages. No such counsel came from Burroughs:

> It is well to let down our metropolitan pride a little. Man thinks himself at the top, and that the immense display and prodigality of Nature are for him. But they are no more for him than they are for the birds and beasts, and he is no more at the top than they are. He appeared upon the stage when the play had advanced to a certain point, and he will disappear from the stage when the play has

> reached another point, and the great drama will go on without him. The geological ages, the convulsions and parturition throes of the globe, were to bring him forth no more than the beetles.

Burroughs, then, was a whole-hearted evolutionist, accepting the view of nature set forth in *The Origin of Species* (1859) and of man's position as given in *The Descent of Man* (1871). It is true that he doubted certain aspects of the theory of sexual selection; but he cheerfully embraced the larger tenets and implications of Darwinism, and put them to use in his writing.

When one recalls that the great biologist Louis Agassiz rejected Darwin's hypothesis and insisted on the immutability of species, and that so respected and influential a writer as James Russell Lowell dismissed evolution by calling it "a poor substitute for the Rock of Ages," * Burroughs' acceptance of Darwin may appear to have been a bold and unconventional move. Actually, however, Burroughs was on the side of his own great mentors; his response was in keeping with the trend shown by earlier nature writers and scientists. Even Emerson, secure in his Transcendental faith, followed scientific developments with sympathy and interest. In his second essay entitled *Nature* (1844) he considered the implications of recent geological discoveries in these characteristic terms:

> Geology has initiated us into the secularity of nature, and taught us to disuse our dame-school measures, and exchange our Mosaic and Ptolemaic schemes for her large style. We knew nothing rightly, for want of perspective. Now we learn what patient periods must round themselves before the rock is formed; then before the rock is broken, and the first lichen race has disintegrated the thinnest external plate into soil, and opened the door for the remote Flora, Fauna, Ceres, and Pomona to come in. How far off yet is the trilobite! how far the quadruped! how inconceivably remote is man! All duly arrive, and then race after race of men. It is a long way from granite to the oyster; farther yet to Plato and the preaching of the immortality of the soul. Yet all must come, as surely as the first atom has two sides.

Thoreau scarcely lived long enough to consider fully Darwin's *Origin of Species*, but a remark recorded by Emerson in his journal

* Quoted by Dirk J. Struik, as part of an excellent short discussion of the evolution controversy in his *Yankee Science in the Making* (Boston: Little, Brown and Company, 1948), pp. 309–314.

indicates that Thoreau sided with Darwin in the controversy which immediately developed in America:

> Agassiz says, "There are no varieties in nature. All are species." Thoreau says, "If Agassiz sees two thrushes so alike that they bother the ornithologist to discriminate them, he insists they are two species; but if he sees Humboldt and Fred Cogswell [a kindly, underwitted inmate of Concord Almshouse], he insists that they came from one ancestor."

There are, furthermore, several hints in Thoreau's formal prose that he responded affirmatively to earlier evolutionary doctrine; and at least one entry in his journal may show a direct reaction to Darwin: "How the [grackles] sit and make a business of chattering! for it cannot be called singing, and no improvement from age to age perhaps. Yet, as *nature* is a *becoming*, their notes may become melodious at last."

Almost thirty years earlier, in 1832, Constantine Rafinesque had postulated a similar "becoming" when he wrote of "the great universal law of *perpetual mutability* in everything" * — clearly an anticipation of later evolutionary theory. Even William Bartram, unsystematic though he was in many ways, recognized the principle of interrelationship and evolution among birds, noting that various bird "tribes" (species) have certain characteristics in common because they have "descended or separated" from a parent stock.

However, the problem of the development of species — including one called *Homo sapiens* — is only part of the evolutionary question. The sections quoted from Burroughs suggest that he was primarily interested in neither Genesis nor genera, but rather in the "cruel" or "merciless" process whereby nature achieved the changes postulated in the theory. He had no trouble embracing the idea that nature is the scene of a constant struggle for life; and here again he was on the side of his major predecessors. In the *Travels* William Bartram frequently described the struggle for survival among various creatures, and did so without moralizing about the matter. Life as it is lived "in the state of nature" was something Bartram accepted without question, as simply the truth as he had seen it. And what Bartram saw, Wilson and Audubon and Thoreau saw also. Among wild things, birds espe-

* Quoted by Bernard Jaffe, *Men of Science in America* (New York: Simon and Schuster, 1946), p. 126.

cially are creatures of intense but precarious life; no one can study them closely without realizing the multitudinous hazards of their brief span, the constant struggle against the natural enemies which beset their way. And so it was that John Burroughs, heir to a century-old tradition of nature study, could see this aspect of evolution in its proper setting and prespective, and accept it without pain or hesitation.

It should not be supposed, however, that Burroughs allowed himself to be dominated by evolutionary doctrine. Theodore Dreiser's Frank Cowperwood saw human life mirrored in a fierce and symbolic (if biologically absurd) struggle between a squid and a lobster, and on the basis of the analogy achieved his own rise to power. Dreiser himself, depressed and unsettled by sudden contact with the philosophical and evolutionary writings of Huxley and Spencer, saw humanity at the mercy of natural "chemism" and determinism. To such ideas Burroughs did not subscribe, nor did he endorse the harsh tenets of Social Darwinism, as represented in America by William Graham Sumner. More than anything else, his temperament precluded such allegiances. Just as Burroughs could continue to speak of birds in personalized and even sentimental terms, despite his patina of Darwinism, so he could hold to traditional standards in human relationships, whatever his views of man's place in nature. Burroughs was at heart a person of kindliness and humility, who, with his greatly admired friend Walt Whitman, based his ethics on "the institution of the dear love of comrades."

❧ ❧ ❧

Between *Wake Robin* (1871) and *The Light of Day* (1900), Burroughs published nine books: *Winter Sunshine* (1875), *Birds and Poets* (1877), *Locusts and Wild Honey* (1879), *Pepacton* (1881), *Fresh Fields* (1884), *Signs and Seasons* (1886), *Indoor Studies* (1889), *Riverby* (1894), and *Whitman: A Study* (1896). Reading through this list, one finds Burroughs constantly broadening his range, developing his powers of expression, extending his sympathies. In one way or another, each of these books concerns nature; but literary criticism or philosophy impinges on many of the essays, and forms the dominant theme of a number of them. In literary histories, Burroughs is commonly put down as a nature essayist; but it should not be forgotten that his first efforts as an author were concerned with philosophy, nor that his first book (not reprinted in its original form in the collected works) was *Notes on Walt Whitman as Poet and Person* (1867). Criticism, whether of literature or of thought, was for Burroughs an enduring preoccupation.

The philosophical problem to which Burroughs usually addressed himself was, broadly, the dispute between science and religion. *The Light of Day*, a collection of essays written in the latter 1880's, sets forth the opinions either stated or implied in several earlier volumes—and does not truly resolve the ambiguity of Burroughs' outlook. The conflict between the mystical and the scientific aspects of his temperament continues. When Burroughs is discussing the reverential awe inspired by contemplating nature, he speaks of God in terms of a believer; but when he considers the God of formal religion, it is to deny His existence. The confusion is not simply the result of loose terminology; it springs from the fundamental ambivalence of a man who could neither accept traditional notions of God nor embrace an uncompromising atheism. On the evidence of *The Light of Day*, Burroughs was not even a proper agnostic. When Huxley coined the term, he meant it to apply to a person who was unable to affirm or deny God's existence; but Burroughs, though a defender of Huxley, claimed for himself the privilege of both affirmation in emotional terms and denial in terms of the intellect. The result is a book that is rich in human interest but poor in systematic philosophy; and with it as a criterion, one may deny Burroughs a place among important American philosophers and do him no injustice.

There seems less justification for ignoring Burroughs as a literary critic than for dismissing him as a philosopher. Because his range was wide, taking in authors of diverse interests, many of his literary essays are of no concern here; but much of his criticism relates directly to the subject of bird literature, and provides a fair sample of his work. In *Birds and Poets*, both the title essay and "The Flight of the Eagle" contain valuable insights into the poetry of nature, especially with regard to Whitman. Similarly useful is the long essay "Nature and the Poets," in *Pepacton*. *Indoor Studies* contains one of the best essays on Thoreau ever written—solid, perceptive, sympathetic in the truest meaning of that term, and lacking only the full sense of Thoreau's tragedy, his utter seriousness in speaking of desperation. "Gilbert White's Book" in the same volume is an excellent appreciation of *The Natural History of Selborne*, showing among other things the sympathy for English nature which Burroughs had earlier demonstrated in *Fresh Fields*.

However, it is on the basis of his treatment of Whitman that Burroughs the critic must stand or fall. He met Whitman in Washington late in 1863, and from then on he was Walt's friend, exponent, apologist, and even literary adviser. To these privileges and duties he brought many advantages. He was, like Whitman, the offspring of a New York farm family, with no great formal education but wide emotional sympathies. He knew and loved the same outdoors, the same climate, the same trees and birds that Whitman knew. Even at the time of the first meeting, he was an avowed man of letters, and as such he could appreciate Whitman as a fellow worker. Finally, he had that proper combination of humility and independence which makes for a fruitful association between a lesser writer and a greater one. There was no repetition here of the "long tragedy" of the Emerson-Thoreau relationship; Whitman was a loving but not demanding friend to Burroughs from beginning to end, and Burroughs remained Whitman's fervant champion and disciple.

The fact that Burroughs was always a partisan, never a detached critic, where Whitman was concerned, may work to his disadvantage. *Notes on Walt Whitman as Poet and Person* is less a work of criticism than a celebration; and even "the final survey and revision" embodied in *Whitman: A Study* can scarcely be called a balanced and judicious estimate. Burroughs never pretended it was such. Near the close of the book he said:

> I have accepted Whitman entire and without reservation. I could not do otherwise. It was clear enough to me that he was to be taken as a whole or not at all . . . Whitman brings us no cunning handicraft of the muses: he brings us a gospel, he brings us a man, he brings us a new revelation of life; and either his work appeals to us as a whole, or it does not so appeal. He will not live in separate passages, or in a few brief poems, any more than Shakespeare or Homer or Dante, or the Bible, so lives.

To some degree, the reader of *Whitman: A Study* needs to adopt a similar attitude. By virtue of his friendship with the poet, Burroughs spoke with an authority few could equal, and achieved insights not granted to critics standing at a greater distance; but *Whitman: A Study* depends on its thesis, not its supporting evidence. The reader's general estimate of the book will at last be contingent on whether he does or does not agree that Whitman was the great poet Burroughs says he is.

10 *American Bird Poetry: Whitman and Others*

In the essay "Birds and Poets" Burroughs mentioned a number of American verses in which birds are featured. He praised Bryant's "To a Waterfowl" and "Robert of Lincoln," Wilson Flagg's "The O'Lincoln Family," Emerson's "Titmouse," Trowbridge's "Pewee," Celia Thaxter's "Sandpiper," and a few others; and he especially emphasized the merits of Whitman's "Out of the Cradle Endlessly Rocking." The essay first appeared—under the title "The Birds of the Poets"—in 1874. It did not deal with many of the poets who were then writing, nor did Burroughs subsequently revise the essay to include poets who appeared later in the century. But he was not attempting a full survey of the subject; his literary interests were eclectic, not scholarly, and neither here nor elsewhere did he exhaust the subject of American bird poetry.

Yet only if one wishes to consider verses of the lowest artistic merits—the kind of thing which appears in "The Poet's Corner" of the newspapers or in second-rate periodicals—is the subject especially large. The truth is that American poetry has few good bird verses to show. There is almost nothing in it comparable to the great bird poems of Shelley, Wordsworth, or Keats, and few treatments of birds in passing that can compare with excerpts from Milton, Marvell, Vaughn, Dryden, Pope, Thomson, Burns, Cowper, Crabbe, or Blake. American birds are richly represented in prose; in poetry, generally, they are slighted or ignored.

Anne Bradstreet, the seventeenth-century New England poetess, is usually considered the first writer of nature verse to appear in America. In a sense, however, hers was a typical and prophetic case; for she, like so many later American poets, was dominated by English models and even by English scenery and wild creatures. Her diction is quite in the Elizabethan manner, faithfully echoing the sort of verse to be found in *The Paradise of Dainty Devices* (1576–1606), *A Gorgeous Gallery of Gallant Inventions* (1578), *The Arbor of Amorous Devices* (1597), and similar English miscellanies. Furthermore, the birds she mentions — the nightingale, the lark, the phoenix, the ostrich, the stork — are derived from her early years in England or from reading, not from observation in America. Scarcely a native bird is mentioned. Anne Bradstreet was a sensitive and often charming writer, but to call her the first American nature poet is to compromise the term.

In the eighteenth century appeared Philip Freneau, who wrote not only a great deal of interesting political verse but also a few noteworthy nature poems. These few were not, however, on the subject of birds. Two verses to insects, "To a Caty-did" and "On a Honey Bee," are the best of his work on nature, with "The Wild Honeysuckle" also a creditable effort. Freneau's scattered bird references were nearly always in general terms.

Alexander Wilson, who was a poet of some note in his native Scotland, continued writing verses after coming to America, and included a few on the subject of birds in his *American Ornithology*, the best of which concerns the osprey. But none of his efforts on birds can compare with his earlier dialect poems, and all of them would certainly have dropped into obscurity if they had not been included in his great ornithological work. There was nothing in Wilson's verses to set them apart from many similar efforts of the time. Such periodicals as the *Port Folio* of Philadelphia and *The Monthly Anthology* of Boston carried verses on nature, commonly neither better nor worse than Wilson's, and like his, imitative in form and diction, conventional in ideas, and generally amateurish in technique.

One might almost apply the same strictures to the nature verse of William Cullen Bryant; but whatever the poverty of his resources, Bryant was a true and dedicated poet with an undeniable lyric gift. "To a Waterfowl" is scarcely remarkable for either its art or its ideas; yet it survives, perhaps because of its very transparency and simplicity. It is a poem which makes no rigorous demands. It merely presents a clear picture, and points a popular, romantic moral of love for wild things, and of trust in the Being whose guidance is vouchsafed both bird and man. The bird — never specifically identified — does not inspire the poet's praise; it is the analogy, "the lesson . . . given" of God's love, which is important. Shelley and Wordsworth wrote passionate lyrics to an inspiring songbird; Bryant wrote a moral homily about a far-off duck or goose.

Bryant's "Robert of Lincoln," addressed to the bobolink, is both more artful and more specific than "To a Waterfowl," but has never enjoyed the vogue of the latter. Elsewhere in his voluminous works Bryant mentioned other birds, often in general terms — "river-fowl," "sea-bird," "ground-bird" — and at other times aptly and specifically; but only in the two poems cited did he achieve bird verse of particular merit.

At first glance, the most famous American bird poem would appear to be Edgar Allan Poe's "The Raven." Famous it is; but this verse is rather too special in its use of a bird to fit into the present study, even under the larger rubric of nature poetry. "The Raven" concerns not nature but the death of a beautiful woman, and her lover's sorrow; the bird serves mainly as a device to reiterate the fact of tragic loss, and as such is less a natural creature than the product of literary calculation. In "The Philosophy of Composition" Poe himself has related that this particular species was selected as "a *non*-reasoning creature capable of speech" — the parrot being Poe's first thought, "but . . . superseded forthwith by a Raven, as equally capable of speech, and infinitely more in keeping with the intended *tone*." The raven's somber plumage and ominous reputation were convenient for the author's purposes, but fundamentally the bird was employed neither as the principal subject of the poem, nor as its primary inspiration, but merely as a literary mouthpiece uttering a single melancholy word. Birds utilized in a similar manner, as fanciful, symbolic, or allegorical figures, may be found elsewhere in American writing; however, they tend to fall outside the range of this book.

Considering its general interest in nature, the Transcendentalist group turned out fewer bird poems than might be expected. Thoreau's sparse list of first-rate verse—"Sic Vita," "Free Love," "Smoke," "Haze," perhaps "Inspiration"—included nothing on birds, and the work of his friend Ellery Channing was similarly barren in this respect. Although in the course of his long life Channing wrote numerous verses with nature as the general subject, he rather reprehended Thoreau's pursuit of wildlife data, and consequently his own bird references tended to be general and conventional. Emerson, as Burroughs pointed out, wrote one excellent bird poem, "The Titmouse," celebrating his favorite bird, the chickadee. But it remained for Jones Very, the nearly mad poet and religious mystic who composed "a century of sonnets," to produce any considerable body of Transcendental bird verse. All too often Very's poetry is marred by inversions, forced rhymes, and excessively pious sentiments; but at its best it is simple and direct, as in "The Humming-Bird";

> Like thoughts that flit across the mind
> Leaving no lasting trace behind
> The humming-bird darts to and fro,
> Comes, vanishes before we know.
>
> While thoughts may be but airy things
> That come and go on viewless wings,
> Nor form nor substance e'en possess,
> Nor number know, nor more or less.
>
> This leaves an image, well defined,
> To be a picture of the mind;
> Its tiny form and colors bright
> In memory live, when lost to sight.
>
> There oft it comes at evening's hour,
> To flutter still from flower to flower;
> Then vanish midst the gathering shade,
> Its momentary visit paid.

One can scarcely ascribe to these verses any great literary merit. The most that can be said for them, and for other verses which Very wrote to the robin, the junco, the petrel, the English sparrow, and the cedar waxwing, is that they indicate Very saw his birds clearly and affectionately, and with a sense of their individuality. Had his power of expression been more commensurate with his ability to observe and understand wild creatures, Very might have produced nature poetry of considerable distinction.

Of all major American poets, Whittier was the most genuinely rural. He did not sojourn in the country; he lived there. Consequently it is surprising to discover that he knew relatively little about birds—especially when his poetry makes plain the fact that he knew flowers and trees quite well. His *Poems of Nature* are often highly evocative; his love of nature is genuine and moving; but his birds, with few exceptions, are treated in general terms, or else are featured in legends, as with "The Robin" and "How the Robin Came."

Longfellow made charming use of a bird legend in "The Poet's Tale," one of the *Tales of a Wayside Inn.* This is not an animal fable in the manner of Chaucer's "The Nonnes Preestes Tale," in which Chauntecleer, Pertelote, and the fox bandy words; rather it is a parable illuminating the relationship between birds and men. The farmers of Killingworth, angered by the theft of a little grain, decide to exterminate the birds of the vicinity; but this "very St. Bartholomew of Birds" results in a grievous plague of caterpillars, and the birds have to be restored to the area to save the farms. Although Longfellow treats his readers to a rather startling mixture of British and American species, his telling of the legend has undeniable grace and felicity. Of Longfellow's other verses to birds, the most noteworthy are the lines in "Evangeline" describing the mocker's song, and the first six stanzas of "Birds of Passage," concerning autumn migration.

After reading through Lowell's poetical works in search of birds, one turns with relief to his bird essay, "My Garden Acquaintance." His verses contain an occasional apt reference, for example to the bobolink in "Under the Willows" and to the Baltimore oriole in "The Nest"; but in general his bird verse is marred by conventionality in both diction and outlook. His essay, on the other hand, is altogether a winning performance—urbane, humorous, happy in choice of detail, accurate, and inclusive. Although it begins as a discussion of White's *Selborne*, it mainly concerns the birds found around Lowell's home at Elmwood. It is anthropomorphic in an offhand way, but not in the least sentimental. On the evidence of this essay, both the author's wide knowledge of birds and his affection for them are entirely plain; and the picture given of the formidable Mr. Lowell perched high on a pine branch, with his penknife freeing young blue jays from a tangle of nest string, is one not soon forgotten.

"My Garden Acquaintance" strongly suggests that had Lowell chosen to do so, he could have become one of America's foremost nature essayists. He preferred to expend his talents in other ways; but even this one essay is enough to demonstrate an important fact about the use of birds in American literature. Lowell's bird essay is excellent of its kind, while his bird verse is usually undistinguished. His knowledge and love of birds emerged clearly and persuasively in his prose, but found little expression in his verse. What is true of this one author may be extended to apply to American writing generally. Bird prose, and especially the bird essay, is an indigenous product, a sturdy native growth that has flourished under American skies; bird poetry, from Chaucer and Shakespeare to Shelley and Keats, is in the central tradition of the great literature of England, and has struck but shallow roots in the new land.

❧ ❧ ❧

If Walt Whitman is the notable exception, it is in one way only. He wrote a great bird poem, to be sure—the only one produced in nineteenth-century America; but he did so by disavowing the old forms and attitudes, and speaking in his own distinctive idiom. "Out of the Cradle Endlessly Rocking" as little reflects "To a Skylark" as "When Lilacs Last in the Dooryard Bloom'd" echoes "Adonais." Nor is the difference merely one of poetic form or diction. Shelley's bird is "an unbodied joy," a messenger of gladness; Whitman's mocker is a herald of love and loss and death. The general mood of "Out of the Cradle" is close to that of Keats's "Ode to a Nightingale"—but again with a vital difference. Keats is overwhelmed by the bird's joy, he is "too happy in [its] happiness," and by contrast is made the more deeply aware of his own sadness. Keats brings his own experience to the nightingale's innocence; Whitman is bereft of his innocence by the knowledge the mockingbird imparts.

"Out of the Cradle Endlessly Rocking" is intense spiritual autobiography. The boy who was Whitman went forth one May and found mockingbirds building in the seaside briars; he watched the pair at their nesting, "never disturbing them, Cautiously peering, absorbing, translating"; at length he discovered that the female bird had disappeared, "May-be kill'd, Unknown to her mate"; and then all the summer he listened to the male bird singing alone, calling in vain to the lost one. In that song, and in the response of the night sea, the boy found knowledge and release; he wept strange tears, and knew he had learned truths never again to be evaded or denied.

> For I, that was a child, my tongue's use sleeping,
> Now I have heard you,
> Now in a moment I know what I am for — I awake,
> And already a thousand singers — a thousand songs, clearer, louder,
> and more sorrowful than yours,
> A thousand warbling echoes have started to life within me,
> Never to die.
>
> O you singer solitary, singing by yourself — projecting me;
> O solitary me, listening — nevermore shall I cease perpetuating you;
> Never more shall I escape, never more the reverberations,
> Never more the cries of unsatisfied love be absent from me,
> Never again leave me to be the peaceful child I was before what
> there, in the night,
> By the sea, under the yellow and sagging moon,
> The messenger there arous'd — the fire, the sweet hell within,
> The unknown want, the destiny of me.
>
> O give me the clew! (it lurks in the night here somewhere;)
> O if I am to have so much, let me have more!
>
> . . . . .
>
> Whereto answering, the sea,
> Delaying not, hurrying not,
> Whisper'd me through the night, and very plainly before daybreak,
> Lisp'd to me the low and delicious word DEATH;
> And again Death — ever Death, Death, Death,
> Hissing melodious, neither like the bird, nor like my arous'd child's
> heart,
> But edging near, as privately for me, rustling at my feet,
> Creeping thence steadily up to my ears, and laving me softly all over,
> Death, Death, Death, Death, Death.

A long section in the middle of the poem is given over to the mockingbird's song, rendered not in approximate phonetic verbalizations, but rather in words that carry the meaning of the poem forward. Whitman made a conscious effort to follow the mocker's song mannerisms, especially in repeating monosyllables at the beginning of certain phrases. However, as Burroughs remarks, there is little use in trying to make strict ornithology of this poem. It submits to no such limitation and distortion. "Out of the Cradle Endlessly Rocking" is no mere bird-watching report; it is the history, told in powerful poetic terms, of a boy's awakening to self-knowledge and an awareness of death, through the agency of a mockingbird's loss.

Death and a bird are again juxtaposed in Whitman's great threnody, "When Lilacs Last in the Dooryard Bloom'd." Now it is the man who is dead and the poet who mourns, while the bird, the hermit thrush, sings "death's outlet song of life." The death carol near the end of the poem makes no attempt to imitate the song pattern of the thrush; it is a "tallying song," an echo aroused in the poet's soul by thoughts of Lincoln. The bird here does not provide the central theme, but rather a counterpoint, "with voice of uttermost woe." The scent of lilac, the sight of the star, the song of the thrush – these are intertwined to symbolize the tragedy, to recall the loss, and also to reconcile the poet, and comfort him in bereavement.

This poem is surely one of the greatest dirges in English, and not to be shaken from its place by minor criticisms. Nevertheless it is relevant to suggest here that "When Lilacs Last in the Dooryard Bloom'd" is less successful in its use of a bird than "Out of the Cradle Endlessly Rocking." There is about the former an air of contrivance, as though the bird had been introduced to provide a plausible echo for the death carol. The thrush here is not presented in personal and immediate terms, as was the mockingbird. Indeed, John Burroughs stated that the hermit thrush was not originally chosen by Whitman, but suggested by Burroughs himself. A change Whitman made in "Starting from Paumanok" lends credibility to the statement. As first published in 1860 (under the title "Proto-Leaf") the first stanza mentioned only one bird, the mocker; but the version appearing in 1867, four years after Whitman met Burroughs, contained this new line:

And heard at dusk the unrival'd one, the hermit thrush from the swamp cedars.

Whitman's lack of personal acquaintance with the hermit thrush is further indicated by the fact that in "Lilacs" he shows it singing at night, which is not that bird's habit.

Burroughs provided Whitman with the data for one other bird poem, "The Dalliance of the Eagles." It is a minor effort. "To the Man-of-War Bird," a poem concerning a species Whitman could scarcely have seen except during his stay in New Orleans in 1848, is not much better. Whitman wrote only one great poem centering on a single bird; elsewhere his most appropriate and evocative bird references were those made in passing, for example as items in his famous catalogues of natural features. In the first edition of *Leaves of Grass* (1855) these lines appeared in the opening poem (later called "Walt Whitman" or "Song of Myself"):

My tread scares the wood-drake and wood-duck on my distant and day-long ramble,
They rise together, they slowly circle around.
. . . . I believe in those winged purposes,
And consider the green and violet and the tufted crown intentional;
And do not call the tortoise unworthy because she is not something else,
And the mockingbird in the swamp never studied the gamut, yet trills pretty well to me,
And the look of the bay mare shames silliness out of me.

The wild gander leads his flock through the cool night,
Ya-honk! he says, and sounds it down to me like an invitation;
The pert may suppose it meaningless, but I listen closer,
I find its purpose and place up there toward the November sky.

. . . . .

Does the daylight astonish? or the early redstart twittering through the woods?

. . . . .

In vain the buzzard houses herself with the sky,
In vain the snake slides through the creepers and logs,
In vain the elk takes to the inner passes of the woods,
In vain the razorbilled auk sails far north to Labrador,
I follow quickly . . . . I ascend to the nest in the fissure of the cliff.

. . . . .

Where the quail is whistling betwixt the woods and the wheatlot,

. . . . .

Where the mockingbird sounds his delicious gurgles, and cackles and screams and weeps,

. . . . .

Where the hummingbird shimmers . . . . where the neck of the long-lived swan is curving and winding;
Where the laughing-gull scoots by the slappy shore and laughs her near-human laugh;
Where beehives range on a gray bench in the garden half-hid by the high weeds;
Where band-necked partridges roost in a ring on the ground with their heads out;

. . . . .

Where the yellow-crowned heron comes to the edge of the marsh at night and feeds upon small crabs;

. . . . .

The spotted hawk swoops by and accuses me . . . . he complains of my gab and my loitering.

A person interested in birds need only glance at these excerpts to realize that Whitman was something of a student of ornithology. Not merely are the references accurate and appropriate; the birds themselves are quite uncommon as subjects for poetry. There is no mention of the robin, the lark, the nightingale, the oriole, the bluebird, the jay; instead Whitman gives us such unusual species as the wood duck, the redstart, the buzzard, the razorbilled auk, the laughing gull, and the yellow-crowned night heron. Of these at least two, the heron and the auk, are rare visitors to Long Island; it seems scarcely likely that Whitman knew them from observation. Where, then, did he get his information?

In 1844 the ornithologist J. P. Giraud, Jr., published *The Birds of Long Island.* A study of this work dispels most of the mystery of Whitman's esoteric bird references. Not all of the quoted passages can be traced to Giraud, but the parallels are too numerous to be coincidental. Following the order of the excerpts from "Song of Myself," the pertinent sections from Giraud are these:

> Often when following those beautiful and rapid streams that greatly embellish our country, in pursuit of the angler's beau ideal

> of sport, have I met with this gaily attired Duck [wood duck]. As if proud of its unrivalled beauty, it would slowly rise and perform a circuit in the air, seemingly to give the admiring beholder an opportunity of witnessing the gem of its tribe.
>
> Late in autumn . . . the Canada Geese are seen in our section of country, sailing high in the air . . . They generally continue flying during the night, but occasionally alight and await the day . . . The hoarse honking of the gander is so familiar to the inhabitants of our country, that it is impossible for them to arrive among us without making their visits known.
>
> [The redstart] is common in the woods and along the roadside, as well as in the swamps and meadows; indeed, wherever its insect prey abounds this active bird is seen, mounting to the tops of the highest trees, or darting rapidly through the low underbrush, uttering as it passes from twig to twig a sprightly twitter . . . It arrives among us in the latter part of April, and returns southward late in September.
>
> [The razorbilled auk] breeds in great numbers on the Gannet Rock in the Gulf of St. Lawrence, on the shores of Newfoundland, and the western coast of Labrador, chiefly in the fissures of rocks.
>
> This handsome Gull arrives on the shores of Long Island in the latter part of April. It is quite a common species, and well known by the name of Laughing Gull, so called from its notes resembling the coarse laugh of a human being.
>
> [The "Common American Partridge" has] a band from the base of the bill, curving down the sides of the neck . . . When roosting, they adopted the form of a ring, with their heads out, and lying thus in a close body, received the mutual warmth of each other.
>
> The Yellow-crowned Heron . . . is chiefly nocturnal, keeping in the marshes during the day, and feeding mostly at night . . . According to Catesby, it is quite common in the Bahama Islands, where it is said to feed principally on small crabs, and its flesh is highly esteemed.

Of course Whitman cannot be charged with plagiarizing in the reprehensible sense. He uses Giraud as Thoreau uses Wilson and Audubon, in order to know what he is talking about in things avian. He adapts Giraud's rather graceless prose to the needs of his poetry, and in so doing provides a hint of the highly functional nature of his special poetic idiom. Given that idiom, the ornithological data serve well; but they would appear hopelessly angular and obtrusive if thrust into more conventional poetic forms.

There is no reason to assume, on the basis of the parallels cited, that Whitman had small powers of personal observation. Certainly he took little from Giraud when he wrote "Out of the Cradle Endlessly Rocking"; except for the line "And their nest, and four light-green eggs, spotted with brown" (most of it lifted verbatim), the poem speaks in terms of intense personal experience. Whitman's prose jottings further verify his interest in first-hand study. While his bird notes in *Specimen Days* may lack precise nomenclature, they nevertheless ring true for the species intended—particularly in descriptions of songs, always of special concern to Whitman. Consider this note for March 16, 1878:

> Fine, clear, dazzling morning, the sun an hour high, the air just tart enough. What a stamp in advance my whole day receives from the song of that meadow lark perch'd on a fence-stake twenty rods distant! Two or three liquid-simple notes, repeated at intervals, full of careless happiness and hope. With its peculiar shimmering slow progress and rapid-noiseless action of the wings, it flies on a way, lights on another stake, and so on to another, shimmering and singing many minutes.

This is a notably just and vivid picture. The ornithologist could take exception only to the phrase "full of careless happiness and hope"; otherwise Whitman's observations are accurate beyond cavil. Yet it is clear that mere precision is neither the virtue nor the intent of this passage. We see the meadowlark plain, to be sure—but the terms are poetic, not scientific. It is the poet who finds such remarkable words (in this context) as "liquid-simple notes" and "peculiar shimmering slow progress." Similarly, there is more poetry than science in descriptions of birds found elsewhere in *Specimen Days*; for example, in "Crows and Crows," "Bird-Whistling," "Swallows on the "River," and "A Hint of Wild Nature."

In an entry for May 14, 1881, Whitman summed up his outlook on ornithology, and nature study generally, in these words:

> Home again; down temporarily in the Jersey woods. Between 8 and 9 A.M. a full concert of birds, from different quarters, in keeping with the fresh scent, the peace, the naturalness all around me. I am lately noticing the russet-back, size of the robin or a trifle less, light

> breast and shoulders, with irregular dark stripes — tail long — sits hunch'd up by the hour these days, top of a tall bush, or some tree, singing blithely. I often get near and listen, as he seems tame; I like to watch the working of his bill and throat, the quaint sidle of his body, and flex of his long tail. I hear the woodpecker, and night and early morning the shuttle of the whip-poor-will — noons, the gurgle of the thrush delicious, and *meo-o-ow* of the cat-bird. Many I cannot name; but I do not very particularly seek information. (You must not know too much, or be too precise or scientific about birds and trees and flowers and water-craft; a certain free margin, and even vagueness — perhaps ignorance, credulity — helps your enjoyment of these things, and of the sentiment of feather'd, wooded, river, or marine Nature generally. I repeat it — don't want to know too exactly, or the reasons why. My own notes have been written off-hand in the latitude of middle New Jersey. Though they describe what I saw — what appear'd to me — I dare say the expert ornithologist, botanist or entomologist will detect more than one slip in them.)

Quite aware of the problem of accuracy, Whitman nevertheless was determined not to be put off by it. Emerson deprecated close study as harmful to the true philosophical perception of nature; Whitman refused it in order to retain "a certain free margin" for poetic enjoyment and understanding. Poetry had first claim; afterward came ornithology, which could mislead a person into being "too precise or scientific about birds." Whitman never disavowed intimate and loving observation; in this same passage the brown thrasher ("russet-back") is admirably delineated, and throughout Whitman's poetry there are equally apt references to birds. Whitman went direct to nature for his insights; he even turned to an ornithologist for his separate facts; but he retained a poet's freedom from the tyranny of mere information. "Nature will not be stared at," said Margaret Fuller — something Henry Thoreau may have learned too late, but Walt Whitman doubtless understood from the beginning.

11 *End-of-the-Century Prose*

Had John Burroughs added a sequel to "Birds and Poets" at the turn of the century, it would not have been a long one. He might have mentioned Sidney Lanier, whose best efforts were two verses to the mockingbird and one to an owl and a robin; Emily Dickinson, whose poetry included several verses to birds; Frank Bolles, who wrote an entire volume composed of fourteen blank-verse poems to the birds of Chocorua; or even Harriet E. Paine, whose verses in *Bird Songs of New England* may often echo Thoreau, but also indicate considerable first-hand knowledge of her subjects. The list, however, is not impressive, nor are the poems themselves especially good. No great bird poem was written in America in the latter decades of the nineteenth century. The anthologist who included only two Americans, Bryant and Whitman, in his *Poems about Birds from the Middle Ages to the Present Day* (c. 1922) was rudely just.

To return for a moment to John Burroughs' prose. It is amusing to find Burroughs calling *Riverby* (1894) "probably my last collection of Out-of-door Papers"; he was subsequently to publish nearly a score of books, many of them on outdoor subjects. But *Riverby* serves very well as a summing up for the purposes of this study. By this time Burroughs had achieved considerable renown, and this book, the product of his middle years, is one of the fullest and richest of his works. Much of his earlier evolutionary rigor has disappeared, but its chastening influence remains, largely precluding sentimentality. A tendency toward anthropomorphism is still evident (especially in the fourth chapter, "Bird Courtship") but it is leavened by a quiet humor. Perhaps the most noteworthy change from earlier books is to be seen in Burroughs' attitude toward killing wild creatures. In *Wake Robin* he had told of participating in the least sportsmanlike of deer hunts, that conducted by jack-lighting; in *Riverby* he deplored deer hunting and wrote, "a man in the woods, with a gun in his hand, is no longer a man,—he is a brute. The devil is in the gun to make brutes of us all." Again and again he goes out of his way to help birds and animals; the man who formerly insisted on the cruelty of nature now rescues from death a chimney swift, a chipmunk, a young woodchuck, a baby rabbit. This is a different Burroughs from the author of *Wake Robin* and *Birds and Poets*.

The metamorphosis is clearly expressed in Burroughs' own words:

> We love nature with a different love at different periods of our lives. In youth our love is sensuous. It is not so much a conscious love as an irresistible attraction . . . We eat the pungent roots and barks, we devour the wild fruits, we slay the small deer. Then nature also offers a field of adventure; it challenges and excites our animal spirits. The woods are full of game, the waters of fish; the river invites the oar, the breeze, the sail, the mountain-top promises a wide prospect. Hence the rod, the gun, the boat, the tent, the pedestrian club. In youth we are nearer the savage taste, the primitive condition of mankind, and wild nature is our proper home. The transient color of the young bird points its remote ancestry, and the taste of youth for rude nature in like manner is the survival of an earlier race instinct.
>
> Later in life we go to nature as an escape from the tension and turmoil of business, or for rest and recreation from study, or seeking solace from grief and disappointment, or as a refuge from the frivolities and hypocrisies of society. We lie under trees, we stroll through lanes, or in meadows and pastures, or muse on the shore. Nature "salves" our worst wounds; she heals and restores us.
>
> Or we cultivate an intellectual pleasure in nature, and follow up

> some branch of natural science, as botany, or ornithology, or mineralogy.
>
> Then there is the countryman's love of nature, and pleasure in cattle, horses, bees, growing crops, manual labor, sugar-making, gardening, harvesting, and the rural quietness and repose.
>
> Lastly, we go to nature for solitude and for communion with our own souls. Nature attunes us to a higher and finer mood. This love springs from our religious needs and instincts. This was the love of Thoreau, of Wordsworth, and has been the inspiration of much modern poetry and art.

The early Burroughs had attracted many readers, but it was the later Burroughs, conferring by the benison of nature "escape" and "rest" and "solace" and "refuge" and "communion," who became famous. This was "John o' Birds," the nature lover, who in the 1890's was lecturing to Wellesley girls and Yale boys, to women's clubs, to schools; the "Sage of Slabsides" who happily received crowds of Vassar students in his picturesque retreat; the literary figure who listed among his friends and acquaintances Whitman, Howells, Stedman, Gilder, Warner, van Dyke, Muir; the future public personage, already corresponding with such diverse political figures as Robert Ingersoll and Theodore Roosevelt. Not since Audubon had a naturalist achieved this sort of fame; and never before had the birds of America been granted so renowned a champion. Audubon was first an artist, then a scientist and writer; Burroughs was primarily an advocate, a propagandist, a zealot in the cause of nature, and only secondarily an essayist, philosopher, or critic. Perhaps he did not see himself thus; but such was his great function in terms of American society, and his great service to it.

❧ ❧ ❧

Burroughs' noted friend "John o' Mountains," John Muir, who wrote with such engaging enthusiasm that one wishes he had spent more time at his desk and less in rambling over the North American continent, published only one book in the nineteenth century, *The Mountains of California* (1894). It contained one chapter on birds, entitled "The Water-Ouzel," originally published in *Scribner's*

Monthly for February 1878 as "The Humming-Bird of the California Water-Falls." Written in his usual spirited prose, it mainly concerns the ouzel, but also mentions (with no great exactitude) various other birds found during the winter in Yosemite. Muir shows great affection for his birds, and speaks of the ouzel in terms of rhapsody. Something of the flavor of his style can be caught from the concluding lines, in which Muir declares that ouzels interpret "throughout the whole of their beautiful lives . . . all that we in our unbelief call terrible in the utterances of torrents, as only varied expressions of God's eternal love."

Muir published another bird article, "Among the Birds of the Yosemite," in the *Atlantic* for December 1898. It is somewhat more subdued and straightforward than "The Water-Ouzel," and deals with a more diverse group of species. Something about this group calls forth an interesting comparison. Muir emphasizes the larger and heavier birds—ducks, geese, grouse, quail, the bigger woodpeckers—and has far less to say about the smaller ones. This is not the usual way with the bird essayists who write of eastern avifauna; they tend to discuss the small, colorful, active songbirds, such as are found in the dooryards, the suburbs, the fields, and the woodlands. Muir may have felt that the western mountain country was on too grand a scale for this kind of familiar writing, and demanded the bigger, sturdier birds as appropriate subjects. In regions where (in the words of Clarence King) "a thousand up-springing spires and pinnacles pierce the sky in every direction," the smaller species may seem merely trifling.

Bradford Torrey and Frank Bolles were two writers in the eastern tradition—or, more properly, the northeastern tradition, established by Thoreau, Flagg, Higginson, and Burroughs. Both began by publishing first in the *Atlantic*, and both devoted their earlier books largely to New England nature. Torrey's initial essay was called "With the Birds on Boston Common," Bolles' "The Equinoctial on the Ipswich Dunes"—titles which patly indicate the early geographical orientation of the authors.

Torrey's first collection of essays was *Birds in the Bush*, published in Boston in 1885. He explained his title thus:

> The interest they [the birds] excite is of all grades, from that which looks upon them as items of millinery, up to that of the makers

> of ornithological systems, who ransack the world for specimens, and who have no doubt that the chief end of a bird is to be named and catalogued, — the more synonyms the better. Somewhere between these two extremes comes the person whose interest in birds is friendly rather than scientific; who has little taste for shooting, and an aversion for dissecting; who delights in the living creatures themselves, and counts a bird in the bush worth two in the hand.

This seems a suitable point of view for a nature essayist, and suggests the later Burroughs. Unhappily, Torrey's conception of "friendly interest" in birds embraced both sentimentality and a strong tendency to personalize his subjects. In the third chapter, "Character in Feathers," he makes miniature human beings of his birds; "Phillida and Coridon" is full of arch references to bird "wooing" and "marriage"; and a statement from Wallace's *Natural Selection,* holding that all birds struggle to survive, Torrey quickly overrides by his assertion that they are nevertheless "happy" because they never suffer ennui, their days are full, they have a simple outdoor life, "a kind of perpetual picnic."

In later chapters of *Birds in the Bush* he muted his anthropomorphism considerably, and also abandoned such literary affectations as the use of archaic words — "nowise," "withal," and "on this wise," for example. His second book, *A Rambler's Lease* (1889), is perhaps his best. In his humorous familiarity and gentle self-deprecation Torrey reminds one of Charles Lamb, and his warm affections and enthusiasms are, like Lamb's, ingratiating. Torrey's writing has little intellectual density; it makes few demands; it is not sinewy and provocative, like Thoreau's, but limpid, graceful, and genial. "New England Winter" and "A Pitch-Pine Meditation" are two chapters that try for philosophical implications, but they are less successful (and less characteristic) than those that deal with wild creatures intimately observed and affectionately described.

The problem of viewing his wild subjects in human terms is not one which Torrey pretends to have solved. Near the end of *A Rambler's Lease* he says, "It is my private heresy, perhaps, this strong anthropomorphic turn of mind, which impels me to assume the presence of a soul in all animals, even in these airy nothings [butterflies]; and having assumed its existence, to speculate as to what goes on within it."

The Foot-Path Way (1892) is wider in geographical range than the two earlier books, and more technical in its studies of individual birds. Detailed investigations of separate species, as in "A Widow and Twins," "The Male Ruby-Throat," and "Robin Roosts," serve to remind us that Torrey was an ornithologist as well as a writer. At the first meeting of the American Ornithologists' Union, in 1883, Torrey was made an associate member; he was a resident member of the Nuttall Ornithological Club between 1884 and 1886; and his work was published not only in the *Atlantic*, but also in *The Auk*, *Bird-Lore*, and *The Condor*. However, the penalty he paid for his technical interests may be discovered in certain chapters of *The Foot-Path Way*, where increased exactitude and emphasis on data mark a concomitant decline in literary style.

A Florida Sketch-Book (1894), *Spring Notes from Tennessee* (1896), and *A World of Green Hills* (1898) are records of Torrey's excursions in the South. A reading of these books at once suggests a contrast between Torrey and Burroughs; for while the latter complained of feeling out of place anywhere except in his New York hills, Torrey, on the evidence of these books, was alert and sympathetic wherever he journeyed. Nor was his sympathy merely for the new avifauna; he appreciated and effectively described the distinctive climate and scenery of the southern states, and showed a democratic interest in the people he encountered. These books are important in the present inquiry because they represent the first major work on southern nature since Bartram, Wilson, and Audubon; but in the literary sense they are important in showing Torrey's increasing skill in delineating human character.

By 1900, Bradford Torrey's best work was behind him, although he continued writing for some years. Frank Bolles, on the other hand, flourished as an author only between 1891, when his first nature article was published in the *Atlantic*, and 1894, when he died. For Bolles writing was not a professional activity, but an avocation and means of escape from the weight of his duties as Secretary of Harvard University. If we may judge from his remarks in passing, and from the chapter "My Heart's in the Highlands" in his second book, the Secretary in those days served both as a glorified bookkeeper and an unofficial dean of men. Bolles enjoyed his work, but was ever willing to close up his office in University Hall and go off on week ends to the hills around Cambridge, or to the Ipswich dunes, or down the Musketaquid, or — during longer vacation periods — to Cape Cod or the mountains of New Hampshire.

Descriptions of these journeys make up the bulk of his first book, *Land of the Lingering Snow* (1891). Most of the chapters are quite short, hardly more than sketches of short excursions. Many of them are parochial in the less happy sense of the term, making reference to the Belmont Hills and Roxbury and the Memorial Hall tower with an assurance other writers might use when speaking of Paris or the Alps or the Acropolis. However, Bolles was a keen observer, especially of climate and birds, and this book, for all its narrow range, communicates in an unpretentious way the pleasures of his outdoor studies.

At the North of Bearcamp Water (1893) is a better book, principally because it is broader in scope and less bound by chronology. Bolles leaves behind him "the foul breath of the Charles and Alewife Brook, open sewers of filthy towns," and flees not merely to the nearby hills, but to the White Mountains, where his best chapters are laid. A new interest in people appears, and the author's keenly sensuous enjoyment of the outdoors is conveyed with a power seldom found in his first book. Bolles does not often attain the literary facility achieved by Bradford Torrey, but on the other hand in certain reflective passages he hints at emotional depths Torrey never manifested.

The promise of this second book was never subsequently fulfilled. Bolles' last book of prose, *From Blomidon to Smoky* (1894), was issued posthumously, without having benefited from the author's revisions; and it is a mixed bag of travel pieces, conventional nature essays, and detailed studies of barred owls and yellow-bellied sapsuckers. The range of these chapters is indicated by the fact that they appeared first in publications as diverse as *The Auk*, *Popular Science Monthly*, *New England Magazine*, and the *Atlantic*. In some of the essays there are further suggestions of a brooding emotional power, but they tend to be lost in the clutter. *Chocorua's Tenants* (1895) was, as noted earlier, a book of verse concerning the birds living near Chocorua in the White Mountains.

By the end of the century several women authors had entered the field of nature writing, and at least four of them, Olive Thorne Miller,

Mabel Osgood Wright, Florence A. Merriam, and Neltje Blanchan, should be mentioned here as minor literary figures. Their particular service to birds, however, came in the area of education, and in this connection they will be treated in some detail in Chapter 14.

In the broadest sense, all the prose writers so far discussed were engaged in a form of public education. By intent or by accident all of them contributed to an awareness of nature which grew with the century. Perhaps in providing Americans with a refuge from their own increasingly urbanized and industrialized society, and turning their eyes back to what Whitman called the "primal sanities" of nature, they were merely responding to the demands which that society created; but again, they may have helped form an outlook which, except for their efforts, would have been lacking. This much at least is certain: the bird essay, originating in the work of Bartram and Gilbert White and the great ornithologists, drawing its greatest inspiration from the writings of Thoreau, and attaining its special literary form and popular status in the work of Flagg, Higginson, Burroughs, Torrey, and Bolles, was a form of expression which burgeoned in the nineteenth century and which in the final decades became widely disseminated. Thoreau was a great writer, and Burroughs a famous one; and, with other writers of like mind, they made the love of birds a famous cause.

"Fifty — or even thirty — years ago such an argument [for conservation] would have carried little weight, but the love of wild nature, the deep and ever growing interest in the bird and plant life around us, first aroused by Thoreau and afterwards fostered by the writings of Burroughs, Bolles, and Torrey, have spread widely among all classes of our people" — so wrote the ornithologist and teacher William Brewster in 1898, in the midst of the struggle toward which all these writings tended, the fight to conserve America's birds.

12 *The Beginnings of Conservation*

Sometimes [robins] will disappear for a week or two, and return again in greater numbers than before; at which time the cities pour out their sportsmen by scores, and the markets are plentifully supplied with them at a cheap rate. In January, 1807, two young men, in one excursion after them, shot thirty dozen. In the midst of such devastation, which continued many weeks, and by accounts extended from Massachusetts to Maryland, some humane person took advantage of a circumstance common to these birds in winter, to stop the general slaughter. The fruit called pokeberries . . . is a favorite repast with the Robin, after they are mellowed by the frost. The juice of the berries is of a beautiful crimson, and they are eaten in such quantities by those birds, that their whole stomachs are strongly tinged with the same red color. A paragraph appeared in the public papers, intimating, that from the great quantities of these berries which the Robins had fed on, they had become unwholesome, and even dangerous food; and that several persons had suffered by eating of them. The strange appearance of the bowels of the birds seemed to corroborate this account. The demand for, and use of them ceased almost instantly; and the motives of self-preservation produced at once what all the pleadings of humanity could not effect.

Alexander Wilson, in American Ornithology, *1808*

The movement to conserve those birds not properly classified as game can trace its beginnings in America to such fugitive acts as the one here related by Wilson. "Some humane person," determined "to stop the general slaughter," seized upon a singular stratagem to attain his ends, and, momentarily at least, saved the robins from further decimation. (The circumstantial account Wilson gives leads one to wonder if the person was not his friend William Bartram, or even Wilson himself.) When "the pleadings of humanity" failed, and no laws were in effect to save the birds, artifice was successfully employed. Although the history of bird conservation in the nineteenth century culminates in concerted actions by powerful and dedicated groups, it begins with separate acts of protest by individuals.

What, we may ask, prompts a man to go to such quixotic lengths to save a few robins? By what convictions is he motivated? What good is likely to proceed from his action? Does he properly represent "the pleadings of humanity," or is he merely a sentimentalist or a crank? In short: what explains or justifies this man's act?

Part of the answer must be sought in the general history of man's relation to birds. If we may judge by paintings which have come down from the Stone Age, birds were food for men from the beginning—and, in addition, subjects for artistic expression. On his cave walls Paleolithic man drew the figures of birds, perhaps in order to prosper the hunt, perhaps also in order to represent creatures noticed and remembered. Thus the relics of prehistory suggest what history verifies: from earliest times birds have been items of human diet, and also objects of human regard.

To be sure, they share this regard with many other creatures, as various as flowers and crocodiles; but birds have special attributes not granted any other form of life. With minor exceptions, birds and men are the only singing animals, and nowhere does man's unique faculty of complex speech seem more closely approximated than among birds. Again almost alone among warm-blooded creatures, birds have the altogether remarkable ability to fly above the earth—a power which for many thousands of years was vouchsafed men only as they were transfigured into spirits or gods. By this power birds may arrive from the far places of the world, and in their appointed time depart again; they may visit the enchanted lands, and return; they may fly toward the sun, but need not, like Icarus, fall back defeated. What man has wished for, time out of mind, the bird commands by a mere flick of its wings.

On the negative side there is the fact that seldom indeed has any bird directly threatened human life. Many men have been killed by plants, by insects, by fish, by serpents, by the carnivorous mammals, and legend has multiplied those deaths; but very few have been killed by birds. Thus bird legends and superstitions—as of the phoenix, the pelican, the roc, the barnacle goose—tend to be bizarre rather than fearsome, and the general tradition of folk belief concerning birds centers around their familiar and more or less harmless attributes and activities. Thomas Babington Macauley asserted that men love nature when it no longer endangers them. Very early it must have been realized that little danger is to be expected from birds, and much pleasure. The literature of man's response to birds, from the Bible and Aesop to modern times, is largely a literature of affectionate analogy, and of innocence and cheer, and love, and wonder.

So the man who in 1807 acted to save the robins was no mere crank. He was a person responding to one aspect of the traditional relationship between men and birds, just as the sportsmen who poured from the cities were responding to another. The "humane person" saw the birds as friends; the hunters looked upon them as food. These are the basic terms in the ambivalent human attitude. They may be extended on the one hand to include the belief that birds are entitled to protection because they are vessels of divine grace, or creatures of special beauty and inspiration, or because killing them is an act of cruelty; and on the other, to embrace the idea that birds should be killed in revenge for depredations, or in the spirit of mere sport, or for the sake of private ornithological collections, or for personal adornment. On such opposing terms as these, the battle for conserving the birds of America was joined.

Between these two contending philosophies, however, there arose at length a third or moderating attitude, holding that if birds were to be killed for food or sport, the killing should be regulated, in order that no species be exterminated. This attitude, at least in America, was late in developing. John Josselyn sounded what was perhaps the earliest warning about diminishing American game birds when he noted the scarcity of turkeys and pigeons in the latter half of the seventeenth century; but until the middle of the nineteenth century, protective laws were few and scattered. In 1708 New York established a closed season for heath hens, ruffed grouse, quail, and wild turkeys in a certain few counties, and in 1791 woodcock were added to the protected list. In 1818 Massachusetts, in order to prevent the wanton destruction "at improper times" of "birds which are useful and profitable to the citizens either as articles of food or instruments in the hands of Providence to destroy many noxious insects, grubs and caterpillars, which are prejudicial or destructive to vegetation, fruits and grain," passed a law protecting grouse and quail from March 1 to September 1, and woodcock, snipe, larks, and robins from March 1 to July 4.

Two years later, New Jersey established closed seasons for woodcock, "moor-fowl," grouse, and quail and in 1838 somewhat increased the length of these seasons. Massachusetts added the heath hen to the protected list in 1831, and in 1837 prohibited all shooting of this bird for four years. Virginia protected wildfowl against night shooting and hunting with large-bore guns in 1832, but a similar law passed by New York six years later, prohibiting the use of battery guns, quickly became a dead letter. Initial efforts at protecting certain game birds were made by Delaware in 1839; Rhode Island in 1846; Missouri and Wisconsin in 1851; California and Illinois in 1852; Alabama and North Carolina in 1854; Indiana, Iowa, Louisiana, and Ohio in 1857; Maine and Minnesota in 1858; Michigan and Pennsylvania in 1859; and Nebraska and Texas in 1860. Lest too much importance should be attached to this listing, however, it needs to be remembered that many of these statutes were limited in their application to small areas, and enforcement in many cases was lax. In addition, few of the laws protected more than a minor fraction of possible species.

Except for the Massachusetts law of 1818 relating to robins and larks, and a similar Rhode Island law of 1846, no protection whatever was extended to American songbirds until 1850. In that year both Connecticut and New Jersey enacted legislation prohibiting the killing of a wide variety of non-game birds—in the latter state, for example, "the night or mosquito hawk, chimney swallow, barn swallow, martin or swift, whippowil [*sic*], cuckoo, kingbird or bee martin, woodpecker, claip or high hole, catbird, wren, bluebird, meadow lark, brown thrusher [*sic*], dove, firebird or summer redbird, hanging bird, ground robin or chewink, bobolink or ricebird, robin, snow or chipping bird, sparrow, Carolina lit [*sic*], warbler, bat, blackbird, blue jay, and the small owl." In 1851 Vermont passed a similar law, and in 1855 Massachusetts extended year-round protection to robins, thrushes, linnets, sparrows, bluebirds, bobolinks, yellowbirds, woodpeckers, and warblers. "Similar acts were passed . . . shortly after by other States, until in 1864 they were in force in the District of Columbia and twelve States, comprising all of New England, and New York, New Jersey, Pennsylvania, Iowa, Michigan, and Minnesota." *

Taken at face value, these laws represented a very considerable advance in conservation of birds. Such adjectives as "harmless," "small," and "insectivorous" were used to designate the protected species, indicating that an effort was being made to distinguish between game birds and other species. However, an examination of the various state regulations reveals numerous weaknesses, the most obvious of which is the fact that large groups of birds were still given no protection, either as game or non-game species — for example, herons, gulls, terns, owls and raptores, and numerous shorebirds. Nor were all the state laws as inclusive in their actual lists as those of New Jersey and Connecticut, or even that of Massachusetts. In its first game law of 1858, Maine extended protection only to larks, robins, partridges, woodpeckers, and sparrows, and then only for four months in the spring. The Pennsylvania law in force in 1864 protected only the bluebird, swallow, martin, or other insectivorous bird — "insectivorous" being so nebulous a classification as to encourage private interpretation. Also, some of these statutes contained clauses which weakened their effectiveness. The New Jersey law prohibited a person from killing the enumerated birds "except upon his own premises," and both the New Hampshire and Massachusetts laws allowed towns and cities to suspend provisions by voting to do so.

Furthermore, protection given to non-game birds was very largely confined to the northern states, and therefore applied to migratory birds only for the spring and summer months. During their passage through the southern states, or during their winter residence there, numerous species were subjected to unrestrained shooting, and thus much of the effect of protective legislation elsewhere was lost.

The most immediate problem, however, was enforcing such statutes as did exist. The ornithologist Joel A. Allen, writing in 1876, analyzed the difficulty in these terms:

> In too many cases [bird protection laws] fail of their objective

* T. S. Palmer, *Legislation for the Protection of Birds Other than Game Birds*, Bulletin No. 12, revised ed., Division of Biological Survey, United States Department of Agriculture (Washington, 1902), p. 15.

from the want of an intelligent public opinion to ensure their enforcement. In the immediate vicinity of the larger cities it may be unsafe for pot-hunters and ambitious youngsters to openly indulge in the indiscriminate slaughter of the smaller song-birds, or to shoot grouse or woodcock out of season, but in the rural districts the case is generally far otherwise. Here the country lads and idlers destroy at all times such birds as their fancy or their love of "sporting" may dictate. The petty inroads upon the garden or grain-field made by a few species of otherwise highly beneficial song-birds is considered ample cause for a murderous onslaught upon a dozen or two of our most useful and ornamental species of birds, and the numbers annually killed in this way throughout the country is undoubtedly rapidly diminishing the representatives of a considerable number of our practically harmless birds. The indiscriminate destruction of the nests and eggs of all the birds found in the suburbs of our larger towns by the irrepressible urchins of the lower classes, merely in wanton cruelty, is, however, an evil of no small magnitude and one not easy to remedy . . .

The custom that has prevailed in the rural districts ever since the settlement of the country of shooting certain kinds of thrushes, jays, sparrows, and blackbirds, and even some of our most useful species of flycatchers, because they now and then steal a few berries or cherries from the garden, or destroy a few young blades of corn or other grain, or now and then seize upon a luckless bee in procuring their varied insect diet, has undoubtedly caused a needless and harmful decrease in the number of the feathered inhabitants of our orchards, gardens, fields and pasture-lands, far more, doubtless, than has resulted from the changes naturally attending the agricultural development of the country. The numerous game protective associations that have originated during the last few years are doing much for the proper limitation of the destruction of game and fish, but the decrease of the smaller song-birds does not so strongly appeal to their self-interest.

Allen realized that the laws on the books of various states were not enough, and that something more was needed if the birds were to be saved. His recommendation, quite prescient in a sense, was this:

Societies should be formed whose express object should be the protection throughout the country of not only these practically innocent and pleasure-giving species, but also the totally innoxious herons, terns and gulls, whose extirpation is progressing with heedless and fearful rapidity. Perhaps no more legitimate or appropriate work than this could engage the attention of the associations for the

> "Prevention of Cruelty to Animals." Unless something is soon done to awaken public opinion in this direction, and to enlist the sympathies of the people in behalf of our persecuted birds, the close of the next half-century will witness a large increase in the list of the wholly extirpated species, and a great decrease in numbers of others that are now comparatively abundant.

Not only the "innocent and pleasure-giving species," but also the "herons, terns and gulls," and many other threatened birds, were soon to be the concern of powerful protective organizations. Presumably Allen referred to The American Society for the Prevention of Cruelty to Animals, formed in 1866, in recommending an organization to carry on the work of saving the birds; but this society was to give only incidental service in the struggle. The two most effective organizations were to arise, appropriately enough, among scientists, writers, and common citizens whose main interests concerned not livestock and work animals and pets, but wild nature, and more especially, birds.

The ornithologist is almost inevitably a conservationist. Not merely does his profession largely depend on the continued presence of an avifauna worth studying; his choice of a lifework plainly implies a high regard, even a love, for the birds themselves. Ornithology is scarcely for those who seek riches or power; it is preëminently a calling for the dedicated person, the scientist who risks giving up certain common rewards of society in order to follow his own star. Ferdinand Rosier grew rich, and died a highly respected and successful merchant; his partner John James Audubon withdrew in failure from mercantile pursuits, and for the rest of his unconventional life, whether in poverty or affluence, fame or disrepute, he lived for birds. Alexander Wilson endured the "dull drudgery" of school teaching only in order to prepare for a highly uncertain career as an ornithologist. Men who are thus devoted to birds will not willingly see them exterminated.

Wilson's comments on the slaughter of robins for the market have been given above. Elsewhere Wilson defended the economic value of woodpeckers; pointed out (by way of correspondence from his versatile friend Dr. Samuel L. Mitchell) the threat of extinction for the heath hen; and anticipated the extermination (in our time nearly accomplished) of the ivory-billed woodpecker, by noting its restricted habitat. Even more remarkably, this least superstitious of men approved those folks beliefs which, by attributing supernatural powers to birds, protected them against slaughter.

Of course Wilson shot birds for specimens, but not without regret. The following passage refers to the ruby-crowned kinglet, but might be applied to many other birds Wilson was obliged to kill in the pursuit of his study:

> I have often regretted the painful necessity one is under of taking away the lives of such inoffensive useful little creatures, merely to obtain a more perfect knowledge of the species; for they appear so busy, so active and unsuspecting, as to continue searching about the same twig, even after their companions have been shot down beside them.

With Audubon the apparent contradiction between shooting birds and holding them in affectionate esteem is especially pronounced. Audubon was always fond of hunting, and even his ornithological collecting often seemed to partake as much of sport as of science. In the first part of "The Florida Keys" there is a description of collecting done in a particular reprehensible manner, by shooting into flocks of birds to kill as many as possible. Audubon gives us a straightforward account of this reckless slaughter of massed pelicans, cormorants, godwits, and other birds, without any noticeable disapproval. Yet a page or two later in this volume of *Ornithological Biography* Audubon condemns a "mischievous" hunter who shoots a crow aimlessly "and leaves the poor creature to die in the most excruciating agonies"; and this is followed by a sober and obviously sincere plea for an end to the systematic killing of "our poor, humble, harmless, and even most serviceable bird, the Crow." Elsewhere in the volume occurs a more general statement on bird destruction, in which Audubon regrets that "several species of our birds are becoming rare, destroyed as they are, either to gratify the palate of the epicure, or to adorn the cabinet of the naturalist." Scattered among Audubon's bird biographies are many similar expressions of disapproval for indiscriminate shooting.

Audubon's "Delineations" gave him an opportunity to treat conservation themes at some length. "The Eggers of Labrador" is a particularly effective account, mordantly describing acts of depredation by men whose natures were, in Audubon's eyes, piratical and debased, and whose wasteful cruelty could have but one result—"the entire disappearance of the myriads of birds that made the coast of Labrador their summer residence." Concern for the vanishing American wilderness also appears in several of the "Delineations," and indicates that the ornithologist had an outlook not limited merely by the status of bird life. His talk with Daniel Boone permitted him to quote the old woodsman as follows:

> "But ah! Sir, what a wonderful difference thirty years makes in a country. Why, at the time when I was caught by the Indians, you would not have walked out in any direction for more than a mile without shooting a buck or a bear. There were then thousands of buffaloes on the hills in Kentucky; the land looked as if it never would become poor; and to hunt in those days was a pleasure indeed. But when I was left to myself on the banks of Green River [about 1810] . . . a few *signs* only of deer were to be seen, and, as to a deer itself, I saw none."

In "The Ohio" Audubon himself adopted the same mood of nostalgia as he reflected upon the vast changes which settlement had brought to the midwestern lands, and he concluded:

> Whether these changes are for the better or for the worse, I shall not pretend to say; but in whatever way my conclusions may incline, I feel with regret that there are no satisfactory accounts of the state of that portion of the country, from the time when our people first settled it. This has not been because no one in America is able to accomplish such an undertaking. Our IRVINGS and our COOPERS have proved themselves fully competent to the task. It has more probably been because the changes have succeeded each other with such rapidity, as almost to rival the movements of their pen. However, it is not too late yet; and I sincerely hope that either or both of them will ere long furnish the generations to come with those delightful descriptions which they are so well qualified to give, of the original state of a country that has been so rapidly forced to change her form and attire under the influence of increasing population . . . They will analyze, as it were, into each component part, the country as it once existed, and will render the picture, as it ought to be, immortal.

Audubon wrote this passage about 1830. Within a few years Washington Irving was to publish *A Tour of the Prairies,* a vivid, humorous, and picturesque narrative of personal experiences in the West, and *Astoria,* a collaborative effort relating the history of John Jacob Astor's attempt to build a fur-trading empire in the Columbia River area. Both works made interesting reading, but neither escaped Irving's preoccupation with persons and events to deal with the new lands in the manner envisioned by Audubon. As for James Fenimore Cooper, three of his best known works on the wilderness, novels centering around the career of Leatherstocking, had already been published. The first of them, *The Pioneers* (1823), had used a scene of passenger pigeon slaughter to deplore the destructiveness of settlers—in Natty Bumppo's words, "This comes of settling a country!" *The Last of the Mohicans* (1826), dealing with Bumppo's earlier years, was less directly concerned with the inroads of the white men, but gave an unforgettable picture of Indian life in the wilderness. In *The Prairie* (1827) the aged Bumppo was shown in full retreat before the settlers, driven by "the sound of the axe . . . from his beloved forests to seek a refuge, by a species of desperate resignation, on the denuded plains that stretch to the Rocky Mountains."

Unfortunately for Audubon's hopes, Cooper subsequently devoted much of his energy to other literary concerns, returning to Leatherstocking only to consider his younger days, in *The Pathfinder* (1840) and *The Deerslayer* (1841). When Cooper again wrote of passenger pigeons, in *The Chainbearer* (1845), it was to draw an analogy between avian stupidity and "the tyranny of numbers" in American politics; but the romantic conception of the trackless frontier had already been established in American thinking by his earlier Leatherstocking books, and Audubon's comments on the disappearing wilderness fell upon ears previously attuned. Unquestionably, the conservation movement in the latter half of the century drew some of its strength from the love of untamed nature which Cooper's books, especially those concerning Natty Bumppo the great woodsman, had engendered in America—and which Audubon's writings had confirmed and enhanced.

13 *Federal and State Bird Books*

Although John James Audubon was the most famous and perhaps the last of the "public ornithologists," ornithology had been a matter of public concern in America before the appearance of the works of Audubon or even Wilson, in connection with governmental survey and exploring parties; and this concern was intensified in the second half of the nineteenth century, resulting in the publication of many ornithological works sponsored by the federal government.

The earliest exploration of the vast new territory of Louisiana, acquired by the United States in 1803, was that carried out by William Dunbar and Dr. George Hunter in the following year. At Jefferson's direction, they undertook a voyage up the Red, the Black, and the Washita rivers, and recorded their discoveries in a journal. Numerous water and forest birds are mentioned, but there is no systematic treatment of the avifauna encountered, nor is there any evidence of collecting. Pike's expedition to the Arkansas and Red rivers (1806) and the much more important expedition of Lewis and Clark (1802–1806) have been discussed in connection with Alexander Wilson; briefly, neither journey resulted in significant ornithological studies, although William Clark made a conscientious effort to collect bird notes.

Two expeditions led by Major Stephen H. Long, one to the Rocky Mountains in 1819 and 1820, the other to the source of "St. Peter's River" in 1823, gave special attention to the gathering of ornithological data, but the results were not conspicuously successful.

What appears to be the first major work of ornithology produced under the auspices of the federal government was that resulting from the Wilkes expedition to the South Seas, 1838 to 1842. The phrase "to the South Seas" gives but a narrow idea of the itinerary; actually this exploring party, starting in six naval vessels from Hampton Roads in August 1838, proceeded to the Madeira and Cape Verde islands, thence to Rio de Janeiro, around Cape Horn, up the coast to Callao in Peru, southward to skirt Antarctica, westward to the South Pacific islands, Australia, and New Zealand, back to the northwest coast of the United States, westward again to the Philippines, thence to Singapore and the Cape of Good Hope, and across the Atlantic to reach New York in June 1842. Several scientists were included in the expedition, and their discoveries filled a number of the volumes of report authorized by Congress.

The eighth volume of the series, concerning mammals and birds, was originally projected as the work of Titian Peale, who had accompanied the party. However, Peale and Charles Wilkes, the commander, fell to quarreling over certain matters of publication, and when the Peale volume appeared in 1848, it received little support from Wilkes. Studying the details of this squabble, one finds it difficult to decide between the proud Mr. Peale and the arbitrary Captain Wilkes; but one regrets that the result of the quarrel was the virtual stillbirth of Peale's work (issued in fewer than a hundred copies) and the temporary abandonment of the plan to issue a folio atlas illustrating the text.

Wilkes persevered, however, and at length called in John Cassin, a Philadelphia ornithologist, to rework the text and assemble material for the atlas. Both volumes were published in 1858. If Peale had been seeking revenge for Wilkes's treatment, he obtained it here. Not merely were most of the bird engravings taken from Peale's paintings; even the completely revised text frequently employed his descriptive notes on species. Yet the Cassin work was a considerable improvement over the earlier version, especially in the classification of specimens, many of which Peale had left unnamed. Since nearly all of the birds discussed were exotic species, these volumes made no important contribution to the study of American birds; but they are significant mainly as they represent an impressive early achievement in ornithological works sponsored by the United States government.

The Wilkes publications did not comprise Cassin's first effort in assembling ornithologies from the data of exploring parties. In 1855 he had reported on the birds encountered by the United States Naval Astronomical Expedition to the Southern Hemisphere (1849–1852), and a year later had edited the ornithological notes collected on Commodore Perry's famous voyage to the Orient (1852–1854). Again the birds were nearly all exotics, described in a few brief notes on habits and occurrence. In the case of Perry's expedition, no scientist was present to collect specimens and data; the artist of the party, William Heine, contributed the bulk of the information, mainly noteworthy as the first ornithological material gathered by an Occidental on the larger islands of Japan. A few colored illustrations added to the interest of both productions; but neither work was in any way exhaustive for the vast areas traversed by these naval parties.

In 1856 Cassin also published another, more detailed work resulting from federal exploration activity. *Illustrations of the Birds of California, Texas, Oregon, British and Russian America . . . and a General Synopsis of North American Ornithology* drew upon a number of surveys required by the acquisition of Texas, New Mexico, Arizona, and California in the 1840's, and by the settlement of the Pacific Northwest. It appears that Cassin published this volume at his own risk, not under direct governmental subsidy; but in the Preface he acknowledged his debt to various official surveying parties when he said:

> [With these new territories] numerous Government expeditions for the purpose of exploration and survey have been necessary, and have been dispatched with the utmost promptness and vigilance of the public good . . . and have almost invariably been accompanied by officers specifically charged with making observations and collections in Natural History. The Smithsonian Institution also has exerted an influence in the highest degree favorable and important in the development of the Natural History of this country, as in other departments of science and literature.

In this work Cassin was dealing with American rather than foreign birds, although again he concentrated on a relatively small number of species, giving "descriptions and figures of all North American birds not given by former American authors," while considering others only in the synopsis. One of the more interesting features of this volume was the art work of George White, whose colored lithographs were usually much superior to the general run of bird illustrations of the period.

Cassin published this work too early to receive the full benefit of a remarkable series of explorations carried out at the direction of the United States government between 1853 and 1856. Conducted in order "to ascertain the most practicable and economical route for a railroad from the Mississippi River to the Pacific Ocean," these surveys fostered the most important studies of American birds since Audubon. Nor were such ornithological results achieved by accident, as in the case of Perry's voyage; the numerous parties organized to investigate railroad routes were charged from the start with the task of gathering data for subsequent reports on various aspects of natural history. A broad sense of public responsibility, a "vigilance of the public good," as Cassin put it, animated this enterprise. Thomas Jefferson had instructed Meriwether Lewis to include among "objects worthy of notice" in the expedition records "the animals of the country generally, and especially those not known in the United States." A similar spirit moved the government half a century later, although now the need was less to discover what lay west of the Father of Waters than to tie the sprawling American territories together with iron rails.

Joseph Henry, a physicist of international reputation and the secretary of the Smithsonian Institution, described the scientific organizing and functioning of the survey parties in these words:

> During the first organization of the parties for the survey of a railroad route to the Pacific, application was made to the Smithsonian Institution by the officers in charge, for instructions and suggestions in reference to the investigation of the Natural History of their respective lines. These were cheerfully furnished, as in accordance with the objects of an establishment intended for the increase and diffusion of knowledge. The specimens in Zoology, as collected, were transmitted from time to time to the Institution, and properly preserved until the return of the parties. A series of special

> reports was prepared by the naturalists of the expeditions; but as these were necessarily disconnected and incomplete, it was deemed advisable to furnish a general systematic report upon the collections as a whole; and this being sanctioned by the War Department, the materials were entrusted to competent individuals for this purpose, the necessary drawings being made by a skilful artist within the walls of the Institution.

The "general systematic report" to which Henry refers had the over-all title of *Reports of Explorations and Surveys to Ascertain the Most Practicable and Economical Route for a Railroad from the Mississippi River to the Pacific Ocean, Made under the Direction of the Secretary of War, in 1853–6*; the ornithological portion appeared as the second part of the ninth volume of the series, in 1858, and is usually referred to as Baird's *General Report*. Spencer F. Baird, assistant secretary of the Smithsonian, was the volume's chief editor and was aided by Cassin and George N. Lawrence of New York.

This portly quarto volume utilized data and specimens from fifteen separate survey groups, twelve of which had been sent out by the War Department, two by the Department of the Interior, and one by the State Department. In addition, private collections and studies were also employed, since this work, despite its title, was not limited to the birds found west of the Mississippi River, but embraced the avifauna of the continent. Indeed, when the volume was privately reissued (with some additions and corrections, but unaltered in essentials) in Philadelphia in 1860, its title was changed to *The Birds of North America*, indicating its proper range.

Alexander Wilson had described two hundred and sixty-two species, Audubon five hundred and six; Baird's *General Report*, the earliest work attempting to encompass the present boundaries of the United States, listed seven hundred and thirty-eight. Whole new areas had been added to the nation since the two great pioneers had finished their work; and where Wilson had only the journey of Lewis and Clark to draw upon, and Audubon that of Townsend, Baird had fifteen official survey parties, each one contributing specimens, information, or both. Baird also had the help of two expert assistants, the sponsorship of the federal government, and the resources of the national museum, the Smithsonian. Ornithology had ceased to be the work of great individuals and had become a coöperative enterprise, indeed a public one.

Almost inevitably, such joint authorship and such imposing support carried its penalty—in a word, dullness. There are a thousand pages in the *General Report*, and thirty-eight chromo-lithograph plates in the atlas; but neither the text nor the illustrations bear the stamp of an arresting personality. Certainly Baird, Cassin, and Lawrence packed far more information into their volume than was available to Audubon, and their mistakes do not cry out for correction as do Audubon's. Yet it is most unlikely that any plate from the *General Report* was ever framed for a gallery of art, or that any author could ever say, as Thoreau of Audubon, "I read in Baird, Cassin, and Lawrence with a thrill of delight."

In 1859 Baird published *Birds of the Boundary* as part of the report rendered by the Interior Department's Mexican boundary survey party. He had already employed the data gathered by this group in his *General Report*; this later work was scarcely more than a listing of species, but included twenty-five colored illustrations of new birds. These plates, plus the original ones from the *General Report*, plus thirty-eight new ones, went into the atlas for *The Birds of North America*.

The *General Report* was the most important ornithological work issued by the federal government in the nineteenth century, but it was by no means the last one. In the early 1870's numerous geological and geographical surveys were made west of the hundredth meridian, and were reported in seven volumes between 1875 and 1889. The fifth volume (1875) contained H. W. Henshaw's *Report upon the Ornithological Collections Made in Portions of Nevada, Utah, California, Colorado, New Mexico, and Arizona*. This work, with nearly four hundred pages of letterpress and fifteen colored illustrations, was the most complete if not the most detailed report yet to appear on the birds of the Southwest. The introductory letter to the volume listed not only the various survey parties involved, but also indicated how considerable was the support extended to this enterprise by numerous biological scientists not connected with the federal service. Robert Ridgway's lithographs, generally quite well designed and reproduced, added color to an otherwise sober and straightforward work of science.

Two works by Elliott Coues, one of the most prolific naturalists of the century, appeared under the auspices of federal geological surveys. *Birds of the Northwest* (1874) and *Birds of the Colorado Valley* (1878) were issued as miscellaneous publications of the United States Geological Survey of the Territories. In a sense they represent a reversion to the manner of Audubon, since they bear the stamp of a person with a well-developed ego and considerable powers of expression. But at times Coues's irascible self-confidence becomes rather overbearing, for example in the long discussion of swallow hibernation in the Colorado volume, where those who deny the hibernation theory are berated for failing to accept "evidence." Coues was no Audubon; he was more often irritating than ingratiating; but his personality helps relieve the general dead-levelness common to governmental publications.

None of these ornithological reports resulted from independent efforts exclusively devoted to the study of birds (although, as with Cassin and Baird, they could result in privately published volumes). All of them were connected in one way or another with wider public enterprises. Not until 1885 was there a federal organization concerned with birds alone, and then it came in, so to speak, by the back door. The Division of Entomology of the Department of Agriculture in 1885 established a section of economic ornithology, which a year later became the Division of Economic Ornithology, and in 1896 the Division of Biological Survey. The original purpose of this organization was to investigate the relationship between birds and agriculture; numerous studies were published on the subject, including *The English Sparrow in North America* (1889), *The Hawks and Owls of the United States in Their Relation to Agriculture* (1893), *The Common Crow of the United States* (1895), *Food of Woodpeckers* (1895), and *Food of the Bobolink, Blackbirds, and Grackles* (1900). But the limits imposed by economics were soon transgressed, and by the end of the century the Biological Survey had begun to publish studies on broader questions of public policy in relation to birds.

* * *

The federal government did not pioneer in American economic ornithology; several states had concerned themselves with the problem before the formal work of the Department of Agriculture began to appear. Indeed, the first noteworthy ornithologies of any sort to be issued at public expense were those authorized by certain states, not those which resulted from federal sponsorship. Henry Thoreau began his career as a nature writer by reviewing natural history reports (including Peabody's section on birds) submitted to the Massachusetts legislature in 1838 and 1839. Another Massachusetts survey, a "Geological Examination of the Commonwealth," had been authorized as early as 1830, and included a bird list by Ebenezer Emmons in its report of 1833. The second annual report of the Ohio Geological Survey (1838) contained a catalogue of birds by Dr. J. P. Kirtland. None of these early productions was important as a detailed work of ornithology, but all three of them reflected a measure of interest in birds on the part of state governments.

James E. De Kay's *Birds* [*of New York*], perhaps the most remarkable of the state bird books, appeared in 1844, as part of a survey of the state's natural features and resources. A substantial quarto, handsomely printed and bound, it contained not only three hundred and fifty-three pages of text but also one hundred and forty-one hand-colored plates with three hundred and eight figures. De Kay's notes on the species, while not lengthy, were especially interesting for the attention devoted to the problem of field identification. Under the heading "Characteristics" he gave what today would be called field marks, and under "Description" and "Color" he further delineated the bird as it might appear in nature. J. W. Hill's illustrations, although drawn from stiff mounted specimens, aided in the task of identification by being simple and brightly colored. This weighty volume was scarcely adapted to the role of field guide, but nevertheless it was perhaps better suited to that use than any bird book which had yet appeared in America, possibly excepting Nuttall's two-volume *Manual of Ornithology of the United States and Canada* (1832–1834).

De Kay adhered closely to his assigned subject, the birds to be found in his own state, and depended more on his own investigations than on the authority of others. Nearly every species treated was described from an actual specimen in the State Collection or the Cabinet of the New York Lyceum. Furthermore, species which could not be discovered within the state were listed as "Extra-Limital," a means of eliminating various errors or hypothetical species found in Wilson and Audubon. The smew was called "accidental"; the "Ring-tailed Eagle" was classed with the golden eagle and the "Sea Eagle" with the bald; the two color phases of the screech owl were called a single species; the carbonated and Rathbone warblers, claimed by Audubon but not verified since, were put among extra-limital birds. De Kay did not go out of his way to correct errors by other ornithologists, and many of the emendations did not originate with him, but he rigorously excluded those birds whose presence in New York state could not be verified by his own observations or by authentic evidence.

California might have surpassed New York in the matter of a state ornithology had it held to the original plan, authorized in 1860, to compile "a full and complete description of the botanical and zoological productions" of the state. However, funds allocated for the work were suspended in 1868, granted once more in 1870, and finally stopped in 1874, with the result that only the first volume, on the land birds, was issued as a state bird book. This was J. G. Cooper's *Ornithology* (1870), edited by Spencer F. Baird. Subsequently Baird, T. M. Brewer, and Robert Ridgway brought out *A History of North American Birds* (1874), in format and illustrations a continuation of the California volume, but devoted to all the land birds of the continent north of Mexico. Ten years later the same authors published two volumes called *The Water Birds of North America,* avowedly "in continuation of the Publications of the Geological Survey of California," but again taking in very many species not found in that state, and published as Memoirs of the Museum of Comparative Zoölogy at Harvard. A particular consequence of this confused situation was that California was denied full credit for a work which, judging from the excellence of the Cooper volume, would have surpassed all other state bird publications.

Of numerous other ornithologies sponsored by the states, the most complete were *The Birds of Pennsylvania* (1888; revised and enlarged 1890) by B. H. Warren, *The Ornithology of Illinois* (1889–1895) by Ridgway and Forbes, *History of the Birds of Kansas* (1891) by N. S. Goss, *Notes on the Birds of Minnesota* (1892) by P. L. Hatch, *The Birds of New Jersey* (1896) by Charles A. Shriner, and *The Birds of Indiana* (1897) by Amos W. Butler. Many lesser works appeared elsewhere, and in the twentieth century other comprehensive state ornithologies were issued. The works mentioned were only the more impressive evidences of the concern shown by various states for the bird life to be found within their boundaries.

14 *Educating a Wider Public*

The best of the state bird books — for example, those of De Kay, Cooper, and Butler — were general works, not limited to narrow concerns of economics; but several others, particularly those issued by state agricultural or horticultural units, were little more than lists dividing birds into good and bad on the basis of stomach contents. In a sense, the listing of certain species as "good" afforded them a measure of protection from indiscriminate shooting; but this appeared a limited and selfish criterion to many persons whose interest in birds was not bounded by material considerations. Thoreau may have been thinking of a report on the content of birds' stomachs made by J. W. P. Jenks to the Massachusetts Horticultural Society (1858) when in his journal he called for a broader view:

> When the question of the protection of birds comes up, the legislatures regard only a low use and never a high use; the best-disposed legislators employ one, perchance, only to examine their crops and see how many grubs or cherries they contain, and never to study their dispositions, or the beauty of their plumage, or listen and report on the sweetness of their song. The legislature will preserve a bird

> professedly not because it is a beautiful creature, but because it is a good scavenger or the like. This, at least, is the defense set up. It is as if the question were whether some celebrated singer of the human race — some Jenny Lind or another — did more harm or good, should be destroyed, or not, and therefore a committee should be appointed, not to listen to her singing at all, but to examine the contents of her stomach and see if she devoured anything which was injurious to the farmers and gardeners, or which they cannot spare.

Mere economic considerations, Thoreau knew, could not properly protect the birds, especially those of dubious repute to the farmer. Another attitude, one of love for the bird on its own terms and for its own special virtues, was required to transcend the narrow standard of gain. At length even the ornithologists realized that such an attitude could not be engendered merely by their books, their state and federal reports, or their articles in technical journals. If the birds were to be saved from extermination or serious decimation, their cause would have to be argued in the public prints; but not until late in the century did any professional bird scientist begin to publish his own magazine addressed to the general reader.

The nature essayists were more fortunate, being able to reach a wide audience through various regular periodicals. *The Atlantic Monthly* has been mentioned as a noteworthy outlet for creative bird writing. The market for such work, however, was by no means limited to this "Mazagine of Art, Literature, and Politics" published in Boston, Massachusetts. *Harper's New Monthly Magazine,* while its list of outdoor writers was less impressive than that of the *Atlantic,* nevertheless ran nature essays on occasion, many of them about birds. S. T. Frost, F. M. Brewer, Mary Titcomb, Edward Samuels, Mary Treat, and Phil Robinson were among the contributors. *Scribner's Monthly* published two of Burroughs' best essays, "The Birds of the Poets" in September 1873 and "English and American Song-Birds" in January 1882 (by which time the magazine's name had changed to the *Century*); J. A. Allen appeared in the issue of October 1881, and one of John Muir's rare bird articles, "The Humming-Bird of the California Water-Falls," came out in February 1878. In general, this periodical seemed to attract the better nature writers, and by publishing articles on a variety of outdoor subjects, tended to appeal to an audience interested in many aspects of the natural world. In addition, it contained a regular department called "Nature and Science," featuring short articles, occasionally on birds.

These three, the *Atlantic, Harper's,* and *Scribner's* (or the *Century*) were the most important of the monthly periodicals publishing bird articles in the latter half of the century. To their output may be added an occasional essay on birds in *Macmillan's Magazine, Appleton's Journal, The Independent,* and *Harper's Bazar.* It is scarcely possible to assess the effect of such writing in terms of conservation; but it seems plausible to suppose that by keeping the subject of birds alive among their hundreds of thousands of readers, these magazines helped prepare the way for bird-protection work carried out in the final decades.

Little of the writing in these periodicals for adults was hortatory; much of it may have been educational, but it was not didactic or propagandistic. The opposite is true of writing about birds in those magazines directed at a youthful audience. The two most important children's periodicals, the weekly *Youth's Companion* and the monthly *St. Nicholas,* were especially forthright in pleading the cause of bird protection.

At first glance, the early *Youth's Companion* seems little more than a religious paper—an impression buttressed by the subtitle it carried for a time, "A Family Paper, Devoted to Piety, Morality, Brotherly Love—No Sectarianism, No Controversy." When he started the periodical in 1827, Nathaniel Willis, the editor, openly avowed his intention to foster piety among his readers, and during his thirty-year editorship there was no significant change in policy. There were sections entitled "Morality," "Religion," "Benevolence," and the like; there were illustrated stories from the Bible; there were pious tales of lives salvaged by faith, and deaths ennobled by it. Yet by one means or another Willis managed to avoid the more debilitating effects of religiosity, and to give his four-page weekly a breadth not commonly found in tracts intended for children.

Perhaps Willis' basic virtue as an editor was his shrewd use of scissors and paste. Much of his material was lifted from secular works, especially those dealing with far-off places and exotic adventures; such excerpts gave the paper a quality of wonder undoubtedly appealing to children. Furthermore, he included a regular department called "Natural History," in which a wide variety of living creatures were described, not always in strictly accurate terms but generally at the proper level for young readers. It was here that much of the propaganda for conserving birds appeared, sometimes openly, in straightforward moral lessons, at other times as implications to be drawn from the praise accorded the birds discussed. In addition, verses addressed to birds appeared now and then, usually pleading for a merciful attitude toward gentle creatures.

But perhaps the most effective pieces were the didactic narratives, telling of bird-killing adventures and their unhappy consequences. "The Wounded Bird," by T. S. Arthur, is an excellent example of the genre, and it was so well regarded that it appeared at least twice in three years. Out to shoot songbirds go two boys, one of them returning at the end of the hunt carrying a wounded oriole. The boy's mother deplores his act, saying it is "most wicked to hurt or kill any one of God's creatures in mere sport," and the story ends with the boy full of remorse for his evil hunting habits. "The Shooting Expedition, or, A Sister's Influence" tells how two boys are dissuaded by a sister from "killing the harmless songsters of the grove." This kind of moral tale, in which mercy and Christian love oppose the evil habit of killing birds and robbing nests, was of such frequent occurrence in the early *Youth's Companion* as to seem almost a regular feature.

In 1856 Nathaniel Willis relinquished control of the magazine to John W. Olmstead and Daniel S. Ford, who conducted it jointly for ten years, after which Ford assumed full editorial responsibility. Under the new management, and especially under Ford, the *Youth's Companion* changed radically. The section called "Natural History" was dropped, along with various departments of a religious character. No advertising had been accepted by Willis; under Ford's management there appeared advertisements for patent medicines, skin disease cures, corsets, kitchen stoves, and many other items. Indeed, by the 1880's one finds it difficult to decide what audience is being aimed at; few of the advertised products relate to the pre-adolescent, and a good deal of the written matter is either too sensational or too ponderous to be considered proper children's fare. The fact is that Ford was endeavoring to make the paper a general family magazine—an aim which Willis had professed but did not pursue. How well Ford succeeded is indicated in part by the circulation figures. Willis had never reached ten thousand subscribers; Ford had three hundred and eighty-five thousand readers by 1885, and half a million by 1898.

In its outlook on nature the magazine changed also. The moralistic nature story disappeared, and was replaced by the outdoor adventure tale (often involving encounters with fierce wild beasts) or by the straightforward nature essay. John Burroughs contributed a few of the latter variety, but a reader seeks in vain for overt didacticism in them. Burroughs' bird essays in *Youth's Companion* tended to be more chatty and familiar than his work for, say, the *Atlantic*, but they were if anything less concerned with conservation than were his more formal efforts. What is true of Burroughs is generally true of other nature authors in the later *Youth's Companion*; they were interested in telling a good story, but not in pointing a moral.

However, Bradford Torrey became one of the junior editors of the magazine in 1886, and no doubt he was responsible for most of the concern for bird protection shown in the years following. There was still no reversion to the Willis manner, but occasionally there appeared a short narrative or editorial comment on some phase of the conservation problem. Once again it is reasonable to ask whether young people or adults were the intended audience; it is scarcely probable that school children were much interested in fulminations against female apparel, or in statistics of bird slaughter quoted from *The Auk*. Because the *Youth's Companion* had such a wide circulation in the final decades of the century, its potential influence in helping to save the birds was considerable; but its effect during this period was doubtless felt as much among adults as among boys and girls.

St. Nicholas was (in the words of its subtitle) an "Illustrated Magazine for Boys and Girls" from its first issue, November 1873, and its original character did not change during the rest of the century. Although in some ways it was a more mature periodical than the *Youth's Companion* — less concerned, for example, with sensational adventure, broader in its cultural range, and more dignified in its advertising policies — it was and remained a magazine for young people. As such, it did not hesitate to present the case for bird protection in terms children could understand. As early as the second number, *St. Nicholas* embarked on a campaign designed to convince its readers of the value and propriety of the conservation movement. That number carried an article by C. C. Haskin which was "a plea for a large family of our friends who are wantonly destroyed and abused by impulsive persons without good reason, and very often thoughtlessly. . . They are the birds—all of them—from the eagle and the vulture down to the tiniest hummingbird." After mentioning that he had corresponded with *St. Nicholas* "on the subject of the abuse of birds," Haskin went on to propose an organization called "Bird Defenders," with this stated aim:

> *Whereas*—We, the youth of America, believing that the wanton destruction of wild birds is not only cruel and unwarranted, but is unnecessary, wrong, and productive of mischief to vegetation as well as morals; therefore,
>
> *Resolved*—That we severally pledge ourselves to abstain from all such practices as shall tend to the destruction of wild birds; that we will use our best endeavors to induce others to do likewise, and that we will advocate the rights of birds at all proper times, encourage confidence in them, and recognize in them creations of the great Father, for the joy and good of mankind.

In June 1875 appeared "A Story for the 'Bird Defenders,'" by Helen B. Phillips, an anthropomorphic tale of a bereaved robin whose mate had been killed by a thoughtless boy. Becoming aware of the bird's sorrow, the boy felt such remorse for his act that he was willing "to join the army of Bird-defenders." Joseph Kirkland's "The Good Shot," in the issue for June 1880, told how young birds died of hunger in the nest, after a boy had shot the parents. There is no denying either the didactic intent or the emotional impact of the story; it sets out to teach a lesson, and does so quite effectively. A long story by J. T. Trowbridge, "The Scarlet Tanager" (subtitled "A Young Bird-Hunter's Strange Adventures") approached the problem from a somewhat different direction, being concerned with the distinction between proper scientific collecting and random shooting based on temporary boyish enthusiasm. Here the moral lesson was disguised behind a tale of youthful adventure, but few readers could fail to discover what Trowbridge was driving at. Near the end of the story Gaspar Heth, the bird hunter, is rescued by Mr. Pike, the schoolmaster, from entrapment in a hollow tree; in gratitude for his deliverance he pledges himself to support Mr. Pike's campaign to enforce the laws against indiscriminate shooting.

Among many pieces on the subject of birds in *St. Nicholas*, these stories were only the most forthright and propagandistic, intended as they no doubt were for the encouragement of the "Bird Defenders." There is no evidence that the "Defender" group ever became an effective organization; mention of it soon disappeared from the magazine, just as later the larger and more influential "Agassiz Association" (for general nature study) received the magazine's sponsorship for a time, and then dropped away. The truth was that the policy of *St. Nicholas* regarding nature was too broad to be encompassed by any special organization or group. The magazine might willingly plead the cause of bird protection, for example, but its concern with nature generally was one of informed and sympathetic interest not bounded by particular preoccupations. Birds appeared not only in didactic fiction but also in articles, poems, and featured illustrations, and they were less a separate aspect than an integral part of the outlook of this admirable periodical for younger readers.

Harper's Young People, an illustrated weekly, began publication in 1880 with a format and general style suggesting *St. Nicholas* — a similarity which extended to its concern with the outdoors. Many of its nature stories and articles were about birds, and although some were not wholly accurate, and others were guilty of personalizing their subjects rather excessively, by and large they were competently written and well adapted to a youthful audience. However, in the middle 1890's the magazine underwent a metamorphosis, signalized by the change of its name to *Harper's Round Table* (reflecting a desire to inculcate King Arthur's "chivalry, honesty, and uprightness" among young Americans) and further represented by a series of articles by Theodore Roosevelt on "Heroes of America." Stories of war and derring-do began to dominate the magazine — too strenuous a view of life for young readers to enjoy, one may suppose, since they abandoned *Harper's Round Table* in such numbers that in 1899, after a final flourish or two, it vanished like Excalibur beneath the wave.

The list of bird writers appearing in these three periodicals for young people is a considerable one, and includes not merely professional authors like Burroughs, Torrey, Trowbridge, Ernest Ingersoll, and Ernest Thompson Seton, but also the ornithologists H. W. Henshaw and Frank Chapman. Among the women writers, Celia Thaxter in poetry and Florence Merriam Bailey in prose were especially notable. Some of the foremost authors writing in English in the latter half of the nineteenth century appeared in *St. Nicholas* and *Youth's Companion,* and were thus introduced to an audience which, except for such magazines, they might not have reached. So too with the nature writers; through the medium of these periodicals, they brought their message of love and sympathy and respect for birds to that age-group which could profit most from their words, and which might otherwise have remained unaware of birds as objects of affection and concern.

The magazine *Birds,* subtitled "A Monthly Serial Designed to Promote Knowledge of Bird-Life," was started by the Nature Study Publishing Company, Chicago, in 1896. Designed for use in schools, it combined excellent colored photographs of mounted birds with a text "prepared with the view of giving the children as clear an idea as possible, of haunts, habits, characteristics and such other information as will lead them to love the birds and delight in their study and acquaintance." This pioneer bird magazine was initially at least quite successful, and no doubt had considerable influence through its use in public school nature study courses.

* * *

Writing for children commonly falls somewhere between art and utility, the creative and the useful. Often it has a dual aim, to provide amusement or diversion or adventure, and at the same time to give instruction. Such was the case with much of the writing in youth periodicals; such it was also with a certain kind of bird book, basically didactic in purpose and usually slanted toward younger readers or uninformed adults, which appeared rather frequently during the nineteenth century. Books of this sort generally can be classified neither as good art nor as proper ornithology. As a rule, literary histories ignore them as having no artistic merit, and histories of science scorn them as contributing nothing to the study of birds, except perhaps errors and misconceptions. Yet they were printed and read, and had their effect, however difficult to assess; they should not be passed by without a sampling.

These popular books varied considerably in method and approach. The appeal of the odd and the extraordinary was employed in *The Architecture of Birds*, by James Rennie, which originally appeared in London in 1831 as a volume of "The Library of Entertaining Knowledge," issued "under the superintendence of The Society for the Diffusion of Useful Knowledge." It was reprinted in Boston in 1833, and reissued, considerably revised and enlarged, as *Natural History of Birds* in New York in 1842, forming the ninety-eighth volume of "The Family Library" being published by Harper and Brothers. The work was an odd mélange of dubious lore and accurate observation, in general concerning the nesting habits of certain British and American birds. It could scarcely lay claim to being a straightforward work of science for the adult reader; yet with its ponderous Latinate style and its plethora of learned references to various ancient and modern authorities, it could hardly have appealed to children. That its curious "facts" might arouse interest on the part of an adult, or wonder on the part of a child, is not to be doubted; but Rennie surely made few concessions to mere readability, whatever the inherent appeal of his material.

The religious tone characteristic of much bird writing in the *Youth's Companion* appeared also in *The Bird Book*, published in 1844 by the American Sunday School Union, and was reflected in *The Boy and the Birds*, by Emily Taylor, issued in 1849 by the General Protestant Episcopal Sunday School Union. The didactic aim of *The Bird Book* was revealed almost immediately, in this passage:

> Alas! that any should be found who, for mere amusement, can silence [the birds'] soft and joyous notes, mangle their curious frames, or rob and destroy their inimitable dwellings.
>
> To study the instincts and habits of birds, is to become acquainted with some of the most wonderful works of creation, and to open to the mind an inexhaustible store of instruction and entertainment.

The stories following were brief and moralistic, with many citations from Scripture; their obvious purpose was to induce children to love birds and not destroy them. *The Boy and the Birds,* which cited Wilson, White of Selborne, and other authorities, imparted its material by the unusual device of dialogues or dramatic monologues involving a boy and a succession of birds. Originally published in England, it was revised somewhat for American publication to include a few native species.

The Reverend J. Hibbert Langille, in *Our Birds in Their Haunts,* published in Boston in 1884 and reprinted in New York in 1892, attempted to inject into a popular work for adults the religious interpretations of bird life usually confined to children's books. For this he was reprimanded by C. Hart Merriam, whose review in *The Auk* complained of his pious explanations for such phenomena as bird migration. In general Merriam was correct; from the scientist's point of view, Langille's professed aim, "to render as popular and attractive as possible . . . the sum total of the bird-life of Eastern North America," labored under the initial disadvantage of religious preconceptions. In Langille's defense it may be suggested that he scarcely aimed at an audience likely to be outraged by either religious sentiments or technical errors.

What might be called the storybook approach was used in other bird books. The opening sentence of Francis C. Woodworth's *Stories about Birds* (1854) was, "Come, little folks, take a trip with me to Bird Land." In a garrulous and familiar way, Woodworth went on to relate a variety of incidents from the lives of birds, at times employing such authentic sources as Wilson and Audubon, at other times depending on sensational reports (for example, about birds of prey) and flights of fancy. *Among the Birds,* by Edward A. Samuels, published in Boston in 1868, was subtitled "A Series of Sketches for Young Folks, Illustrating the Domestic Life of Our Feathered Friends," and made the most unblushing use of anthropomorphism—"'Oh, you sly thing!' said old grandmother Towhee Bunting," and the like. Ella Rodman Church, in *Our Home Birds* (1877), combined the citing of scientific authorities with a storybook device calculated to make her book attractive to children. An erudite governess, quoting often from Audubon and other ornithologists, was shown teaching her three young charges about various bird neighbors. Her informal manner of presenting information, through conversation interspersed with incidents, doubtless gave the book an appeal which the factual material alone could not have conferred.

❧ ❧ ❧

In the 1880's the work of two noteworthy woman authors, Olive Thorne Miller and Florence A. Merriam, began to appear. Both women were serious students of bird life, and both aspired to literary achievement. Mrs. Miller (whose real name was Harriet Mann Miller) had published general nature books earlier, but her first bird book was *Bird-Ways,* which appeared in 1885. J. A. Allen, reviewing it in *The Auk,* said it easily rivaled "in interest and literary merit" Torrey's *Birds in the Bush* or Burroughs' *Wake Robin* and *Birds and Poets.* He overstated the case. Mrs. Miller wrote well enough to be published frequently in the *Atlantic* and similar periodicals, but simplicity of style and warmth of affection do not necessarily give "literary merit" to a book, and *Bird-Ways* was neither as substantial and complex as Burroughs' work nor as artful as Torrey's.

Mrs. Miller's *In Nesting Time* (1888) began with the assertion that "the sketches of bird manners and customs in this little collection are the record of careful observation, and scrupulously true in every particular." Broadly this was the case, but the observations were made in terms of human life, and the "manners and customs" were interpreted as though proceeding from human motives. Epithets attached to certain birds further suggested this kind of outlook: the orchard oriole was "hot-headed" and "blustering," the jay was a "rogue," the mocker "a tricksy spirit," and so on. *Little Brothers of the Air* (1892) was, like the prior book, largely concerned with close investigations of bird "family life," and was similarly threatened by anthropomorphism. Which is not to say that either book was a mere exercise in misguided sentimentality; Mrs. Miller was too shrewd and accurate an observer and too disciplined a writer to permit such an outcome.

At the beginning of *A Bird-Lover in the West* (1894) Mrs. Miller produced an interesting and sober discussion of finding release from the pressures of daily work by going off to new surroundings, new scenes, new birds. In a genteel way, this passage has a modern ring, dealing as it does with problems faced by those women whose economic emancipation brings them into competition with men and with other women in urban employment. But the mid-twentieth century was yet far off; Mrs. Miller had recourse not to psychiatry but to "a cottonwood grove on the banks of the Minnelowan (or Shining Water)." Here she sought out new western birds, and in the seeking gained the tranquillity of spirit she desired. There is more self-revelation here than in earlier books, and consequently, perhaps, a more noticeable reflective strain, often contrasting with the general buoyancy of her writing. *Upon the Tree-Tops* (1897) seems less a separate volume than extension of *A Bird-Lover in the West*; the same theme of escape from the city is here, and western scenes are once again evoked. The book is padded out with miscellaneous chapters on various bird pets.

Florence A. Merriam (later Florence Merriam Bailey) published her first book, *Birds through an Opera Glass*, in 1889, as the third volume of "The Riverside Library for Young People" issued by Houghton, Mifflin. As the name of the series suggests, this book was primarily intended to introduce birds to a youthful audience. Seventy species which might readily be studied in the northeastern area of the United States were discussed in brief, informal essays. Miss Merriam employed both her own observations and numerous quotations from Lowell, Thoreau, Longfellow, Audubon, and others. The title of the book indicated the trend away from the practice of shooting specimens; the educational intent of the work was emphasized by an identification list and suggested references for further study.

My Summer in a Mormon Village (1894) was less a piece of nature writing than an exercise in the local color genre. In her economical presentation of persons and scenes, and in the sensibility which informs her work, Miss Merriam reminds one of Sarah Orne Jewett, although she has little of the brooding quality to be discovered in the latter's sketches of life in Maine. Her discussion of Mormon polygamy showed a lively sense of the perplexing human situations that arose from the doctrine, and her plea for the Mormon woman's emancipation was based not on feelings of moral outrage but on sympathy for the persons immediately involved.

When Miss Merriam's *A-Birding on a Bronco* appeared in 1896, the irascible Elliott Coues, reviewing it in *The Nation,* dismissed what he called "this booklet" by saying "the same story has been told over and over again by Mrs. Miller and too many others." In a sense he was right; *A-Birding on a Bronco* was generically related to Olive Thorne Miller's western books, and, like them, told of a series of encounters with particular species. But since the review also contained the astounding statement that the pictures of Louis Agassiz Fuertes were "better than Audubon's were to begin with," one may wonder whether Coues was not as obtuse in appreciating Florence Merriam's literary qualities as in comprehending Audubon's art.

Mabel Osgood Wright made up part of her first book, *The Friendship of Nature* (1894), from pieces published earlier in *The New York Times* and the *Evening Post*—a fact which may account for the chronological pattern of the collection. Her work was not, however, journalism in the derogatory sense of that term; *The Friendship of Nature* was made up not of glib reporting but of conventional nature essays, occasionally too literary in approach or too overladen with sensibility, but at their best delicately wrought and highly evocative of the outdoors. In *Birdcraft* (1895) she demonstrated her intimate knowledge of northeastern species by producing a book for the study of birds in the field. The text was, in the words of Frank Chapman, of "exceptionally high character"—spirited but not effusive, practical without being tedious. A color key was included to help in the identification of species treated in the text.

Mrs. Wright's *Tommy-Anne and the Three Hearts* (1896), with its sequel *Wabeno the Magician* (1899), comprised one of the most ambitious works of nature fiction for children published in the nineteenth century—and also one of the best. Tommy-Anne, the young heroine who receives her nickname from her tomboyish enthusiasm for the outdoors, at the start of the story is favored with the gift of magic spectacles, enabling her to look into the secrets of nature and understand the talk of various wild creatures. The general idea of magical powers is of course common enough in fairy stories, but Mrs. Wright put the device to special use. Instead of bestowing supernatural strength, extraordinary sagacity, or unusual control over nature, these magic spectacles merely permit the girl to meet birds and mammals and reptiles and insects at their own level. By this means Mrs. Wright could present her creatures, so to speak, "in character," and not merely as miniature human beings.

The conception is broadly anthropomorphic, but not anthropocentric; Tommy-Anne is a single human visitor in a world where representatives of her species are usually but ignorant intruders. She learns a great deal about the lives of wild things, and she is also made aware of the cruelties and injustices the human being visits upon other creatures. At one point she is made to regret wearing a bird skin on her bonnet, by discovering that the bird was once the mate of a bobolink with which she talks. She is also told of the depredations of her cat; she hears a tale of commercial persecution from the eider duck; she meets the extinct great auk. These two books plainly were intended to teach conservation to children, and, by their sympathetic and appealing presentation of numerous creatures, to instill tolerance and love for all wild things.

Neltje Blanchan (Mrs. Nellie Blanchan Doubleday) published in successive years two complementary volumes, *Bird Neighbors* and *Birds that Hunt and Are Hunted*. The first, brought out in 1897, gave "in a popular and accessible form, knowledge which is accurate and reliable about the life of our common birds"—such was the author's claim. The birds were to be identified by means of several group classifications—color, size, habitat, season—and through detailed descriptions, notes on habits, and numerous colored photographs. This system was considerably modified in the second volume, which concerned "Birds of Prey, Game Birds and Waterfowls." Here the species were grouped only under taxonomical headings, with identification depending on descriptions and photographs.

Olive Thorne Miller, Florence A. Merriam, Mabel Osgood Wright, Neltje Blanchan—these four were the most important woman authors of bird books in the nineteenth century. All of them wrote with grace and some distinction, and yet none of them has a secure place in literary histories. Perhaps they are unfairly neglected; but on the other hand, there may be a certain justice in ignoring them as literary figures, simply because their proper place is elsewhere. Their function in terms of American society was not so much literary as educational; the special perceptions they brought to the study of birds were more valuable in giving instruction than in providing inspiration; they bestowed the gift of sight rather than insight. It was a coincidence, but no mere accident, that within the space of a few years all four of them brought out books whose explicit purpose was to attract and instruct beginners in the study of birds: *Citizen Bird* (1897) by Mabel Osgood Wright (with Elliott Coues); *Birds of Village and Field* (1898) by Florence A. Merriam; *The First Book of Birds* (1899) and *The Second Book of Birds* (1901) by Olive Thorne Miller; and *How to Attract the Birds* (1902) by Neltje Blanchan. Each was a fitting contribution by an expert in the field to the greatly important task of educating young people in things avian.

It is clear that such education was becoming widespread as the century drew to a close. By 1898 G. O. Shields, editor of the magazine *Recreation*, could say, "Thousands of progressive educators have inaugurated courses of nature study in the schools, which include object lessons in bird life." On the other hand, Frank Chapman in a survey of the same year found almost no attention being given to birds in the New York City schools; the single instance he could discover involved the use of "a pigeon or a chicken" as a representative of the class Aves. Yet when he took a broader view of the matter, he found that between 1893 and 1898, "New York and Boston publishers . . . sold over seventy thousand text books on birds," and concluded optimistically that "the ranks of bird students are constantly growing."

Strong corroborative testimony for his statement is provided by the number of bird books for school or college use appearing about this time. In addition to the five mentioned above, the list included the *Pocket Guide to the Common Land Birds of New England* (1895) by M. A. Willcox, professor of zoology at Wellesley; *Bird World* (1898) by J. H. Stickney and Ralph Hoffman, subtitled "A Bird Book for Children" and issued by Ginn and Company as one of a series called "Study and Story Nature Readers"; *Our Native Birds* (1899) by D. Lange, instructor in nature study in the public schools of St. Paul, Minnesota; and *Everyday Birds* (1901) by Bradford Torrey, a work similar to *Bird World* in its level of instruction. Frank Chapman's attractive *Bird-Life* appeared in 1897, and two years later, in order to aid those who were giving courses in bird work, Chapman brought out the *Teacher's Manual of Bird-Life,* containing numerous suggestions on the techniques of instruction and study. Such books, it should be noted, were issued not by minor, specialized publishers, but by large commercial houses, in response to the growing demand for bird texts.

The movement to institute Bird Day in the manner of Arbor Day was a further evidence of interest in bird study in the schools. The observance of Bird Day was suggested in 1894 by C. A. Babcock, superintendent of schools in Oil City, Pennsylvania. Responding to Mr. Babcock's proposal, J. Sterling Morton, Secretary of Agriculture in the Cabinet of President Cleveland, said: "The cause of bird protection is one that appeals to the best side of our natures. Let us yield to the appeal. Let us have a Bird Day—a day set apart from all the other days of the year to tell the children about the birds." In July 1896 the Biological Survey issued a circular recommending the establishment of Bird Day in the schools. The observance of the day in the town of origin, Oil City, received considerable notice, and there is evidence that schools in several other states took up the idea in the latter 1890's. Perhaps because of the essentially verbal character of its rites, and its lack of a symbolic act—such as Grant Wood pictorialized with great charm in his "Arbor Day"—Bird Day never attained the popularity of its older prototype; but it serves to indicate to the later student the growing concern for birds in the public schools, during a crucial period for the conservation movement.

15 *Boys, Pot-Hunters, and Women Enemies of Birds*

The person to be reached by primary and secondary school instruction in wildlife was first and foremost the boy with the gun, shooting birds for the fun of it, or the boy who in moments of enthusiasm for "collecting" took nests, eggs, and adult birds indiscriminately, to no good purpose. Here was a threat to bird life of long standing, and one which became more acute as the century advanced, bringing greater population density, easier transportation, and cheaper firearms. But the boy was not the only threat, nor even the worst; there were many other factors contributing to the decrease of bird life in the nineteenth century, some of them inevitable and irreversible, others amenable to control.

A man named LeGrand T. Meyer, writing in 1889, analyzed the problem (in picturesque if not always dignified language) as follows:

> What is the cause of this extermination, you are ready to ask? Let me enumerate the artificial causes, taken from trustworthy observations and statistics.
>
> First, the "Pot-Hunters." Those human fiends that from day to day tramp the happy feeding grounds of game birds . . . The Pinneated Grouse and Quail . . . were once one of the most com-

> mon game birds east of the Mississippi River, now nearly extinct among the New England and Middle States. For a market supported by bloated epicures and sensualists, they have done their work thoroughly . . .
>
> Second, for Fashion. Those ladies (?) that from their ill-concealed vanity yearly sign the death warrants of millions of birds simply because they possess an attractive plumage. Recently, an item in an exchange read "Lady Gemini appeared in the reception room with a dress decorated with patches of three thousand Brazilian Hummingbirds!" Not long ago I saw a woman in a cable car wearing a hat with the heads of, by actual count, twenty-one Quails. Do you think they were taken from those slaughtered for the market? Impossible.
>
> One human resemblance, living near the seacoast of South Carolina, supplied, for a New York milliner, three thousand Roseate Terns; so that locality, once resoundant with happy parental cries of this graceful "Sea Swallow," is silent . . .
>
> Third, our Amateur Naturalists. Many of the present embryotic [*sic*] Ornithologists believe that in order to become Audubons or Bairds, they must slaughter indiscriminately every species met, and every nest must be robbed, under the transparent veil of science.

Mr. Meyer's tone was choleric, but his ideas were not far off the mark. Ten years later the biologist William T. Hornaday, in a report to the New York Zoological Society, reached somewhat the same conclusions, although he lengthened the list of factors tending toward bird destruction and provided a statistical analysis to buttress his arguments. By means of a questionnaire sent to authorities in every state, he discovered that in twenty-eight states, the District of Columbia, and Indian Territory bird life had decreased an average of forty-six per cent during the period 1883–1898. Four other states showed an increase, three reported no change, and ten failed to report. As to the cause of decrease: according to answers Hornaday received, the four major factors were the inroads of sportsmen, the wholesale slaughter by market hunters, various depredations by boys, and killing for plumes and other millinery ornaments. Also on the list were factors having to do directly with population growth (which amounted to perhaps twenty million persons in the fifteen years in question), urbanization, and extension of agriculture and lumbering. Another factor, "Italians and others, who devour song birds," was a consequence of increasing immigration from lands with a tradition of eating anything in feathers, and would tend to disappear with the integration of the newcomers within the society.

Little, certainly, could be done about the broad problems arising from the increase in population. From the beginning of the colonial period, the number of people occupying the American land rose continuously; the primeval forests were progressively destroyed; the swamps were drained, the prairies and plains broken by the plow, the uplands converted to grazing range. In consequence, intricate ecological relationships, many thousands of years in the making, were altered or destroyed in the course of a few decades, or even within a few years. Conservationists were unable to check or reverse these huge changes; survival of the birds essentially depended on the adaptability of each species to the new requirements. When Audubon and Wilson noted the special wilderness conditions required by the ivory-billed woodpecker, they implicitly foreshadowed the disastrous dwindling of its numbers as those conditions disappeared before settlement and lumbering. But on the other hand, Wilson's hint that the ivory-bill's relative, the pileated woodpecker, would share the same fate was not borne out; the latter bird managed to adapt to second-growth forests, and survived. Even a bird as spectacularly abundant as the passenger pigeon faced the basic problem of a changing habitat, and unable to meet the test, perished. What all the market hunters could not have done, the biological inflexibility of the species itself accomplished. The terms for survival were harsh: either adapt to the new conditions, or go under.

With the benefit of hindsight, one may assume that by the end of the nineteenth century the vast majority of American species had verified their capacity for survival in a land thickly settled by human beings from across the Atlantic. Many had learned to avoid the new dangers; the wild turkey no longer "sallied by our doores," but kept to the remote areas; the ruffed grouse, "fool hen" to early settlers, had acquired a salutary wildness; the canvasback duck, relentlessly hunted for the market, had learned new ways to survive. Other birds had actually taken advantage of the changed situation, leaving the woods for the suburbs, abandoning hollow trees for chimneys, moving from cliffs to the beams of barns, and so forth. Again, there was very little that conservationists could do about such developments; whether the bird as a species could find proper conditions for survival depended on more factors than could be subjected to direct control.

To say this is not to imply that immediate dangers facing particular species were also beyond the range of human action. Almost any of the game birds, if hunted ruthlessly enough, could be extirpated over wide areas and the species reduced to insignificant numbers, mere fugitive reminders of former abundance. So too with certain song-birds; a large enough corps of boys, systematically shooting birds and robbing nests, might strip a given region of its smaller species, at least for a season or two. Situations of this sort were properly the concern of persons interested in bird protection; here, at least, effective action could be taken. Sportsmen, market hunters, and boys, three of the four main causes of decline given in Hornaday's report, could be held in check by laws establishing shorter game seasons and smaller bag limits, and giving complete protection to non-game birds — and of course by enforcing these laws rigorously, and supplementing their effects by education.

But consider the fourth cause of bird decrease — "Plume-hunters and milliners' hunters," in Hornaday's words, or, as Meyer more bluntly put it, "for Fashion." Wilson and Audubon had mentioned nearly every factor which appeared on the Hornaday list many decades later, but neither had spoken of the threat of fashion. That threat was, in fact, new; it was not a problem of any importance in the times of Wilson and Audubon, but one which loomed up suddenly in the latter decades of the century, and provided conservationists with not only their most immediate challenge, but also their best rallying point and most colorful public issue.

A study of the famous fashion magazine entitled *Godey's Lady's Book* reveals that the practice of decorating women's hats with parts or entire skins of birds became fashionable about 1875, and dominated millinery styles after 1880. Plumes of various kinds were of older lineage, but they too became of prime importance in the 1880's. Earlier, hats had been relatively simple and dignified, but toward the end of the century, in keeping with other articles of feminine apparel, they became showy, flamboyant, and rather massive, often combining a stuffed bird or two, several plumes, a wreath of flowers or a ruffle of lace, and numerous ribbons in a single creation. It is interesting to compare these hats with other manifestations of style to be found in the fashion magazines—the houses described by such names as "A Plain Gothic Rural Cottage," "Ornamental Italian Cottage," "French Gothic Gamber Dormer Villa," and "Picturesque American Cottage" (a "cottage" in those days commonly had ten or twelve rooms), the weighty pieces of furniture, the ornate items of interior decoration—and consider how truly these graceless, ostentatious affairs reflected both the vulgarity and the naïve enthusiasm of the period, Mark Twain's "Gilded Age" brought up to date. Here was "conspicuous consumption" indeed, in all its vigor and innocence and gross bad taste; and here too was a threat to American birds in keeping with the prodigal and heedless spirit of the age.

Taste in birds seemed to be quite eclectic—or, more accurately, entirely random. Frank Chapman in the course of two late afternoon walks in 1886 was able to discover forty different species on the hats of women shopping in downtown Manhattan. They included such unlikely birds as the blackpoll warbler, the northern shrike, the kingfisher, the saw-whet owl, and the ruffed grouse. Of the total species, twenty-two were passerine or perching birds, four were gallinaceous game birds, three were woodpeckers, and the rest were miscellaneous representatives of several different orders.

In this last group appared what were perhaps the most surprising birds of all—two terns, the green heron, the laughing gull, and the grebe. The plumage of such species apparently became increasingly popular; a handbill issued by a New York merchant some years later called for "prime, nicely cured, clean and dry round skins" of several other large water birds, including the following (with prices paid): royal tern 35¢, "Wilson's Tern" (common tern) 35¢, "Sea Swallow" (one of the smaller terns) 35¢, herring gull 40¢, "Blackheaded Least Tern" (breeding plumage) 25¢, "Greyheaded Least Tern" (immature) 12¢, herring and laughing gull wings, 15¢ a pair, and royal tern wings, 15¢ a pair. The merchant then added:

> I also solicit your valued shipments for HONEY, WAX, WHITE HERON (White Crane) EGRET PLUMES, LARGE BLUE CRANE SKINS WITH WINGS, ALLIGATOR SKINS, BEEF HIDES, GOAT, SHEEP, DEER SKINS and FUR. Also GREEN TURTLE and SALT WATER TERRAPIN to be shipped about the middle of November next.

And then a puzzling footnote:

> DON'T SHIP FOLLOWING: Small Blue Crane, Night Heron, Brown Egret, Surf Snipes, Water Turkey and Grosbeak.

This last signified, we may suppose, nothing more than a glutted market for the birds mentioned.

Nor was this quite the complete roster of wanted species. W. E. D. Scott, after making a tour of the Florida rookeries, wrote a series of articles for *The Auk* in 1887, revealing that the millinery hunters killed not only egrets, herons, gulls, and terns, but also cormorants, pelicans, frigate birds, ibises, and spoonbills. Agents for the plumage trade employed large parties of gunners to do their work, and paid prices ranging from ten cents for the back plumes of the Louisiana heron to five dollars for the roseate spoonbill.

Here, then, were the outlines of the problem facing the protectionist who opposed the slaughter of birds for millinery. A great variety of songbirds contributed to hat decoration, resulting in alarming decreases in many states; but as a general rule, these birds had too wide a nesting area, too sparse a distribution, and too much adaptability to be killed in such numbers as to threaten the species with extermination. Much the same was true for the miscellaneous victims, the game birds, owls, grebes, and a few others; they might be seriously decimated by the millinery trade, but because of remote nest sites, secretive habits, and scattered distribution, they were not likely to be entirely extirpated. Like the songbirds, these species had long been hunted, and had managed to escape extermination by one means or another.

But for the gulls, terns, herons, egrets, ibises, the roseate spoonbill, and the brown pelican, there was scant hope of such escape; these showy and locally abundant species, previously subjected to little but "sport" shooting, suddenly became the most accessible and the most lucrative of all millinery birds, and were set upon with such violence that they had little time to adapt their ways to avoid extermination. The particular (and potentially fatal) weakness shared by this group of birds was the habit of nesting in colonies. Audubon's Labrador eggers had taken advantage of this habit to secure vast numbers of eggs from the ancestral nesting grounds of alcids; the hunters in the eighties and nineties did the same thing in order to kill adult plume

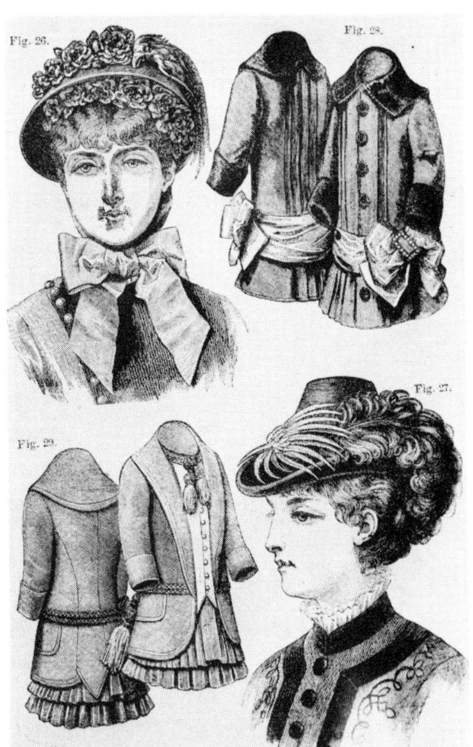

35. *Godey's Lady's Book,* February 1883: "Fig. 26. – Bonnet of sapphire-blue velvet, trimmed with flowers, and a gay-colored bird, flowers inside the brim. Fig. 27. – Hat for lady, made of felt trimmed with velvet, a long feather, and a bird's head."

WHAT WAS CHIC by way of dead birds, dead kittens, et cetera, in the latter decades of the nineteenth century, is indicated by these plates from the women's magazines (Figures 35–40).

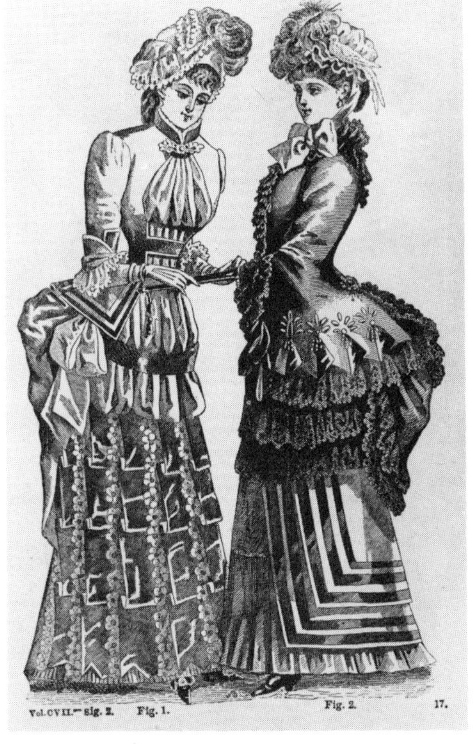

36. *Godey's* for July 1883: "Fig. 2. – Walking dress of cigar-colored foulé . . . very bouffant in back. Bonnet of crape, trimmed with feathers shaded with pale pink, and a bird at one side."

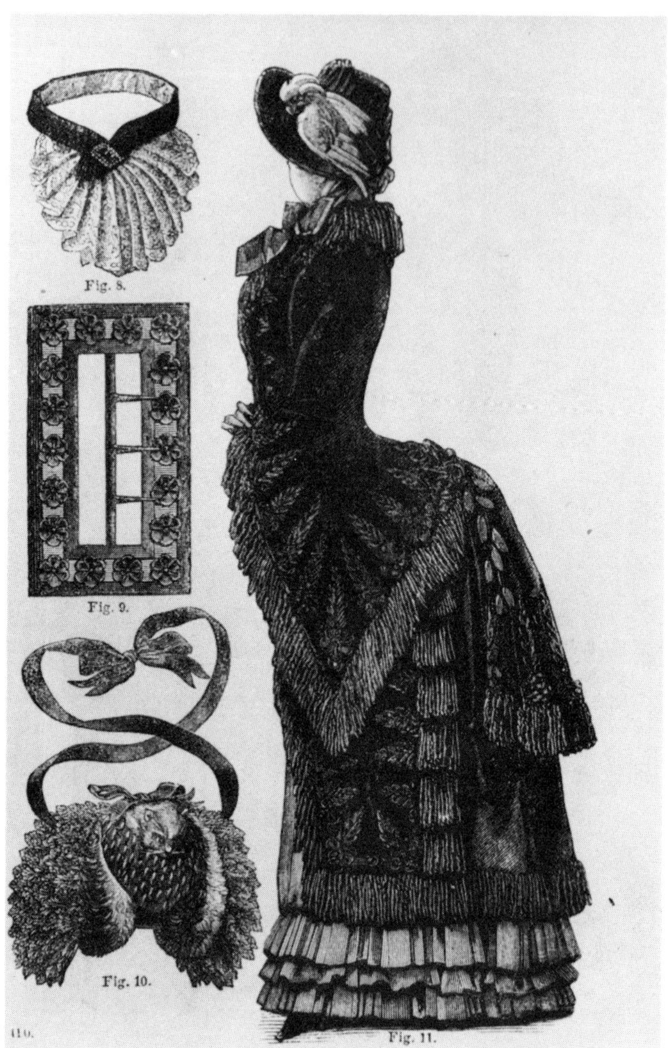

37. *Godey's* for November 1883: "Fig. 10. – Black velvet muff; in the center of the muff there is a kitten's head. . . Fig. 11. – Visiting costume . . . Black velvet bonnet, trimmed with large bird and lace."

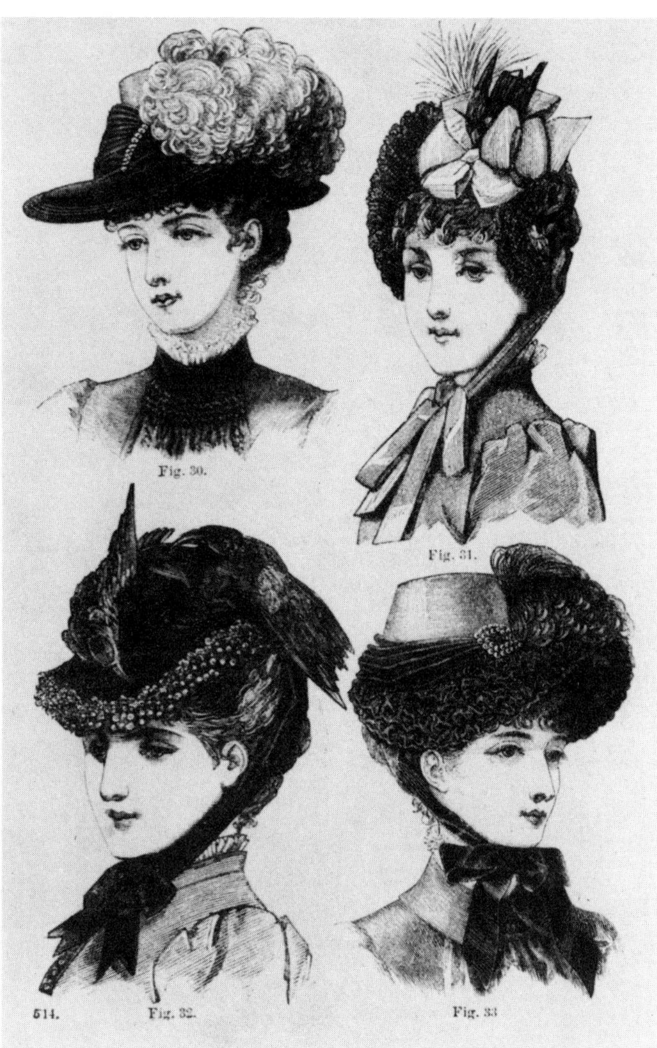

38. *Godey's* for December 1883: "Fig. 31.—Bonnet of ruby velvet, trimmed with lace, ribbon bows, birds, and aigrette. Fig. 32.—Bonnet of black velvet, trimmed with jet, birds, and velvet."

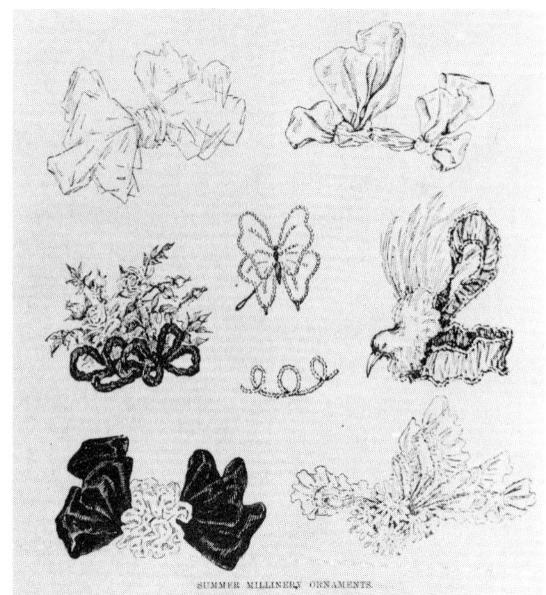

39. *The Delineator*, August 1898: "Summer Millinery Ornaments . . . Taffeta silk in any preferred shade is shirred on a cord on each side and looped in fancy style, a white bird resting against the standing loop." (Center, right.)

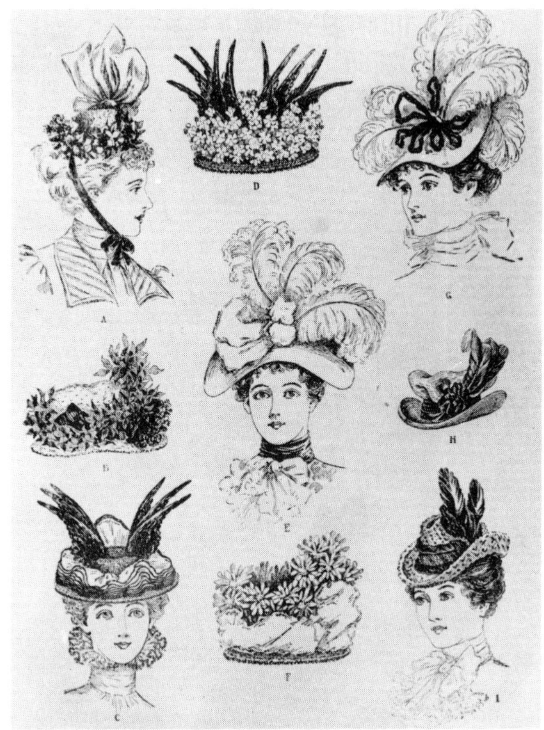

40. *The Delineator*, August 1898: "Figure C. – Particularly stylish is this hat of fancy straw . . . [with] many frills of taffeta ribbon . . . rising in the back between Mercury wings. Figure D. – This stylish hat is profusely trimmed with wild roses . . . and rising from their midst are Mercury wings that lend a most attractive air. Figure E. – In exquisite taste is this coquettishly bent hat of white Leghorn, with its trimming of white plumes and chiffon. . . The simple yet thoroughly elegant arrangement of the decorations lend to it a most *distingué* air."

birds at the point of greatest concentration. In the case of the egrets, there was a special reason for invading the rookeries; only during the nesting season did the birds carry the graceful nuptial plumes, the "aigrettes" which at the peak of demand were worth their weight in gold. The fact that such slaughter of the adults caused death by starvation to countless nestlings was scarcely a deterrent to the hunters; but it supplied the protectionists with one of their strongest motives for ending the millinery traffic, and with one of their most effective public arguments.

16 *Rescue at Hand*

It appears that the first formal protest against millinery shooting was made by J. A. Allen, writing in 1876:

> The herons, nearly useless as food, have suffered an immense decrease in number, mostly through very natural causes, but often through wholly reprehensible acts of wantonness. Many have of late been destroyed for their feathers where, in Florida especially, the havoc made with these poor defenseless birds is a subject of painful contemplation and a disgrace to the age. The poor birds are attacked at their breeding grounds, and hundreds are slain in a few hours by single parties, whose only use of them is to secure the beautiful plumes with which nature has unfortunately adorned them. In this way colony after colony is broken up, the greater part of the birds being actually killed on the spot, often leaving nestlings to suffer a lingering death by starvation . . . The effect of the wholesale destruction that for the last few years has prevailed in Florida and other portions of the Gulf States, is already apparent in the rapid decrease there of these beautiful birds.

This was an isolated voice, a lone warning which went unheeded for some years. But meanwhile there was in the making an event of first importance to the professional ornithologist—the founding of the

American Ornithologists' Union. Until the A.O.U. was formally organized, there was no national organization for the serious student of birds; the Nuttall Ornithological Club of Cambridge, Massachusetts, at first an informal group, later a fully organized association with its own quarterly bulletin, served the purpose until 1883. In that year the A.O.U. was formed—appropriately enough, as a direct outgrowth of the Nuttall Club. J. A. Allen was elected president, a position he retained until 1890.

Much of the work of the A.O.U. was of a strictly professional character, and is of little concern here. There was a Committee on the Nomenclature and Classification of North American Birds, charged with the complex task of establishing a canon of taxonomy (published in 1886 as the first "A.O.U. Check-List"); a Committee on Avian Anatomy; a Committee on the Geographical Distribution of North American Birds, later merged with another formed at the same time, the Committee on the Migration of North American Birds. *The Auk*, a quarterly journal, began publication in 1883 as a continuation of the Nuttall Club bulletin. No special activity of the A.O.U. was without relevance to broader questions concerning American bird life, but only with the formation of the Committee on the Protection of North American Birds did professional ornithologists directly enter the field of conservation.

William Brewster, one of the founders of the Nuttall Club and its president for over forty years, was the moving spirit behind the organization of this committee. In the words of William Dutcher, a member of the group and later president of the National Association of Audubon Societies:

> To Mr. Brewster should be given the credit of raising the first note of alarm when the non-game water birds of this country were being killed for millinery ornaments. He was the first man to call attention to this fact, and from his statement at a meeting of the Ornithologists' Union in 1883 has come all of the non-game protection work in the country, and the marked improvement in game conditions.

As noted, in "raising the first note of alarm," J. A. Allen had preceded Brewster by some years, but nevertheless Dutcher was essentially right. Brewster's remarks at the second annual A.O.U. meeting resulted in the decision to form the protection committee; and, though ill health forced him to resign the chairmanship in 1885, Brewster continued to serve for many years. In this as in other work, he proved himself an unusual person. Indeed, from the testimony of contemporaries regarding his professional abilities and personal force, and from reading his works, we may conclude that Brewster was a man who might have been something of a "public ornithologist" in the earlier tradition, had he so desired. Such was not his wish; he was content with his work as a curator of the Museum of Comparative Zoölogy at Harvard, with his occasional articles and books, with his public activities in behalf of bird protection, and with his influence on generations of Harvard students (including one man who wrote home that the Brewster museum had "the *finest private collection of American birds in the world*!"—young Franklin Roosevelt).*

Much of the influence of the Committee on the Protection of North American Birds could be attributed to the simple fact of its existence as an agency of the powerful American Ornithologists' Union, and to its distinguished membership, which included, besides Brewster, such notable scientists as Sennett, Bicknell, Grinnell, Dutcher, and J. A. Allen. But in the field of immediate action, the committee's most influential achievement was the publication of two bulletins for general distribution. The first of these, "Destruction of Our Native Birds" (1886), was particularly useful. J. A. Allen contributed a long general discussion of bird slaughter, including an estimate that five million American birds were being sacrificed annually to adorn women's hats. The section following gave more detailed statistics: one dealer obtained eleven thousand bird skins from South Carolina in three months, a single Long Island village collected seventy thousand skins in four months, a New York exporter contracted to supply forty thousand skins to the Paris market in a single summer, forty thousand terns were killed on Cape Cod in one season, and so on. William Dutcher wrote of the destruction of birds in the vicinity of New York City, and included two fashion notes from the newspapers, praising certain ladies (one of whom apparently wore an entire crow "among the curls and braids of her hair") for their ex-

* *F.D.R. His Personal Letters: Early Years* (New York: Duell, Sloan & Pearce, 1947), p. 370.

cellent taste in dead birds. George B. Sennett discussed the trade in wild bird eggs, a reminder that millinery was only the most pressing of several protection problems.

Near the end of the bulletin appeared what was perhaps its most important feature, a suggested text (later known as the "A.O.U. Model Law") for state laws to protect birds. This concrete proposal, written not by sentimentalists or ill-informed legislators, but by professional ornithologists, was relatively brief and to the point. The first section made unmistakable the separation between game and non-game birds, by classifying the former as including only the Anatidae, the Rallidae, the Limicolae, and the Gallinae (roughly, ducks and geese; rails and coots; shore birds; and turkeys, grouse, pheasants, and quail), with all others to be completely protected, with the single exception of the English sparrow. Here was a clear and rigid dichotomy: four particular groups of game birds on the one hand, the entire remainder of our indigenous avifauna on the other. Under such a law, no special prohibition against millinery hunting, for example, need be instituted, simply because most of the victims of such hunting were protected as non-game birds.

The second section of the law prohibited any person from taking or needlessly destroying eggs or nests of any game or non-game bird, again excepting the English sparrow. The third, fourth, and fifth sections granted scientific collectors immunity from the prior provisions, on condition that they secure proper certification (renewable each year) from competent and responsible persons or groups. The sixth section concerned the English sparrow, and the seventh repealed all contrary provisions of earlier laws.

Such was the A.O.U. Model Law, aptly so called not merely for its function as a prototype to be followed, but also for its appropriate brevity and concreteness. With certain modifications, it was widely adopted in the early twentieth century, affording among other things a uniformity of legislation from state to state which is likely to be rare in our federal union.

At the time the Model Law was propounded, however, no such happy outcome was in sight. Indeed, within a few years the protection committee itself had lost heart, as was reflected in its brief annual reports to the A.O.U. By 1890 only New York and Pennsylvania had passed legislation patterned on the Model Law, and even this was a short-lived victory, since both states soon modified or repealed the statutes. What J. A. Allen took to be "the markedly improved sentiment respecting bird-slaughter for millinery purposes" achieved by 1890 was no more than a momentary lull in a losing battle. In 1891 the only real progress reported by the committee concerned the protection of terns on Muskeget Island; in 1892 and 1893 no report whatever was rendered. The protection committee was reorganized in 1894 under Frank Chapman, and again the following year under William Dutcher, but there seemed no hope that the cause could prevail against the pressures of feminine fashion.

A further reason for gloom in 1895 was the fact that an organization called the Audubon Society, begun in 1886 "for the protection of wild birds and their eggs," had vanished from the scene, apparently for good. Originating in an editorial in *Forest and Stream* for February 11, 1886, and incorporated in August of that year by George Bird Grinnell, J. A. Allen, and others, the society received immediate and enthusiastic support from such prominent persons as Whittier, Holmes, Henry Ward Beecher, Charles Dudley Warner, and Celia Thaxter. By the end of the year, sixteen thousand members were enrolled; by August 1887, more than thirty-eight thousand. The monthly *Audubon Magazine* was started in January 1887, sponsored by the Forest and Stream Publishing Company. All signs seemed to point to a successful career for an organization serving a worthy cause. Yet by 1889 the magazine had ceased publication and the society had almost completely disbanded, its efforts apparently expended in vain.

An analysis of this failure was made in 1904 by William Dutcher. He noted that the society started with the initial disadvantage of central organization and direction, although its efforts were in general to be utilized to secure action not at the national but at the state level. A single corporation, the Forest and Stream Publishing Company, had assumed the burden of support, and the task proved too demanding both in funds and in effort. *Forest and Stream*, superficially a magazine merely for sportsmen, was actually one of the first periodicals to expose the evils of the trade in birds for millinery, and to call for preventive action; but it was not suited to the role of sponsoring a national organization whose single purpose was bird protection. An analogy can be drawn between the Audubon Society of *Forest and Stream* and the "Bird Defenders" and the "Agassiz Association" of *St. Nicholas*; in each case, superimposing a special organization upon the framework of a general periodical proved unworkable.

Dutcher also mentioned the fact that very little support had been received from the American press, that protective laws were not forthcoming, and that no warden system had been projected to ensure the observance of such laws as might be passed. His summary of the situation existing in 1895 was this:

> At the close of the year 1895 the low tide of bird protection had come and the end of the first cycle was at hand. The A.O.U. Protection Committee was discouraged and hopeless, feather-wearing was as rampant as ever, the legislatures of the states of New York and Pennsylvania, where the model law had been enacted, had amended or repealed the same, and bird legislation was as defective as it was before the protection movement began; the Audubon Society had practically ceased to exist, and the "Audubon Magazine" was no longer published. Truly it might be said that the cause of bird protection seemed hopeless, for the movement that had started so brilliantly in 1883 was seemingly dead after a short career of twelve years.

Within a year the tide had begun to flow once again. In January 1896 there was organized in Boston the Massachusetts Audubon Society, with William Brewster as president, and in October in Philadelphia the Pennsylvania Audubon Society. In 1897 similar organizations were formed in New York, New Hampshire, Illinois, Maine, Wisconsin, New Jersey, Colorado, Rhode Island, Minnesota, and the District of Columbia. By the end of the year 1900 the Audubon Society—with a total membership of forty thousand—was established in twenty states, and a national federation of these independent groups was in the making.

This time the movement was to survive and flourish, not die out in a few years, as had happened earlier. These state societies were autonomous units, joined in a common cause but supported and directed by the local membership and the state committees. Some of them were large, active, and enthusiastic, while others were too small to carry out effective work; but none of them depended on leadership or financial subsidy at the national level. Until the formation of the National Committee, the main unifying force, other than the general principle of bird protection, was Frank Chapman's magazine *Bird-Lore*, a bi-monthly started in February 1899 for "the study and protection of birds," and including a regular Audubon Society department under the editorship of Mabel Osgood Wright.

Two aspects of these new Audubon societies were especially noteworthy. It takes but a quick perusal of the early records to reveal the predominance of women in the membership rolls—which suggests, among other things, that the "clubwoman" with her leisure-time activities is not entirely a product of the twentieth century. The first issue of *Bird-Lore* carries this report:

> A score of ladies met in Fairfield on January 28, 1898, and formed "The Audubon Society of the State of Connecticut." Mrs. James Osborne Wright was chosen president and an executive committee provisionally elected, representing so far as possible at the beginning, the State of Connecticut . . .
>
> The Society has had two lectures prepared, one by Willard G. Van Name, entitled "Facts About Birds That Concern the Farmer," illustrated by sixty colored lantern slides, and one by Mrs. Mabel Osgood Wright, on "The Birds About Home," illustrated by seventy colored slides. A parlor stereopticon has been purchased for use in projecting the slides . . .
>
> An illustrated lecture by Mrs. Kate Tryon, having been given in Bridgeport, November 19, under the auspices of Miss Grace Moody (local secretary), Mrs. Howard N. Knapp, and Mrs. C. K. Averill. While Mr. Frank M. Chapman lectured before a large audience at the Stamford High School, on December 2, under the auspices of Mrs. Walter M. Smith, the local secretary of that city.
>
> Harriet D. C. Glover,
Cor. Sec'y and Treas.

This feminine invasion may not have been entirely welcome in some quarters; the A.O.U. member who complained about "Audubonites and fad protectionists" and derided the Audubon woman who "declines to wear mangled bird-remains on her hat or as trimming for her clothing" was perhaps not entirely alone in his manly dismay.

Another feature of these early state societies was, if we may judge from the pioneer Massachusetts group, the public prominence and social respectability of the persons enrolled. The list of vice presidents of the Massachusetts Audubon Society began with Charles Francis Adams, writer and sometime president of the Union Pacific Railroad, and Mrs. Louis Agassiz, a founder and president of Radcliffe College; also included were Mrs. John L. Gardner, Mrs. Julia J. Irvine, president of Wellesley, Sarah Orne Jewett, Henry L. Higginson, Senator George F. Hoar, and Bradford Torrey. A goodly representation of what has been called Proper Boston—which broadly includes Proper Brookline and Proper Milton—may be discovered on the list of founders. The impression is strong that the Audubon Society formed in 1886 enlisted many enthusiasts but failed to attract a sufficient number of substantial citizens, whereas these later groups, being properly local, appealed to that sense of civic pride and public responsibility which is held in high repute among the gentry.

Early reports submitted to *Bird-Lore* show that the programs of the state societies centered on obtaining the passage of the Model Law or other protective legislation, conducting campaigns against the use of birds on hats, sponsoring lectures, school courses, Bird Day observances, and other educational efforts, and securing areas to be set aside for bird sanctuaries. There was also coöperative action on the national scale, beginning with attempts to secure passage of the Lacey Bill in 1897. Introduced by Representative John F. Lacey of Iowa on July 1 of that year, it passed the House in modified form, but in the Senate an analogous bill sponsored by Senator Hoar was added as an amendment, and the bill died for lack of agreement in conference. The Lacey Bill alone passed both houses of Congress when reintroduced in 1900, becoming law on May 25. Briefly, it forbade the importation of "any foreign wild animal or bird except under special permit," and prohibited interstate commerce in such importations, and also in "the dead bodies or parts of any wild animals or birds" which had been killed in violation of state laws. In effect, this bill gave the Department of Agriculture control over the traffic in birds shot for millinery, so long as such shooting violated laws in force in the separate states.

The usefulness of the Lacey Bill depended, therefore, on the local situation with regard to bird protection. It has been mentioned earlier that various state regulations were in effect in the latter part of the century, but were poorly observed, ambiguously worded, and lacking in uniformity from state to state. The Model Law, on the other hand, was brief and clear, and promised to standardize the criteria of bird protection for the entire nation. To secure the passage of this measure was necessarily a primary objective of the Audubon associations.

As William Dutcher later noted, it was frequently a long and disheartening task to lobby for the Model Law at the state capitals. Initially, indeed, it appeared nearly a fruitless endeavor; by the end of the year 1900 only five states, as widely separated as Arkansas and Vermont, had passed the law, and two of these five had done so before the new Audubon Society existed. New York state, which had previously passed and then repealed the Model Law, in 1900 adopted a more restricted measure, the Hallock Bill, which made possession of the plumage of non-game birds illegal. Four or five years of work by the Audubon societies had seemingly come to very little.

These efforts, however, were sufficient to arouse millinery merchants to action. When Senator Hoar's bill for the protection of songbirds was reintroduced in Congress in December 1899, *The Millinery Trade Review* responded with a demand that "every man or woman connected with the millinery trade" help to crush "this most iniquitous and childish measure," or face the loss of employment. Then in April 1900 the Millinery Merchants' Protective Association sought to treat, so to speak, with the enemy, by drawing up an armistice agreement. Its main provisions were these:

> [The milliners pledge themselves] not to kill or buy any more North American birds from hunters or such people who make it a business to destroy North American birds . . . This does not refer to plumage or skins of barnyard fowls, edible birds, or game birds killed in their season, nor to the birds or plumage of foreign countries *not* of the species of North American birds . . . In return for this pledge, we expect the Audubon Society and the Ornithological Union to pledge themselves to do all in their power to prevent laws being enacted in Congress, or in any of the States, which shall interfere with the manufacturing or selling of plumage or skins from barnyard fowls, edible birds and game birds killed in their season, and all birds which are not North American.

Frank Chapman, in presenting this proposal to the several Audubon societies for their decision, urged serious consideration for it. He seemed to feel that the milliners had made a major concession, and in his editorials relating to the proposal, he appeared to favor accepting it. One can only speculate whether he recognized the perils not merely of compromising so dramatic a public issue, but more especially of becoming a party to an agreement so imprecisely worded. In many areas "edible birds" was still a term of considerable latitude, taking in any bird which might be shot and offered for sale. Furthermore, under some state laws the term "game birds" signified a large number of species (including songbirds) not designated as game in the Model Law. Finally, it was already plain to persons investigating the techniques of the millinery trade that various tricks of dyeing and rearranging plumage made it very difficult to determine the species used. It was reasonable, therefore, to doubt that every milliner would honor the agreement in complete good faith.

As it turned out, however, the Audubon groups rejected the proposal, declaring that "to sanction, even passively, the killing of birds anywhere would violate the cardinal principles of the Societies." Knowledge as well as sentiment lay behind this declaration, since protectionists had been aware for some years that much of the plumage used in the millinery trade came from foreign countries. When egrets in the United States were driven close to extermination, the rookeries in Central and South America were raided; a fashion for white "Mercury wings" resulted in the slaughter of two million ptarmigan between 1894 and 1897 in the Province of Archangel, Russia; a desire for exotic plumage caused great inroads among certain species in India and China; and even the common birds of Europe were killed in large numbers for millinery, despite efforts of several European protective organizations. When the Audubon societies rejected an armistice with the Millinery Merchants' Protective Association, they in effect refused to compromise a supra-national principle for the sake of a partial respite for American birds.

Whatever his misgivings, Frank Chapman went along with the decision to spurn the milliners' offer. Had he been able to foresee the near future, he would scarcely have given that offer a second thought; the first several years of the new century saw the virtual rout of the plumage merchants before the protection movement, and the initial resurgence of the persecuted species. In a scant five years from the time the Audubon societies refused "to pledge themselves to do all in their power to prevent laws from being enacted in Congress, or in any of the States" against the plume trade, the Model Law was in force in thirty-three states, and the federal government, in the person of that amateur ornithologist and friend of the Audubon movement, President Theodore Roosevelt, had established several reservations for the express purpose of protecting birds and other wildlife from persecution.

When Audubon warden Guy M. Bradley was shot to death by a plume hunter on Oyster Key, Florida, in the summer of 1905, protectionists were given a harsh reminder that the time for victory celebrations was not yet. Nor would the time ever come, in the sense that every problem of bird protection and conservation could be put down as solved. Law and public pressure (plus perhaps a wholly arbitrary shift in the restless winds of fashion) brought the millinery trade in birds to an end; but other problems, as diverse as the failure of eel grass and the excessive use of DDT, would arise in later years. Nevertheless the twentieth century was scarcely a decade old before the cause of bird protection had triumphed in its first great test, and by 1914 William T. Hornaday could look back upon the victory as an accomplished fact:

> In the beginning of the craze for stuffed birds and wild birds' plumage on women's hats, all kinds of bright-colored song-birds, terns, gulls, herons, egrets, spoonbills, ibises and the flamingo were used. The small birds were mounted entire, and the larger species were used piecemeal. The slaughter for millinery purposes called forth, as the special champion of birds, the Audubon Societies, state and national. Their first work consisted in prohibiting the use of song-birds, and in stopping the killing of gulls and terns. The Audubon people stepped in at a time when a furious and bloody general slaughter of our gulls and terns was in progress, and they literally brought back to us those interesting and pleasing species. But for their efforts, there would to-day be only the merest trace of the long-winged swimmers along our Atlantic coast.*

"The Audubon people stepped in" — true enough. Except for the

* William T. Hornaday, *Wild Life Conservation in Theory and Practice* (New Haven: Yale University Press, 1914), pp. 22–23.

endeavors of the Audubon societies and allied groups, numerous threatened species of American birds might have perished for lack of a champion. That they did not so perish, but did instead survive to flourish once more, is written into the history of the twentieth century.

But now, at the end of the present inquiry, let us stand off and take a longer view of what they had done. The Audubon movement achieved its victory through the agency of law, and law, as the Eighteenth Amendment would shortly prove, must accord with the common outlook or become a dead letter. The observance of any law in a democracy finally depends on the desire on the part of both the citizenry and the enforcement agencies to see it observed. Simply as special pressure groups, lobbying assiduously in the corridors and committee rooms of the state capitals, the Audubon societies might have pushed the Model Law through the legislatures; in Washington they might have induced a president ignorant of birds to set aside sanctuaries or sponsor protective legislation; but, having done so, they alone could not have put these measures into effect.

Yet of course they were not alone; they were part of a wider movement, an older outlook, a continuing cultural trend. They had, for example, their own educational programs and publications — things not unique or discrete, but part of what had been, part of a larger whole embracing *St. Nicholas* and the "Bird Defenders," Nathaniel Willis and *Youth's Companion*, the Sunday School unions and the popular bird books, and going back to that most winsome of teachers, Aesop the fabulist. They had as fellow-members such literary figures as John Burroughs, Bradford Torrey, Sarah Orne Jewett, Mabel Osgood Wright — and Henry Thoreau, Walt Whitman, William Cullen Bryant, White of Selborne, Wordsworth and Shelley and Keats, Shakespeare and Chaucer and Aristophanes. They had the painter Louis Agassiz Fuertes — and John Gould and Audubon, and Bewick and Wilson and Catesby, and Dürer and Pisanello and Roeland Savery, and the Egyptians who painted on the walls of temples and tombs, and Stone Age men who limned birds on the sides of caves. They had Frank Chapman and William Brewster — and Baird and his great mentor Audubon, Wilson and his loyal friends Bartram and Peale, Mark Catesby and his Swedish correspondent Linnaeus,

Francis Willughby and his editor John Ray. They had Theodore Roosevelt and George Hoar—and Edward Everett and Daniel Webster, and Thomas Jefferson, and Frederick II, Holy Roman Emperor, and by tradition at least, King David and Solomon his son. "The Audubon people" were in a sense merely some thousands of Americans joined in special groups to achieve particular ends; but in another, broader sense, they were the inheritors and custodians of a great and complex tradition of science and art and literature, and of a tradition even older and deeper in human experience, the simple love of birds.

Selected Bibliography

Footnotes in this book have purposely been kept to a minimum; but for those who may wish to investigate further any of the subjects considered, a list of references, arranged under chapter headings and in the order the works or their authors are mentioned within a chapter, is provided below.

1. NEW LANDS, NEW BIRDS

John Ray, ed. and trans. *The Ornithology of Francis Willughby*. In Three Books. London, 1678.

Mark Catesby, F.R.S. *The Natural History of Carolina, Florida, and the Bahama Islands, Containing the Figures of Birds, Beasts, Fishes, Serpents, Insects, and Plants.* 2 vols. London, 1731–1743. Appendix, 1748.

Elsa Guerdrum Allen, "The History of American Ornithology before Audubon," *Transactions of the American Philosophical Society*, new series, vol. XLI, part 3 (October 1951), pp. 387–591.

William and Mabel Smallwood. *Natural History and the American Mind.* New York, 1941.

Bernard Jaffe. *Men of Science in America.* New York, 1946.

Thomas Jefferson. *Notes on the State of Virginia.* Philadelphia, 1801.

Benjamin Smith Barton. *Fragments of the Natural History of Pennsylvania.* Philadelphia, 1799. This first and only edition put out by Barton is quite rare, but a reprint was issued by the Willughby Society in London in 1883, edited by Osbert Salvin.

2. PIONEER AND PROPHET: ALEXANDER WILSON

William Bartram. *Travels Through North and South Carolina, Georgia, East and West Florida* (1791). An American Bookshelf Series, ed. Mark Van Doren. New York, 1928.

John Latham. *A General Synopsis of Birds.* 3 vols. London, 1781–1785. Supplements, 1787 and 1801. See also Latham's *Index Ornithologicus*, 2 vols., London, 1790.

Frank L. Burns, "Alexander Wilson," *The Wilson Bulletin*, vol. XX, nos. 1, 2, 3, 4; vol. XXI, nos. 1, 3, 4; vol. XXII, no. 2. Oberlin, Ohio, March 1908–June 1910.

George Edwards. *A Natural History of Birds, Most of Which Have Not Been Figur'd or Describ'd.* 4 vols. London, 1743–1751.

William Turton, ed. and trans. *A General Synopsis of Nature, through the Three Grand Kingdoms . . . by Sir Charles Linné.* 7 vols. London, 1806.

Thomas Pennant. *Arctic Zoology.* 2 vols. London, 1784–1785. Supplement, 1787. See also a work by Pennant now referred to as the *Unpublished Collection towards an Account of the Zoology of Virginia,* in the library of the Museum of Comparative Zoölogy, Harvard University.

Thomas Bewick. *History of British Birds.* 2 vols. Newcastle, 1797, 1804.

Mathurin Jacques Brisson. *Ornithologie, ou méthode, contenant la division des oiseaux en ordres, sections, genres, espèces et leurs variétés.* 6 vols. Paris, 1760.

Le Comte de Buffon. *Histoire naturelle des oiseaux,* 10 vols. Paris, 1771–1786. The folio edition; there were others in smaller format.

Wilson's American Ornithology, ed. T. M. Brewer. New York, 1852. One of several printings of the Brewer edition, first issued in Boston in 1840.

Collection of Wilsoniana (letters, verses, cost accounts, etc.). Library of the Museum of Comparative Zoölogy, Harvard University.

3. THE "AMERICAN ORNITHOLOGY"

Alexander Wilson. *American Ornithology; or, The Natural History of the Birds of the United States.* Illustrated with Plates Engraved and Colored from Original Drawings Taken from Nature. 9 vols. Philadelphia, 1808–1814. The first edition, in so-called imperial quarto size; not to be confused with Ord's later edition, incorrectly dated in duplication of first edition.

James S. Wilson. *Alexander Wilson.* New York, 1906.

Jeremy Belknap. *The History of New Hampshire.* 3 vols. Boston, 1792.

Charles Lucien Bonaparte, "Observations on the Nomenclature of Wilson's Ornithology," *Journal of the Academy of Natural Sciences,* Philadelphia, April 1824–September 1825.

Witmer Stone, "Some Unpublished Letters of Alexander Wilson and John Abbot," *The Auk,* October 1906.

Alexander B. Grosart. *The Poems and Literary Prose of Alexander Wilson.* Paisley, Scotland, 1876.

4. A MEETING OF CONSEQUENCE

John James Audubon. *Ornithological Biography; or, An Account of the Habits of the Birds of the United States of America; Accompanied by Descriptions of the Objects Represented in the Work Entitled The Birds of America, and Interspersed with Delineations of American Scenery and Manners.* 5 vols. Edinburgh, 1831–1839.

Walter Faxon, "Early Editions of Wilson's Ornithology," *The Auk*, April 1901.

Frank L. Burns, "Miss Lawson's Recollections of Ornithologists," *The Auk*, July 1917.

Proceedings of the American Philosophical Society, vol. I, no. 13 (August, September, October 1840). George Ord's charges of plagiarism against Audubon appear on pp. 272–273.

6. BIRD ART AND AUDUBON

John James Audubon. *The Birds of America.* 4 vols. London, Published by the Author, 1827–1838. The elephant folio edition.

Herbert Friedmann. *The Symbolic Goldfinch: Its History and Significance in European Devotional Art.* Washington, D. C., 1946.

Bernhard Degenhart. *Antonio Pisanello.* Vienna, 1940.

Gian Alberto Dell'acqua. *Pisanello.* Milan, 1952.

Casey A. Wood and F. Marjorie Fyfe, eds. and trans. *The Art of Falconry*, being the De Arte Venandi Cum Avibus of Frederick II, Palo Alto, California, 1943.

Carl A. Willemsen. *Die Falkenjagd, Bilder aus den Falkenbuch Kaiser Friedrichs II.* Leipzig, 1943.

Jean Anker. *Bird Books and Bird Art.* Copenhagen, 1938.

Donald Culross Peattie, ed. *Audubon's America.* Boston, 1940.

Roger Tory Peterson, "Bird Painting in America," *Audubon Magazine*, May 1942. Mainly concerns work of the twentieth century.

Collection of Wilson's original paintings (from which the *American Ornithology* engravings were made) in the Museum of Comparative Zoölogy at Harvard.

Collection of early Audubon watercolors in the Houghton Library, Harvard.

7. LITERARY BIRDMAN: HENRY DAVID THOREAU

Henry D. Thoreau, "Natural History of Massachusetts," *The Dial*, July 1842.

F. B. Sanborn, ed. *Familiar Letters of Henry David Thoreau.* Boston, 1894.

Francis H. Allen, ed. *Notes on New England Birds by Henry D. Thoreau.* Boston, 1910. An expert and convenient compilation of all major bird references from Thoreau's journals.

Thomas Nuttall. *A Manual of the Ornithology of the United States and Canada.* 2 vols. Cambridge, Massachusetts, 1832; Boston, 1834.

Bradford Torrey, ed. *The Journal of Henry David Thoreau.* 14 vols. Boston, 1906.

Edward Waldo Emerson and Waldo Emerson Forbes, eds. *Journals of Ralph Waldo Emerson.* 10 vols. Boston, 1909–1914.

George Turbervile. *The Booke of Faulconrie or Hauking, for the Onely Delight and Pleasure of all Noblemen and Gentlemen.* London, 1575.

Izaak Walton. *The Compleat Angler* . . . with original memoirs and notes by Sir Harris Nicolas. 2 vols. London, 1860. This edition collates the first edition with Walton's later much expanded work.

Gilbert White. *The Natural History of Selborne* . . . with an introduction and notes by E. M. Nicolson. New York, *ca.* 1930. This volume follows the first edition (1789) and eliminates the "Antiquities" section.

Gilpin's Forest Scenery, ed. Francis George Heath. London, 1879. This volume follows the text of the third edition (1808) as corrected by Gilpin himself.

Oliver Goldsmith. *An History of the Earth and Animated Nature.* 8 vols. London, 1774.

William Yarrell. *A History of British Birds.* 3 vols. London, 1839–1843.

William MacGillivray. *History of British Birds.* 5 vols. Edinburgh, 1838–1852.

N. Bryllion Fagin. *William Bartram, Interpreter of the American Landscape.* Baltimore, 1933.

The Writings of Henry David Thoreau. 10 vols. Boston, 1894.

8. EMERSON AND OTHER WORTHIES

The Works of Ralph Waldo Emerson. 14 vols. Boston, 1883.

Thomas Wentworth Higginson. *Outdoor Studies* [*and*] *Poems.* Boston, 1900. The sixth volume of his *Writings*; an earlier version, called *Outdoor Papers,* appeared in 1863.

Wilson Flagg. *A Year with the Birds.* Boston, 1881. A final version of Flagg's work on birds, with many of the pieces taken from earlier volumes.

9. "JOHN O' BIRDS": JOHN BURROUGHS

John Burroughs. *Notes on Walt Whitman as Poet and Person.* New York, 1867.

——— *Wake-Robin.* New York, 1871.

——— *The Writings of John Burroughs.* Boston, 1905. This "Riverby Edition" appeared in 14 volumes, but was later augmented (under the same general title and format) by several other titles.

Theodore Dreiser. *A Book About Myself.* New York, 1922.

10. AMERICAN BIRD POETRY: WHITMAN AND OTHERS

The Works of Anne Bradstreet. New York, 1932.

Poems of Freneau. New York, 1929.

Selden L. Whitcomb, "Nature in Early American Literature," *Sewannee Review,* February 1894.

The Poetical Works of William Cullen Bryant. New York, 1916.

Ellery Channing. *Poems of Sixty-Five Years.* Philadelphia, 1902.

Poems and Essays by Jones Very. Boston, 1886.

The Complete Poetical Works of John Greenleaf Whittier. Boston, 1896.

The Poetical Works of Henry Wadsworth Longfellow. Boston, 1884.

The Writings of James Russell Lowell. 10 vols. Boston, 1890. "My Garden Acquaintance" appears in vol. III.

Walt Whitman. *Leaves of Grass.* Philadelphia, 1900. The variorum edition brought out by David McKay.

——— *Complete Prose Works.* Boston, 1898.

11. END-OF-THE-CENTURY PROSE

Poems of Sidney Lanier. New York, 1916.

Selected Poems of Emily Dickinson. New York, 1948.

Harriet E. Paine. *Bird Songs of New England.* Boston, 1882.

H. J. Massingham, ed. *Poems about Birds from the Middle Ages to the Present Day.* New York, *ca.* 1922.

John Muir. *The Mountains of California.* New York, 1894.

Bradford Torrey. *Birds in the Bush.* Boston, 1885.

——— *A Rambler's Lease.* 1889.

——— *The Foot-Path Way.* 1892.

——— *A Florida Sketch-Book.* 1894.

——— *Spring Notes from Tennessee.* 1896.

——— *A World of Green Hills.* 1898.

Frank Bolles. *Land of the Lingering Snow.* Boston, 1891.

——— *At the North of Bearcamp Water.* 1893.
——— *From Blomidon to Smoky.* 1894.
——— *Chocorua's Tenants.* 1895. A book of verse.

12. THE BEGINNINGS OF CONSERVATION

T. S. Palmer. *Legislation for the Protection of Birds Other than Game Birds.* Bulletin No. 12, revised ed., Division of Biological Survey, U. S. Department of Agriculture. Washington, D. C., 1902.

——— *Chronology and Index of the More Important Events in American Game Protection, 1776–1911.* Bulletin No. 41, Biological Survey. 1912.

J. R. Dodge, "Birds and Bird Laws," *Report of the U. S. Department of Agriculture for 1864.* Washington, D. C., 1865.

J. A. Allen, "On the Decrease of Birds in the United States," *The Penn Monthly*, December 1876.

13. FEDERAL AND STATE BIRD BOOKS

Thomas Jefferson and William Dunbar. *Documents Relating to the Purchase and Exploration of Louisiana.* Boston, 1904.

Edwin James, ed. *Account of an Expedition from Pittsburgh to the Rocky Mountains, Performed in the Years 1819 and '20 . . . under Command of Major Stephen H. Long.* 2 vols. and atlas. Philadelphia, 1823.

William Keating, ed. *Narrative of an Expedition to the Source of the St. Peter's River . . . Performed in the Year 1823 . . . under the Command of Stephen H. Long, Major U.S.T.E.* 2 vols. Philadelphia, 1824.

[*Report of the*] *United States Exploring Expedition . . . under the Command of Charles Wilkes, U.S.N.* Vol. VIII: *Mammalia and Ornithology*, by Titian R. Peale. Philadelphia, 1848.

[*Report of the*] *United States Exploring Expedition during the Years 1838, 1839, 1840, 1841, 1842, under the Command of Charles Wilkes, U.S.N.* Vol. VIII (with folio atlas): *Mammalogy and Ornithology*, by John Cassin. Philadelphia, 1858.

[*Report of the*] *United States Naval Astronomical Expedition to the Southern Hemisphere . . . 1849–52.* Vol. II, Appendix F, Part 2: "Birds," by John Cassin. Washington, D. C., 1855.

Narrative of the Expedition of an American Squadron to the China Seas and Japan, Performed in the Years 1852, 1853, and 1854, under the Command of Commodore M. C. Perry, U.S.N. Vol. II, pp. 219–248: "Birds," by John Cassin. Washington, D. C., 1856.

Reports of Explorations and Surveys to Ascertain the Most Practicable and Economical Route for a Railroad from the Mississippi River to the Pacific Ocean, Made under the Direction of the Secretary of War, in 1853–6. Vol. IX, Part 2 (with atlas): *Birds,* by Spencer F. Baird, with John Cassin and George N. Lawrence. Washington, D. C., 1858.

Spencer F. Baird, with John Cassin and George N. Lawrence. *The Birds of North America.* Philadelphia, 1859.

[*Report of the*] *United States and Mexican Boundary Survey, under the Order of Lieut. Col. W. H. Emory.* Vol. II, Part 2, second article: "Birds of the Boundary," by Spencer F. Baird. Washington, D. C., 1859.

Report upon Geographical and Geological Explorations and Surveys West of the One Hundredth Meridian . . . under the Direction of Brig. Gen. A. A. Humphreys, Chief of Engineers, U. S. Army. Vol. V, chapter 3: "Report upon the Ornithological Collections," by H. W. Henshaw. Washington, D. C., 1875.

Elliott Coues. *Birds of the Northwest . . . Ornithology of the Region Drained by the Missouri River and Its Tributaries.* Miscellaneous Publication No. 3, United States Geological Survey of the Territories. Washington, D. C., 1874.

——— *Birds of the Colorado Valley.* Miscellaneous Publication No. 11, 1878. Includes a long bibliographical appendix.

James E. De Kay. *Zoology of New York.* Part II: *Birds.* Albany, 1844.

Geological Survey of California . . . Ornithology. Vol. I: *Land Birds,* Edited by Spencer F. Baird from the Manuscript and Notes of J. G. Cooper. [Printed by Harvard University Press, Cambridge], 1870.

Spencer F. Baird, T. M. Brewer, and Robert Ridgway. *A History of North American Birds. Land Birds.* 3 vols. Boston, 1874.

Spencer F. Baird, T. M. Brewer, and Robert Ridgway. *The Water Birds of North America.* 2 vols. Boston, 1884. Vol. XII of Memoirs of the Museum of Comparative Zoölogy at Harvard College.

L. S. Foster, "A Consideration of Some Ornithological Literature with Extracts from Current Criticism," *Abstract of the Proceedings of the Linnaean Society of New York,* no. 6 (1894).

14. EDUCATING A WIDER PUBLIC

Frank Luther Mott. *A History of American Magazines.* 3 vols. New York and Cambridge, Mass., 1930–1938.

Periodicals: *Youth's Companion,* Boston, first issue April 16, 1827. *St. Nicholas,* New York, first issue November 1873. *Harper's Young*

People, New York, first issue November 4, 1879; became *Harper's Round Table*, April 30, 1895; ceased publication in 1899.

15. BOYS, POT-HUNTERS, AND WOMEN

Le Grand T. Meyer, "Extinction of Our Birds," *The Ornithologists' and Oologists' Semi-Annual*, Pittsfield, Mass., January 1889.

D. Lange. *Our Native Birds*. New York, 1899.

Ludlow Griscom, "The Passing of the Passenger Pigeon," *The American Scholar*, Autumn 1946.

Frank M. Chapman. *Autobiography of a Bird-Lover*. New York, 1935.

W. E. D. Scott, "The Present Condition of Some of the Bird Rookeries of the Gulf Coast of Florida," *The Auk*, vol. IV (1887).

16. RESCUE AT HAND

The American Ornithologists' Union. *Destruction of Our Native Birds*. Articles by several hands, first published as a supplement to *Science*, February 26, 1886, and later reprinted as Bulletin No. 1 of the A.O.U. Committee on the Protection of North American Birds.

J. A. Allen. *The American Ornithologists' Union, a Seven Years' Retrospect*. New York, Published by the Union, 1891.

William Dutcher, "History of the Audubon Movement," *Bird-Lore*, February 1905.

Periodicals: *The Auk*, A Quarterly Journal of Ornithology, Boston and New York, first issue January 1884. *Bird-Lore*, A Bi-Monthly Magazine devoted to the Study and Protection of Birds, New York, first issue February 1899.

INDEX